How Ottawa Spends,

THE SCHOOL OF PUBLIC POLICY AND ADMINISTRATION at Carleton University is a national center for the study of public policy and public management.

The School's Centre for Policy and Program Assessment provides research services and courses to interest groups, businesses, unions, and governments in the evaluation of public policies, programs and activities.

School of Public Policy and Administration
Carleton University
10th Floor Dunton Tower
1125 Colonel By Drive
Ottawa, ON
Canada K1S 5B6
www.carleton.ca/sppa

How Ottawa Spends, 2014–2015

The Harper Government – Good to Go?

Edited by

G. BRUCE DOERN

and

CHRISTOPHER STONEY

Published for
The School of Public Policy and Administration
Carleton University
by
McGill-Queen's University Press
Montreal & Kingston · London · Ithaca

© McGill-Queen's University Press 2014
ISBN 978-0-7735-4444-4 (paper)
ISBN 978-0-7735-8498-3 (ePDF)
ISBN 978-0-7735-8499-0 (ePUB)

Legal deposit fourth quarter 2014
Bibliothèque nationale du Québec

Printed in Canada on acid-free paper that is 100% ancient forest free
(100% post-consumer recycled), processed chlorine free

McGill-Queen's University Press acknowledges the support of the Canada
Council for the Arts for our publishing program. We also acknowledge
the financial support of the Government of Canada through the Canada
Book Fund for our publishing activities.

Library and Archives Canada has catalogued this publication as follows:

How Ottawa spends.
1983–
Imprint varies.
Includes bibliographical references.
Continues: How Ottawa spends your tax dollars, ISSN 0711-4990.
ISBN 0822-6482
ISBN 978-0-7735-4444-4 (2014/2015 edition)
ISBN 978-0-7735-8498-3 (ePDF). – ISBN 978-0-7735-8499-0 (ePUB)

1. Canada – Appropriations and expenditures – Periodicals. I. Carleton
University. School of Public Policy and Administration

HJ7663.H69   354.710072'2   C84-030303-3

This book was typeset by Interscript in 10 / 12 Minion.

Contents

Preface

This is the 35th edition of *How Ottawa Spends*. As always we are greatly indebted to our roster of contributing academic authors and other expert authors from across Canada and abroad for their research, their insights, and for their willingness to contribute to public debate in Canada.

Thanks are also owed to Sheena Kennedy and Mary Giles at Carleton University's School of Public Policy and Administration for their excellent research and technical support and to Ryan Van Huijstee and his colleagues at McGill-Queen's University Press for their always professional editorial and publishing services and expertise.

We also extend our deep appreciation for the scholarly stimulation and encouragement provided by our colleagues at the School of Public Policy and Administration and at the Politics Department, University of Exeter, UK.

G. Bruce Doern and Christopher Stoney
Ottawa

How Ottawa Spends, 2014–2015

1 The Harper Government – Good to Go?

G. BRUCE DOERN AND CHRISTOPHER STONEY

INTRODUCTION

In last year's *How Ottawa Spends*, we characterized the Harper Conservative government as suffering from the mid-term blues but still offering up its long-term policy plans. In 2014–15 our entry point is to ask whether the Harper government is "good to go." Good to go refers to the increasing possibility that it will be out of office after the fall 2015 federal election.

The immediate trigger for the good to go descriptor and prediction was the increasingly direct association of the Senate scandal with the prime minister himself and with the Prime Minister's Office (PMO). "Good to go" was of course the phrase uttered by former PMO chief of staff Nigel Wright to Harper's legal counsel Benjamin Perrin after Wright had spoken to Harper about whether the $90,000 payment to reimburse Senator Mike Duffy for alleged illegal expenses would proceed.[1] Wright sent an email saying "we are good to go from the PM." The exchange emerged after court documents were made public, suggesting to many that Harper was more fully briefed on the Duffy "deal" than he subsequently led parliament and the media to believe during weeks of unrelenting questioning from opposition parties. The ambiguous phrase quickly morphed via social media, regular media, and opposition party coverage into notions that "Harper was good to go" and variously that his government was good to leave office (and indeed that Harper might want to leave as Conservative leader) and that Tory ministerial challengers were beginning to become more public in their criticisms of Harper. Harper has denied repeatedly that he had anything to do with such a payment but this defence did not resonate with his super-controlling prime ministerial style, including his reputation as arguably the micro-manager supreme.

Such triggers and labels for discussing and predicting the possible demise of a government can often turn on very specific high profile events / decisions but they can also emerge in the context of the life cycle of governments in power. Harper is now in his eighth year in office and such periods of long tenure are often precisely the time when Canadian voters, not to mention the media, are anxious to find ways of expressing the normal clarion call of "time for a change." Similar rumblings of discontent had emerged in the latter Liberal Chrétien-Martin era in the 2003 to 2005 period in the wake of the Sponsorship corruption scandal and indeed in Martin's battle within the Liberal cabinet to succeed Chrétien as prime minister.

This chapter explores the probability and possibility of the good to go argument. It does so in two major ways. First we explore the building and immediate context of political-economic forces and policies that are shaping the run-up to a late 2015 fall election. Second we set out and examine the Harper government's priorities as expressed both in its October 2013 Speech from the Throne and in the closely linked and themed Budget Speech of February 11, 2014. In both sections, we relate these priorities and policies to the insights and arguments supplied by our contributing authors both on macro issues and on selected more particular policy and federal departmental realms. Brief conclusions then follow.

POLITICAL-ECONOMIC FORCES AND CONTEXT

With the next election drawing ever nearer, strategies and battle lines are becoming increasingly clear as the parties look to define the issues and shape the political agenda. For the Harper Conservatives they remain focused on the narrative of overseeing an improving economy, job creation and growth and a balanced budget without raising taxes. While the government will be able to point to its achievements in slaying the deficit, and even trumpet a modest surplus by Budget 2015, the recovery has been more sluggish than they would have liked and concern still lingers that further stimulus funding will be required both for public infrastructure and private corporations, particularly those located in the auto and manufacturing sector.

The lack of growth in manufacturing has helped raise the spectre that "Dutch disease" still lingers with much of Canada's recovery being attributed to the exploitation and exporting of natural resources, particularly oil and gas and hence yet a further staples trap in what is an economic and social innovation age. Critics, as well as Finance Minister James Flaherty, have also been concerned about the rising debt levels of many Canadians and the extent to which this is both masking and undermining the economic fundamentals required for a sustained and sustainable recovery. On several occasions Flaherty has exhorted Canadians to reign in their spending and in a controversial move early in 2013 he intervened to prevent banks from lowering interest rates. This move was criticized by some within the Tory party who saw it as direct state interference in the markets and also by members of the public looking to secure lower borrowing and mortgage rates. At times the government's economic policies have appeared schizophrenic, particularly with regard to consumer spending, debt and interest rates but this in large part reflects the mercurial and uneven nature of the recovery.

In spite of the mixed economic signals the government has continued to pump millions of dollars into advertising its own Economic Action Plan (E A P) that will form a key 2015 election plank and that has become the working title of its budget speeches including the 2014 budget (see more below) The unprecedented amounts spent advertising the E A P have continued in spite of poll results showing that public patience with the self promotional messages may be wearing thin to the extent that they are now counter-productive. Public fatigue and cynicism with political branding was exacerbated by the government's investment of $2.5m in promoting the Skills Training Program that did not exist and still required provincial agreement and funding before it could be rolled out. The Canada Job Grant advertising was part of an $11-million fund set aside in 2012 for Employment and Social Development Canada to promote the government as a "job creator." Before the T V ad went to air, the government paid Environics Research Group almost $70,000 to conduct market research. They concluded: "The main message was consistently seen as positive and one that inspired hope … in light of seeing the new ad for the Canada Job Grant, most now believe the Government of Canada is on the right track regarding skills training and the job market in Canada."[2]

In spite of heavy marketing and the relatively positive economic outlook, the government has consistently struggled to press home its message, including the newly minted free trade deal with the EU that was supposed to provide a further "good news" announcement leading up to the Conservative party convention in early November 2013.

The Senate Scandal

Much to Harper's chagrin the year has been dominated by the Senate scandal and in particular the extent of the prime minister's knowledge and involvement. Tory party faithful as well as the broader public, the media and opposition parties, have demanded answers from the P M to questions about his involvement in the $90 thousand given to Senator Duffy. Harper's attempts to obfuscate and dissemble in the face of inquisitorial questioning from the opposition party leaders, the N D P's Thomas Mulcair in particular, have made for gripping theatre at times and may yet produce similar court room drama depending on the result of ongoing police inquiries.

The Senate scandal is politically significant for several reasons. First of all it places the second chamber firmly in the public spotlight and has exposed a clear lack of oversight and entitlement that the Harper government was elected to "clean up" in 2006. After eight years in office little has been done to reform the Senate as the Conservative's promised to do. Over forty new Conservative senators have been appointed by Harper even though he promised he would appoint none. And with some curious high profile appointments by Harper, many believe the Senate to be morally and ethically worse, not better, than when Harper came to power. Senate reform is now clearly on the agenda but unlikely to happen. Even if the Supreme Court rules that reform of the second chamber is legal under the constitution, there is little chance that a majority of the provinces will agree to change or to outright abolition, again thwarting Harper's oft-stated intent.

Second, the Senate scandal and the way it has been handled by Harper and the PMO, has reinforced the narrative of the Harper government as unaccountable, controlling, manipulative and contemptuous of the democratic process. His refusal to answer legitimate questions of fact in the House and the cynical and at times farcical antics of his parliamentary secretary (Paul Collandra MP), who often rose to answer questions on Harper's behalf, regularly made a mockery of Question Period with bizarre anecdotes and personal attacks on opposition members deliberately used to avoid and deflect questions. This may have bought Harper some valuable breathing space in the House but it may have damaging implications in the longer term for Harper's credibility and appeal amongst the electorate.

His declining popularity, indicated by numerous opinion polls, may be further compounded by his willingness to throw MPs, Senators and trusted advisors under the proverbial "bus" when politically expedient to so. This again fuels Harper's image as a ruthlessly cold and calculating politician and opens up the PM and his government from more damaging revelations from Senators Mike Duffy and Pamela Wallin, both former journalists, and perhaps Nigel Wright who has so far maintained a dignified silence in the face of attacks on his reputation, but may yet be required to give evidence under oath. Indeed there are signs that Harper's treatment of Wright has not been popular within sections of the party or amongst certain ministers with potential leadership challengers Peter MacKay and Jason Kenney both coming to his defence in a rare show of cabinet disunity.

Third, the Senate scandal has raised questions about Harper's judgement as well as the political and policy advice he is receiving, and may have further undermined his alleged status as a master tactician and strategist. In particular, questions have been raised about his choice of high profile senators based in Ottawa to represent regions far away from where they reside; a decision that led in part to the subsequent abuse of residency rules and the misuse of travel expenses as the line between senate duties and political fundraising became increasingly blurred. Questions have also been raised about the way an issue primarily about senate expenses was allowed to escalate into a political crisis leading directly to the Prime Minister's Office. Rather than attempting to cover up inappropriate expense claims a more transparent approach from the outset may well have limited the damage to a handful of senators. As always in politics the cover up is more damaging than the initial misdemeanour and by misjudging the Senate scandal the PM and his advisers have allowed it to define the political agenda in the run up to the next election.

A number of other policy lapses also lend weight to the view that Harper's political instincts are waning and have prompted speculation that he may be considering stepping down as leader even before the next election. The decision to shut down service centres for veterans may have been justified in terms of costs and benefits, but the political damage is significant and the way that it was mishandled by Minister of Veterans' Affairs Julian Fantino has alienated important sections of the Conservative base and added to the Harper government's narrative as uncaring and harsh. The apparent leaking of retired General Andrew Leslie's moving expense claims in February 2014 also looks to have backfired and raised further questions about the government's perceived inequitable treatment of military veterans. With General Leslie about to announce his candidacy for the Liberal Party in the next election at the 2014 Liberal convention, disclosure of his moving expenses (about $72,000) was no doubt intended to embarrass the former general. Instead it has also revealed many more instances which, on the back of the senators' expense scandal, have raised public ire and questions about the government's apparent inability to change policies to limit "generous" entitlements after eight years in office. For a party that has spent millions of dollars promoting its brand and policies it is bewildering that it would cause self inflicted wounds with veterans and many of its rank and file supporters who believed the Conservative party would put a stop to the entitlements enjoyed by public servants and military brass under successive Liberal governments.

Even more crucially two further post-budget events and bungled decisions by Harper led to direct and pointed attacks on Harper's personal reputation and leadership. The first was the thorough rebuke Harper received from the Supreme Court of Canada regarding his attempt to appoint Marc Nadon. Nadon as a Quebec appointee had to come from the province's highest courts or the bar and he did not. The Harper government tried to change the Supreme Court Act unilaterally rather than through constitutional processes.[3] And then Harper was also pilloried for having to fire Dimitri Soudas as executive director of the Conservative Party, a loyalist he had appointed only four months earlier but who had been intervening in the electoral riding of his partner and fiancée, Eve Adams, a Conservative MP.[4] In both these decisions Harper garnered more criticism, public and private, from the Tory caucus and local party supporters.

Finally, and somewhat ironically, issues such as the Senate scandal have allowed both opposition leaders to enhance their reputations. Mulcair has been widely lauded for his persistent, focused and at times surgical questioning of the Harper during question period. While less prominent in the House, Liberal leader Justin Trudeau has been able to steal a march on both his rivals, and enhance his leadership credentials, with an audacious move to eject Liberal senators from the caucus. By forcing independent status in the senate on formerly Liberal senators Trudeau has managed to find a pragmatic way to partially reform the senate without having to engage in tortuous constitutional wrangling. As a political ploy this is exceptionally shrewd. It looks like the Liberals are the only party to be responding to the public clamour for reform and it paints Harper into a difficult corner. He must either continue to do nothing, at least until the Supreme Court ruling is handed down, or he must follow Trudeau's lead. Neither option is politically attractive.

In addition to taking decisive action, Trudeau may also be protecting himself and the Liberal Party from further revelations by the auditor general whose report (forthcoming at the time of writing) is expected to implicate other senators in financial misdemeanours. Whatever the motives, the removal of the Senators has been packaged as a positive and democratic reform that will increase the effectiveness of the Senate as an independent chamber of sober second thought and eventually limit the influence of patronage and partisanship. Polling suggests the majority of Canadians see this as a very popular move by Trudeau with over two thirds of respondents indicating they support it and half of the Conservatives polled signalling they would be happy for Harper to follow suit.

By late February 2014 the impact of the Senate scandal, though far from over, and the responses to it, appeared to be having an impact on the popularity of the leaders and the three major parties. A CTV News/Ipsos Reid poll showed the Liberals establishing an eight-point lead over the Conservatives with 37 per cent saying they would vote Liberal, 29 per cent Conservative and 24 per cent NDP while 18 per cent were undecided.[5] Perhaps more worrying for the Conservatives and the NDP, the same poll found that 54 per cent of Canadians say they "agree" (16 per cent "strongly," 38 per cent "somewhat") that they "share Justin Trudeau and the Liberal's values when it comes to where Canada should be headed."[6]

Harper on the International Stage

In addition to sticking to the mantra of economic growth and jobs the Conservative's response to this dramatic shift in fortunes for the Liberal party has been partly to focus on Harper's role on the international stage. In addition to the EU free-trade deal mentioned earlier Harper has continued to travel abroad looking for new markets for Canadian exports and particularly oil and gas and other natural resources. This strategy has highlighted some tensions between the US and Canada over the XL pipeline and more specifically between President Obama and Prime Minister Harper on the causes, extent and seriousness of climate change. With Obama reluctant to commit to the pipeline before the next US elections, both for political and environmental reasons, the Harper government have become increasingly frustrated and vocal, and occasionally strident, as they seek to cement the deal before the next Canadian federal election.

A further high profile tour to Israel in January 2014 was significant for several reasons. Harper was again seen to be operating on a world stage and was accompanied by 208 Canadians representing diverse business interests, Jewish leaders and Christian representatives, plus an official delegation of 30 MPs, senators and officials. For Harper this was a chance to establish his and the party's staunch support for Israel. Although cynics would point out this represented a timely and shrewd domestic fund raising exercise, it also seemed at times to be a very personal and spiritual journey. Harper's address to the Knesset offered unequivocal support of Israel and established Canada as one of its strongest allies in the world. Some Muslim members of the Knesset were visibly angry and walked out during Harper's address and it will be interesting to see how the Canadian stance is viewed at home. Many of the key electoral battlegrounds are populated by immigrants and an increasing number are Muslim. This may have been a factor influencing the announcement that Canada would give Jordan $100m to help with the resettlement of Syrian refugees.

The Harper international agenda, albeit in an arguably less high profile way, is also revealed in chapter 14 in Ruby Dagher's analysis of the Canadian International Development Agency (CIDA) and CIDA's unambiguous shifting of support for the Canadian mining industry from a trade and developmental aid agenda to a trade and export agenda only. CIDA had itself been shifted to be under the control of the 'development' part of the Department of Foreign Affairs, Trade and Development.

Rob Ford and the Federal Battle for Toronto Area Swing Votes

Domestically, Toronto mayor Rob Ford's travails also helped to shift public attention away from the Senate scandal with the media circus providing the prime minister with some relief of sorts. However, Ford's brazen contempt for civic office, in addition to provincial scandals (particularly in Ontario and Quebec) and municipal corruption (e.g. the Charbonneau Commission of Inquiry) has fuelled concern that democracy and ethical standards in Canada are in decline and perhaps in crisis. Harper was quick to try and distance himself and the party from Ford's behavior but this has proved difficult to do so because of close political and personal ties.

Ford has been a strong supporter of Harper and his delivery of "Ford Nation" votes at the last federal election enabled the Conservatives to secure key marginal seats in and around Toronto that ultimately helped secure a majority government. Ford and Toronto have since been well rewarded with billions of dollars in federal funding for subway and other major infrastructure projects. Ford has also received personal endorsements from Harper and his cabinet colleagues as well as numerous photo-opportunities that Conservative strategists may now regret in part because the Ford factor could adversely affect swing ridings in the 2015 federal election where thirty new ridings, thought to be favourable to the Conservatives, will be present for the first time.

In addition, the unrelenting Rob Ford saga in Toronto appeared to highlight bitter cabinet divisions with two of Harper's most powerful cabinet members, Jason Kenney and Jim Flaherty engaging in a "profane dispute" on the floor of the House after the former had called for Mayor Ford to step down.[7] Finance Minister Flaherty, a close family friend of the Fords, confronted Kenney on the floor of the House about Ford. Several colleagues tried to separate the two believing they might come to blows over the dispute. Flaherty later became very emotional during an interview when asked to comment on Mayor Ford and was unwilling to condemn his behaviour and the Cabinet has since remained silent on the matter, although some commentators have suggested the rifts remain and may be linked to deeper cabinet and ideological divisions.

A Tory Backbench Revolt, Declining Democracy, and the "Fair" Elections Act

While the anti-democratic narrative associated with Harper has been reinforced by the Senate scandal and his continued contempt for Parliamentary process, it usually emerges out of concern for his controlling leadership style. In December of 2013, Michael Chong, a backbench Conservative MP, introduced the Reform Act, "an effort to strengthen Canada's democratic institutions by restoring the role of elected MPs through free votes and related measures.[8] Chong maintains his bill was not specifically designed with Harper in mind, but as MacNaughton and Stoney discuss in chapter 5, it was introduced to address public concern and perception that MPs have been reduced to impotent "lapdogs" as political power has continued to centralize in the hands of the PM and PMO.

While the private member bill is unlikely to succeed it has further highlighted concern, this time from within the Tory party ranks, that Canada's democratic system is being stifled by the heavy hand of centralized political control. As if to underline these concerns, in December 2013, the government moved to prevent employees of members of Parliament from discussing aspects of their work. By requiring staff to sign contracts, O'Malley claims this will "restrict their ability to share information – and stifle the kind of whistle-blowing that led to some of the revelations in the Senate scandal."[9]

In February 2014, Canada's Minister for democratic reform Pierre Poilievre tabled Bill C-23, the "Fair Elections Act," on electoral reform intended to introduce new and harsher penalties for violation of elections law, such as occurred in the so-called Tory party "Robocalls" affair, and address other issues and concerns. Many of the proposed reforms have been well received including: lifting the blackout release of election results until all polls close across the country; creating a mandatory public registry for automated election phone calls; increasing penalties for impersonation of election officials or deception that attempts to dissuade people from voting; increasing the political donations limit to $1,500 per person per year, from $1,200, and increasing local and national campaign spending limits by 5 per cent; allowing MPs in a dispute with Elections Canada to keep voting in the House of Commons and sit on committees until a judge rules on the matter; allowing candidates for party leadership to donate up to $25,000 to their own campaign, but makes it an offence for leadership debts to be left unpaid after three years; place tighter rules on voter identification at polling stations, and put an end to "vouching" for a voter not on the voters' list.[10]

More controversial has been the proposal to make the commissioner of elections independent of Elections Canada, and provide greater powers to crack down on election fraud. Currently, the commissioner of elections is appointed by the chief electoral officer, the head of Elections Canada. The chief electoral officer controls the commissioner's staff and budget, and directs investigations, putting the chief electoral officer in the position of both facilitating political candidates and policing them. Poilievre justified the proposed change by arguing that "The referee should not be wearing the team jersey … [i]ndependence is 'Governance 101.' It is normal to separate administration from investigations"[11] when in fact administration and investigation is often combined in many agencies and departments and Parliamentary watchdogs.[12] Opposition reaction to the bill has focused mainly on the process with Mulcair accusing the government of shutting down debate on what are significant and fundamental changes to electoral law. Substantive policy concerns have focused on the easing of election funding and donation restrictions which Mulcair believes will favour the Conservative party as they tend to have a disproportionate number of wealthy donors. While some commentators believe that a more independent commissioner will be a good thing, others question whether it will make any difference if he/she is not empowered to seek out the information required to conduct a proper investigation. Steven Shrybman, the lawyer who represented the Council of Canadians in its case to annul the results of six ridings in the 2011 federal election because of Robocalls said that "the bill would muzzle the chief electoral officer from speaking about voter fraud."[13] Marc Mayrand, the chief electoral officer said the bill would prevent him from speaking about anything beyond how, where and when to vote, and would prevent him from conducting surveys with Canadians on Elections Canada services. Continuing Poilievre's hockey metaphor, he responded, "What I know from this bill is that no longer will the referee be on the ice."[14]

The proposed reforms have raised questions in the House as to why a bill that is supposed to target election fraud is being used to prevent the chief electoral officer from speaking to the media and Canadians.[15] Opposition and media speculation suggests that the changes could be politically driven reflecting Harper's alleged mistrust of Mr Mayrand who has ruled against the government on several occasions, leading some Conservatives to question his impartiality.

The Rise of the Trudeau Liberals and an NDP Decline

For the NDP opposition leader Thomas Mulcair the last year must have been a frustrating one and does not portend well for the election if current trends continue. In spite of dominating performances in Question Period the NDP and its leader has failed to make up significant ground on the Conservatives and lost ground to Justin Trudeau and the Liberals. In addition there are clear signs that the Liberals are polling well in the NDP's power base province of Quebec and with the Quebec Parti Québécois government's rise in popularity as a result of an increasingly divisive values charter agenda, there is also every chance that federally the Bloc Québécois could re-emerge as a political force within the province. Nationally the NDP stands to lose the most if the anti-Harper vote strategically aligns itself with the Liberals as the best chance of defeating the Conservatives.

Chapter 5 by MacNaughton and Stoney focuses in detail on the rise of Justin Trudeau in the broader context of modern politics and the cult of personality. Thus far the Liberal party has relied on Trudeau's star power and charisma to re-establish its credibility both in terms of fundraising and public support. By positioning Trudeau as a "rose between two thorns," one portrayed as angry and tempestuous, the other ruthless and cold, the Liberals hope to attract disaffected Tory and NDP voters as well as the younger voters who may identify more with Trudeau's message of hope and change.

As the election draws nearer the Liberals will face increasing pressure to add some policy substance to their message and signs are that policies are beginning to emerge. In addition to Trudeau's commitment to legalize marijuana and establish a process for choosing independent senators, the Liberal party convention in February 2014 provided a clearer indication of philosophical and policy direction.

As Andrew Coyne suggests, Liberals will likely promise voters "more of the same" on the economy, but with a "more appealing face, literally and figuratively."[16] In addition to promising a more open and transparent style of government some of the emerging themes for changing the face of government include pursuing the sustainable development of Canada's natural resources, ensuring post-secondary education for at least 70 per cent of Canadians and better treatment for immigrants as citizens and not just itinerant workers.[17] In addition, as Trudeau attempts to position himself as the defender of the "middle class" warnings to the rich to "start sharing wealth or prepare for the consequences"[18] suggest that more targeted redistributive fiscal policies and social programs will be tabled although details have still to emerge. Moreover, defining the middle class is always problematical and moreover, the Conservatives repeated effort to show how their policies are aimed at "hard working Canadian families" is a direct competitive form of political discourse. In a CBC interview Trudeau stated that he had no intention of raising any taxes should he be elected prime minister,[19] so it will be interesting to see how he intends to square the fiscal circle. Given the semantics of modern day political rhetoric, this may not rule out "new" taxes and a carbon based tax could be an attractive option were it not for the Liberal's bitter recollection of former Leader Stephan Dion's disastrous "green shift" campaign.

With respect to investment, Trudeau appears to be open to foreign investment in the tar / oil sands and, according to Coyne, sees an opportunity for the federal government to act as a facilitator, bringing together sources of capital and building expertise in transportation, water and climate change mitigation projects. In particular the Liberals would like private sector pension funds and banks to invest strategically in more robust infrastructure.[20] This would help address the growing infrastructure gap and look at longer-term infrastructure needs rather than short-term objectives such job creation and retail politics. This could help renew the urban agenda that the Martin government promoted and invested in a decade or so ago but has since withered under the Conservatives.

It may also underpin important philosophical and ideological differences between the Liberals (and NDP) and the Conservatives with respect to the role of the federal government. By practicing so-called "open federalism" the Conservatives have deliberately scaled back the role and ambition of federal government in a number of policy areas and also in terms of intergovernmental relations and national federal-provincial agenda leadership. At the 2014 Liberal convention it became clear that Liberal party activists are looking for a Liberal government to play a much more prominent leadership role in several policy areas. Among the resolutions put before the convention many called for a wide range of national strategies including: transformative infrastructure, transportation, energy, manufacturing, childhood development, mental health, disability, water, pharmacare, youth employment, science, and innovation.[21] In addition, there were proposals to reverse cuts to employment insurance and old age security, expand the Canada Pension Plan, build a high-speed rail line from Quebec City to Windsor, create a Department of Climate Change, a Secretary of State for Water, a "government institution for peace," and many more.[22]

While there are political-electoral risks in having too little policy there are clearly risks as well in having too much, especially when it is a highly expansive agenda that has somehow to be financed. The costs involved would render many of these measures unrealistic, especially in light of the commitment not to raise taxes, exposing Trudeau to attack for putting forward an unfunded mandate as well as for having too many priorities. When first elected, Harper's minority government strategy was to commit to five oft-repeated priorities. Limited in scope they were highly effective in allowing him to deliver quickly on election promises such as cutting the GST and, by restricting the number of priorities, he also highlighted the relatively complex and shifting agenda of Paul Martin as Liberal prime minister from 2004 to 2006 which would eventually earn him the unfortunate moniker of "Mr Dithers."

In addition to balancing the need to define his own leadership priorities with the need to satisfy party expectations and ambition, Trudeau will have to withstand the attacks on his leadership credibility that will inevitably portray him as a political lightweight who is, in the Tory view, "out of his depth." In this context it may be Trudeau's proclivity for making inappropriate and ill judged comments that pose the biggest threat to the party's electoral chances and his leadership skills will come under further intense scrutiny.

HARPER PRIORITIES: THE 2013 SPEECH FROM THE THRONE AND THE 2014 BUDGET

In the above changing political-economic and democratic context, the Harper government's priorities are revealed in both the October 16, 2013 Speech from the Throne (SFT) and its February 11, 2014 Budget Speech. Coming four months apart, they are both key but also different occasions to fashion and sell agendas and values for the fall 2015 federal election. Not surprisingly the two documents are similar in broad scope and intent. We focus more on the Budget Speech but some initial points about the SFT are also needed.

It is of some interest to note that the SFT both starts and ends with the reference to Canada's coming 150 anniversary as a country in 2017. In the early SFT mention it is linked with a call that Parliament will "relentlessly advance and uphold ideas that are inclusive, honourable, selfless, smart and caring at every turn without fail."[23] At the end of the SFT, the Harper government refers to an array of 2017 celebrations that "our government will join with Canadians in honouring this momentous milestone,"[24] indicating that the government is clearly banking on being in power then. It is only within the context of the 2017 event that the SFT mentions the Senate but noticeable by its absence is mention of the Senate scandal, the event, along with Harper's handling of it and association with it, that has contributed most to his and his government's downfall over the last year. It states merely, instead, that "the status quo in the Senate of Canada is unacceptable."[25]

A second feature of the sft, an event where legislative intentions are more prominent than in budget speeches, are two legislative promises. The first is found in the promise early in the sft that the government "will enshrine in law its successful and prudent approach" by "introducing balanced-budget legislation" that "will require balanced budgets during normal economic times, and concrete timelines for returning to balance in the event of an economic crisis".[26] There is no indication of what might constitute normal economic times or what kind of economic crisis or indeed crises it might have in mind.[27] Moreover, as soon as such macro budgetary reforms are opened for discussion, other issues will emerge. These include the kind discussed by John Lester in chapter 7 regarding the relations between the two spending worlds of normal spending and tax expenditures. Such a debate has not been held in Canada since the Mulroney reform agenda that lead to the closing of numerous loopholes and the establishment of the Goods and Services Tax (gst). The Harper Conservatives have been masters of the political arts of the tax boutique, where numerous small gestures like new tax credits to categories of Canadians have been created in virtually every budget since 2006, including one noted below in the 2014 budget.

A second legislative promise is that the government will "enshrine the polluter pay system into law."[28] This occurs in the sft's resource development section where again "responsible resource development" that "respects the environment" is stressed. This is a somewhat surprising statutory promise because responsible resource development, as the Toner and McKee analysis in chapter 8 shows, has seriously weakened Canada's environmental laws, all of which imply some form of de facto polluter pay principle. Again, this is a statutory promise where the notion of "paying" is left vague as well as the practical issues of "how much" and for "how long." The analysis in chapter 8 of federal water management in the Harper era does not augur well for Harper era environmental promises and policies. Cargnello, Brunet, Retallack, and Slater show a strong initial stated commitment by Harper in the 2006–07 period but then water management like so much else regarding environmental matters disappeared from the government's action plans. In both the 2013 and earlier sfts and budget speeches, the Harper government was far more likely to link the environment to natural resources and national parks and, as we see below, natural heritage and Canada's traditional resource industries. Indeed, in the 2014 priority-setting commitments, one of its only promises was funding for the repaving and upgrading of roads in Canada's national parks. Climate change as an environmental issue is not mentioned.

There are other legislative items in the sft including new rail safety measures in the wake of the Lac-Mégantic rail crash that killed 47 people in an explosive fire and that destroyed key parts of the town centre. A new array of laws and amendments are also promised to continue and extend the Harper agenda of "supporting victims and punishing criminals." Craig Jones' analysis in chapter 4 views earlier features of this Harper agenda as being more a punishment agenda than a justice agenda. It is also in keeping with other analysis that has cast Harper as a Hobbesian prime minister re-erecting and extending the night-watchman state.[29]

The Harper government's de facto environmental agenda has also included an overt attack on some Canadian charities, especially environmental ones. Some have opposed Canada's energy export agenda and as a result the Conservative government ordered Revenue Canada to conduct a broad scale review of many charities regarding whether they were violating their statutory limits on lobbying activity. Chapter 8 examines these threatening kinds of moves but the analysis by Kryvoruchko and Rasmussen in chapter 10 also shows how much broader the political-economic issues are for the valuable role played by both regular charities and those larger ones with foundation status.

Other features of the SFT and its order of priority ranking and political credit claiming are closely similar to the 2014 Budget Speech and hence we will present and deal with them under the Budget Speech per se. As in recent budgets, the Budget Speech by Finance Minister James Flaherty is itself titled *Canada's Economic Action Plan*. In the 2014 version, Flaherty stresses that "this prudent plan builds on our record of strong, sound and consistent fiscal management. It is a low-tax plan to promote jobs and economic growth and support Canadian families. And it is a common sense plan that will see Canada return to a balanced budget in 2015."[30] He went on to remind Canadians that through its action plans, "since the depths of the recession, Canada has led the G-7 in job creation" … and that coming out of the recession Canada "had a triple A credit rating with a stable outlook – which was and still is virtually unmatched among our peers."[31] But he also stressed that the world economy is still fragile.

In order of priority, the speech then set out four expressed priorities (see more details below).

- Balancing the Budget (in 2015 including a surplus in 2015 and higher surpluses in later years);
- Keeping taxes low (showing that since 2006, an average family of four pays $3,400 less in tax in a year);
- Promoting jobs and economic growth (including measures on research and innovation; responsible resource development; and environment):
- Standing up for families and communities (including a Consumers First agenda)[32]

In the related budget documents, including the *Budget in Brief*, there is a summary of both past actions and also some typically smallish new or extended budget items (in a Budget that Flaherty described as "prudent" and "boring").

The budget items are rearranged to some extent in the Budget in Brief as follows (with only a sample of items noted in our illustrative list; for others see the Budget in Brief document);

Connecting Canadians with Available Jobs
- Better aligns training with labour market needs through the Canada Job Grant.
- New generation of Labour Market Agreements for Persons with Disabilities;
- Creates Canada Assistance Loan;

Fostering Job Creation, Innovation and Trade
- Planning and Construction of Windsor-Detroit International Crossing
- Creating new Canada First Research Excellence Fund ($1.5 billion overnext decade);
- Additional $500 million over two years to the Automotive Innovation Fund to support new strategic research and development projects;

Responsible Resource Development, Conserving Canada's Natural Heritage, and Investing in Infrastructure and Transportation
- Providing $28 million over two years to the National Energy Board for comprehensive and timely reviews of project applications and to support the Participant Funding Program;
- Asserting Canada's sovereignty in the North;

Supporting Families and Communities
- Invests $305 million over five years to extend and enhance broadband internet service for Canadians in rural and Northern communities;
- Introduce a Search and Rescue Volunteers Tax Credit in recognition of the important role played by these volunteers;
- $ 390 million over five years to strengthen Canada's food safety system;
- Introducing legislation to prohibit unjustified cross-border price discrimination to reduce the gap between consumer prices in Canada and the United States.[33]

While these are among the aspects of the Harper agenda chosen by the Tories for emphasis in the Budget Speech and the Budget in Brief, other aspects of the fiscal and policy package are not given emphasis but instead are in the longer imposing Budget papers.

Most assessments of Budget 2014 saw it as minimalist endeavour with Harper and Flaherty holding fire until the 2015 Budget when, with a healthy fiscal surplus in place, new election spending and tax reduction measures can be deployed in the run-up to the 2015 fall election.[34] With this strategy in mind, the Harperites in a very different sense saw themselves as good to go for another election victory and majority government.

Slower economic growth, however, had led to projected revenue shortfalls and thus new budget cuts had to be found. One is a slicing of £3.1 billion from the defence capital budget over the 2013–14 through to 2016–17 fiscal years. This is a cut like a lot of capital spending that may not be a cut but rather is moved about in the fiscal future year mists. Moreover, defence spending, including debacles in defence equipment procurement is not something that is a shining example of Conservative fiscal or managerial competence. Another item in budget cuts, which the Harper Budget 2014 was strongly prepared to draw attention to was lower costs due to new requirements for public servants to pay a higher proportion of their pension plan contributions and the government less.

In and around the Budget 2014 event, discussion had emerged as well, about how the Tories were gearing up for their previous election platform promise, namely that when a surplus emerged in 2015, they would introduce a "family tax cut" in the form of tax sharing for couples with dependent children under eighteen years of age.[35] But this tax sharing provision or income splitting had already been criticized as a provision that would only favour richer couples.[36]

More significantly, Finance Minister Flaherty right after his 2014 Budget Speech expressed his opposition to such a plan, indicating in the process a more open rift with Harper than at any time in the government's eight year existence. And then Flaherty resigned as minister of finance on March 18, 2014. Harper's replacement for Flaherty is Joe Oliver who had been the minister of natural resources where he had not garnered a favourable political verdict in large part because of his belligerent approach to environmentalists and scientists in Canada and in the US in the battle over the oil sands and related pipelines. It is only when he was appointed as Minister of Finance that Canadians became more aware of his pre-politics career and qualifications as an investment banker and as a securities regulator in Ontario.

A further post-budget event centred on changes in the rules to federal infrastructure funding. The $14 billion Building Canada Fund had been announced in the 2013 Budget and Flaherty drew attention to it again in his Budget Speech for 2014. But it was two days after the 2014 Budget speech that Prime Minister Harper announced the new infrastructure rules just as the battle over how to spend the billions was about to begin.[37] Interestingly, the Harper speech was referred to on his website, simply as "PM delivers remarks in Gormley," one of his Conservative MP's Ontario riding.[38] Media coverage pointed out that under the new rules, local roads will not qualify for the new fund though they had in previous programs. Municipalities will also not be allowed to use federal gas tax money as part of their one third funding of large projects. And any project costing over $100 million now had to be screened and approved by P3 Canada the federal crown corporation.[39] P3 Canada now had binding powers to decide whether the project had to be a public-private partnership.[40] This P3 screening was a provision that Harper described in Gormley as "an excellent additional tool to allow taxpayers to share risk and thus help get projects completed on time and on budget."[41]

Harper does see himself in different policy contexts as a person interested in good and better common sense public management. Jennifer Spence's account in chapter 12 of the national shipbuilding model for procurement gives the Harper government and key ministers considerable credit for this initiative as a more rational and less inherently political approach to procurement, though stressing that it may not work for other fields and areas of procurement. Amanda Clarke's analysis in chapter 9 also gives the Harper era some credit for fostering or allowing new bottom-up open information and collaboration systems within and across the public service. The Harper government is accurately seen as supra top-down controlling regime but new technologies and information sharing are being fostered within the public service and by the senior public service. Other managerial reform initiatives in the Harper era are also examined in Evert Lindquist's assessment in chapter 6 of Ottawa's search for more parsimonious cost and efficiency reporting, some of which are also driven by the better use of new information technologies and ways of assembling and displaying spending and program information across the government.

The Harper era started, via its 2006 Accountability Act, as a self-proclaimed accountability government but it has morphed into something quite different where accountability and transparency is not the descriptor that would first come to mind. The Rounce and Levasseur analysis in chapter 2 shows the continuing secrecy and non-accountable practices regarding public service cuts. The Lee and Cross assessment in chapter 3 of the first five years of the parliamentary budget officer (PBO) also draws attention to similar barriers and also to the failure of the government to make the PBO into a true parliamentary office in the first place when Harper and PCO officials had instead lodged it within the Parliamentary Library. And most telling of all is the Harper era's concerted effort to muzzle federal scientists and related policy evidence both as an aspect of its hyper attack politics and continuous campaigning strategy and in the nature of its science budget and program cuts. Chapter 13's analysis by O'Hara and Dufour give a compelling account of these attacks on accountability overall and science in particular as do other recent published assessments.[42]

CONCLUSIONS

Fast moving and looming developments in 2013 and early 2014 have led to the above conjecture that the Harper government is "good to go" and could be defeated in a fall 2015 election. The scenario emerges first out of both the entrenched Senate scandal and Harper's personal association with it. But it also gains plausibility with the emergence of Justin Trudeau and his Liberal party leading in the polls and also with the quite normal "time for a change" ethos that seeps into Canadian politics when one party and one prime minister has governed for 8 years and now wants four more (after a 2015 election). The massive electoral defeat of the Marois Parti Québécois government in the April 7, 2014 Quebec election by a resurgent Quebec Liberal Party also now enters the federal and federalist political climate in ways other than just ending the threat of another referendum on Quebec independence.[43] The reaction of all three federal party leaders was obviously a sense of political relief. There is also a sense of changing policy and political calculus for each of Harper, Trudeau, and Mulcair as they contemplate a 2015 federal election.

At the same time, however, the governing Conservatives have an economic agenda that they want to and are capable of defending. As we head into the 2015 election year it seems likely that the Conservative's will stick with Harper as leader unless there are further serious revelations arising out of the police investigation into the Senate scandal or the polls continue to show Trudeau pulling away from the other two main party leaders. It is likely to be Harper's worst nightmare to be defeated by a Trudeau. In spite of the trying events of the last year, it seems that predictions of Harper's metaphorical retirement "walk in the snow" were and are premature and that he will try and continue to transform Canada through an approach perhaps best described as radical incrementalism. At some point Harper's legacy of political and social change in Canada will warrant the moniker of "Harperism" such will have been its impact both at home and internationally.

More immediately he, and the Conservative party, must hope that emphasis on the economy and attacks on the other two parties can outweigh a weak record on the environment and overcome the potentially damaging but accurate narrative of an anti-democratic and at times sinister government. With three main parties in the electoral race and with three contrasting, albeit mainly centrist visions, and quite different leadership and campaign styles on display, it promises to be an important and fiercely contested campaign. If the margin of victory is as tight as the polls predict then it could well be that the thirty new seats created by Elections Canada and thought to favour the Conservatives could determine the outcome of the next election. How ironic if Mr Harper has Canada's chief electoral officer Marc Maryand and his department partially to thank for a third term in office.

NOTES

1 See Tim Harper, "Eight Words in Senate Scandal That Could Stick to Tories." *Toronto Star* (December 2, 2013).

2　Sophia Harris, "Canada Job Grant Ads Cost \$2.5M for Non-existent Program, Commercials Were Part of \$11-million Fund to Promote Government as a Job Creator," *CBC News* (January 13, 2014) http://www.cbc.ca/news/politics/canada-job-grant-ads-cost-2-5m-for-non-existent-program-1.2495196.

3　Jeffrey Simpson, "The Harper Government Deserves the Supreme Court's Rebuke," *Globe and Mail* (March 21, 2014).

4　Lawrence Martin, "The Harper Machine Is in Disarray," *Globe and Mail* (April 1, 2014).

5　CTV News.ca, Andrea Janus (February 20, 2014).

6　Ibid.

7　Evan Solomon, "Jason Kenney's Rob Ford Comment Sparked Profane Rebuke from Jim Flaherty – Toronto Mayor's Admitted Drug Use Causes Conservative Caucus Rift to Erupt on Commons Floor," *CBC News* (December 13, 2013), http://www.cbc.ca/news/politics/jason-kenney-s-rob-ford-comment-sparked-profane-rebuke-from-jim-flaherty-1.2463984

8　http://www.reformact2013.ca/Backgrounder.pdf.

9　Kady O'Malley, "Hill Staff Asked to Sign Lifetime Confidentiality Agreements, Mandatory Standardized Form Meant to Replace 'Ad Hoc' Agreements, Speaker's Office Says," *CBC News* (December 11, 2013).

10　Leslie MacKinnon, "Election Reforms Include End to Blackout on Early Results, Pierre Poilievre also Announces Harsher Penalties for Breaking Canada's Election Laws" *CBC News* (February 4, 2014).

11　Leslie MacKinnon, "Election Reforms."

12　See G. Bruce Doern, Michael J. Prince, and Richard J. Schultz, *Rules and Unruliness: Canadian Regulatory Democracy, Governance, Capitalism, and Welfarism* (Montreal and Kingston: McGill-Queen's University Press, 2014).

13　Mark Burgess, "Tories' Elections Reform Bill Allows for 'Creative Accounting' with Campaign Fundraising, Says a Leading Expert, Also Targets Elections Canada's CEO," *The Hill Times* (February 10, 2014).

14　Ibid.

15　Ibid.

16　Andrew Coyne, "Liberal Plan to 'Reinvent' Party Appears to Be in Disarray," *Postmedia News* (February 21, 2014).

17　Lee Berthiaume, "Trudeau Warns the Rich to Start Sharing the Wealth or Prepare for Consequences," *Postmedia News* (February 22, 2014).

18　Ibid.

19　Ibid.

20　John Ivison, "Trudeau Targets Infrastructure investment – without Tax-and-Spend Liberalism," *National Post* (February 19, 2014).

21　Coyne, "Liberal Plan to 'Reinvent' Party," 13.

22　Ibid.

23　Government of Canada, *Speech from the Throne* (October 16, 2013), 1.

24　Ibid., 12.

25 Ibid.

26 Ibid., 3.

27 On temporal and crisis budgeting, see G. Bruce Doern, Allan Maslove, and Michael J. Prince, *Canadian Public Budgeting in an Age of Crises: Shifting Budgetary Domains and Temporal Budgeting* (Montreal and Kingston: McGill-Queen's University Press 2013).

28 Government of Canada, *Speech from the Throne* (October 16, 2013), 5.

29 See Michael J. Prince, "The Hobbesian Prime Minister and the Night-Watchman State: Social Policy under the Harper Conservatives," in *How Ottawa Spends, 2012–2013: The Harper Majority, Budget Cuts and the New Opposition*, 53–70, eds. G. Bruce Doern and Christopher Stoney (Montreal and Kingston: McGill-Queen's University Press, 2012).

30 Government of Canada, *The Budget Speech* (February 11, 2014), 1.

31 Ibid.

32 Ibid., 2–5.

33 Examples listed are found in Government of Canada, *The Budget in Brief* (February 11, 2014), 5–16.

34 See for example, Matthew Stewart and Daniel Fields, *Federal Budget, 2014–15: Stay Tuned for Next Year* (Conference Board of Canada, February 11, 2014); and William Watson, "No Lobbyist Left Behind by Flaherty's Budget," *Financial Post* (February 13, 2014).

35 See Chantal Hebert, "Flaherty's Discontent Signals Troubles for Stephen Harper," *Toronto Star* (February 12, 2014).

36 Alexander Laurin and J.R. Keselman, *Why Income Splitting for Two-Parent Families Does More Harm than Good* (C.D. Howe Institute, October 4, 2013).

37 See Bill Curry, "Municipalities Caught Off Guard by Details of $14 Billion Infrastructure Fund," *Globe and Mail* (February 13, 2014).

38 See Prime Minister of Canada, "PM Delivers Remarks in Gormley" (February 13, 2014).

39 Infrastructure Canada, *The New Building Canada Fund* (Infrastructure Canada, 2014).

40 For a critical analysis of P3 Canada, see Christian Bordeleau, "Public-Private Partnership Canada and the P3 Fund: Shedding Light on a New Meso Institutional Arrangement," in *How Ottawa Spends, 2012-2013: The Harper Majority, Budget Cuts and the New Opposition*, 145–160, eds G. Bruce Doern and Christopher Stoney (Montreal and Kingston: McGill-Queen's University Press).

41 See Prime Minister of Canada, "PM Delivers Remarks in Gormley" (February 13, 2014), 3.

42 See Professional Institute of the Public Service of Canada, *Vanishing Science* (Professional Institute of the Public Service of Canada, 2014); and Jonathan Gatehouse, "When Science Goes Silent," *Maclean's* (May 3, 2013), 1–8.

43 Graeme Hamilton, "Pauline Marois Loses Riding Then Resigns, as Quebec Liberals Hand Parti Quebecois a Stunning Defeat," *National Post* (April 8, 2014).

PART ONE

Economic and Social Policy Agenda and Challenges

2 Government Retrenchment and Public Service Cuts: A Tale of Two Processes

ANDREA ROUNCE AND KARINE LEVASSEUR[1]

INTRODUCTION

Canadian governments are not immune to deficit situations and when such situations arise, program and public service cost reductions occur. There have been several attempts to reform federal programs and the public service in such deficit contexts. Two important reforms include Program Review (PR) in the mid-1990s and the Harper era Strategic and Operating Review (SOR). Both reforms have been framed differently, but both emphasize deficits, economy, greater efficiency, and service delivery. This chapter comparatively assesses these reforms and uses PR to better understand SOR.

We argue there are important differences both in terms of ideological approaches, size / scope of the impact, and transparency such that the dissimilarities of these processes outweigh their commonalities. We first provide a contextual overview of the reforms, then critically assess the commonalities and dissimilarities of both, and discuss the lessons learned.

CONTEXT

Understanding the economic, ideological, and public service realities is necessary to compare and contrast PR under the Chrétien Liberals and SOR under the Harper Conservatives. These reform processes clearly reflect the different realities of their time.

Program Review

While much of the focus on public sector downsizing is placed firmly on the Chrétien Liberal government under PR, Lee and Hobbs argue that the original workforce adjustment policy was rooted in the first Mulroney Conservative government.[2] Over 26,000 employees were identified as being "affected" under the Conservative plan; however, the workforce adjustment process resulted in a reduction of 4,684 full-time equivalents and an increase in part-time indeterminate, term, and seasonal employees.

Prime Minister Kim Campbell began the implementation of the deCotret Report's recommendations in June 1993, which included the restructuring of ministries and the changing of central agency roles. Campbell reduced the number of federal ministries from 32 to 23, regrouped them, and eliminated six cabinet committees. She also froze public sector wages.

When the Liberals were elected on October 25, 1993, the debt and deficit had risen to a point where government had little choice but to act quickly in order to keep the country's economy from declining. By 1994, budgetary problems – particularly a growing debt (see Table 2.1) – led to higher interest rates, reflecting the decreased confidence global markets had in Canada's fiscal situation, and its debt-financing.[3] Additionally, the country faced a "crisis of governance, which generated demands for a change in the structure and functioning of the federation."[4] These crises led to a process known as "Government Renewal," which included policy reviews, PR (efficiency analysis of existing departments and programs), action plans to reduce duplication of provincial activities, alternate service delivery, and incorporation of new technology to reduce costs.[5]

In its first budget of 1994, the Liberal government committed to reducing the deficit to 3% of GDP (or $13 billion) by 1996–97. In his budget speech, Finance Minister Paul Martin announced a comprehensive review of all departmental programming, known as "Program Review" (PR). The approach of PR was to examine existing programs and departmental activities to determine if the program: was still in the public interest; was a legitimate and necessary role for government; should be realigned with the provinces; should be delivered in partnership with the private / voluntary sector; could be made more efficient; and if it was affordable.[6]

As well as extensive cuts to departmental operating budgets, with savings in government operations to exceed $3 billion, Martin announced a two year extension of the salary freeze and suspension of pay increments within grade.[7] Lee and Hobbs argue that "in the 16 months after the Liberals assumed office (November 1993 until March 31, 1995) the public service was reduced by 15,000 full-time equivalents from 237,200 to 222,400. During the last half-century, no government was able to reduce the Public Service by 15,000 (FTE). Yet the Liberals achieved this in 16 months without any new incentive programs."[8]

Table 2.1
Surplus / deficit in billions 1985–1994

Year	Prime Minister	Surplus / Deficit (In billions)
1985	Mulroney	-33.3
1986	Mulroney	-29.8
1987	Mulroney	-29
1988	Mulroney	-29.9
1989	Mulroney	-29.1
1990	Mulroney	-33.9
1991	Mulroney	-32.3
1992	Mulroney	-39
1993	Mulroney / Campbell / Chrétien	-38.5
1994	Chrétien	-36.6

Source: Finance Canada, Treasury Board Secretariat, Statistics Canada.

While many of these reductions were due to retirements, attrition would not satisfy budget projections. The government argued that spending restraint – not tax increases – would be required to decrease the scope of the debt and the resulting deficit. Martin announced that the "public service will be reduced by some 45,000 positions, of which 20,000 will be eliminated by the summer of 1996."[9]

PR was a reform process carefully managed from the centre of government, mainly due to the need for consistency. Paquet and Shepherd have argued that the process of PR meant a "new rationale for a strong central government has therefore evolved in the form of the need for process and rules. This is the means through which ownership of Program Review has come to be claimed by the Treasury Board Secretariat, not so much by design as by default."[10]

While the minister for public service renewal was responsible for guiding and answering to the changes being made under PR, Treasury Board was responsible for reviewing and implementing the changes, including the reduction of the public service. PR was "conducted entirely by insiders, senior political and bureaucratic officials who were likely to bear the brunt of any serious transformation of the governance system."[11] This approach had significant consequences for officials within the system as well as for the government's commitment to transparency.

These cuts, along with structural and institutional changes to intergovernmental partnerships and social welfare, had the desired impact of reducing the deficit and putting the country on a more secure global economic standing. By 1997, government had eliminated the deficit and begun running a surplus until 2008. However, the reduction in the scope and size of government had tremendous impacts on the morale of those in the public service and on the government's ability to do what it was tasked. The auditor general's report noted that the public service was being asked to do more with fewer resources.[12] While PR solved some of government's problems, it created others that would need to be addressed by future governments.

Strategic and Operating Review

Our analysis centres on the scope of retrenchment under SOR as a source for comparative analysis with PR. SOR is differentiated from strategic review. Strategic review, conducted annually between 2007–2010, assessed the costs of programs for every federal department and agency. Each department "identified its lowest-priority or worst-performing programs, totaling at least 5% of program spending. The money from these activities was then moved to higher-priority programs."[13] These cumulative reviews sought to generate savings of $2.8 billion.[14]

The focus of SOR is broader than strategic review and includes an assessment of salaries, benefits, and outsourcing of work. Treasury Board President Tony Clement conceptualizes SOR as an extension of strategic review, but there is an important difference between the two: "[SOR is] intended to find significant one-time cuts in services, rather than ongoing and permanent cuts as in the case of the former. "Strategic reviews" were introduced to force departments and agencies to find critical savings and to use these savings to align with key government priorities. Such reviews are conducted every four years with the objective of finding five percent savings from low performing, low priority programs and services."[15]

SOR was announced in the 2011 budget as a one-year process with Tony Clement leading a cabinet committee charged with identifying efficiencies in the public service.[16] Focusing on $80 billion of direct program spending, the cabinet committee is meant to find up to $11 billion in savings over five years because of savings related to initial cuts.[17] In 2013, the clerk of the Privy Council created the Deputy Minister Board of Management and Public Service Renewal to shape the public service for the future.[18]

As with the Chrétien government, the Harper government faced significant financial challenges related to national and global economic situations. While the minority government was able to maintain a surplus for 2006 and 2007, deficits began to accumulate starting in 2008 ($5.8 billion). Expenditure restraint, with the goal of balancing budgets, was an evident part of Conservative budgets from 2010 onward.[19] Actions established in the October 2007 Economic Statement and in Budget 2008 focused on spending reductions as well as tax reductions to enable Canada to manage through a period of global economic recession.[20] The slowdown of the US economy required Canada to take action to prevent repercussions for the Canadian economic system. While Finance Minister Flaherty suggested that Canada had been running surpluses, paying down debt, managing inflation, and experiencing low interest rates and low unemployment, it was clear that the Canadian economy was likely to slow down in the coming years.[21]

The Economic Action Plan (E A P) – launched in 2009 – focused on positioning Canada for the global recession.[22] While the E A P would require running temporary deficits in order to boost the Canadian economy, Finance Minister Flaherty initially predicted a return to surplus by 2013. Expanded government activity like the E A P normally requires more public servants and the core public administration also increased in size until 2011 (see Figure 2.1). However, Budget 2010 indicated the potential for a shrinking public service, by freezing the total amount spent on government salaries, administration, and overhead.[23]

While the S O R process is an internal-to-government set of activities (as was P R), there have been many criticisms of both its processes and outcomes. Criticism has come from public sector unions and from Opposition members. In S O R, when positions are to be eliminated in a department or agency, all of the public servants in that classification are considered to be "affected." This means that if 20 out of 100 positions are to be eliminated, all 100 workers will receive notice that they are "affected." Nicknamed the "Harper Hunger Games" by the media, the use of "affected" workers in the process has led critics to suggest the government has "unnecessarily fann[ed] stress and anxiety in the workplace."[24]

Many grievances were filed by public sector unions to contest how employees were informed about the impact of S O R. However, Wayne Wouters disagreed, arguing that through "diligent human resources planning and effective implementation, we have managed the system-wide changes sensitively and responsibly. Workforce adjustment training for executives and managers at all levels equipped them to manage these changes effectively. Management teams also worked closely with bargaining agents to carefully implement the downsizing measures."[25]

Whatever the perspective on the implementation of S O R, 2013–14 is crucial both for S O R and for the public service as a new round of collective bargaining occurs for most of the public sector unions. The prime minister's Advisory Committee on the Public Service also argued that "this will be an important opportunity for both management and labour to think about the kind of employment model they want to build for the future Public Service."[26] Lee argues that these activities, including the cuts, will be "used as a wedge issue in the next (election) campaign."[27]

ANALYTICAL FRAMEWORK: ASSESSING
THE DIFFERENCES AND SIMILARITIES

Depth and Breadth of the Reductions

S O R is designed to secure *operational* savings including staffing costs / benefits and not intended to review program spending and transfer payments.

Figure 2.1
Total core public administration (FTEs) 2005–2012

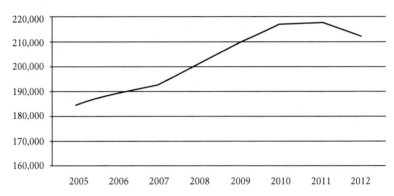

Source: Population of the Federal Public Service by Department, Statistics Canada.

As of March 31, 2012, the overall percent of the total public service population had not declined significantly (Table 2.2). However, more job losses are
expected in the next two fiscal years but this must be seen in the context of the
steady increase in the size of the federal public service between 2006 and 2010
under the Harper government.

Comparatively, PR sought to reduce government spending by $29 billion
with a reduction in the public service of 45,000 positions. Prima facie, these
numbers reveal the magnitude of cuts under PR compared to SOR.

Planned spending for key departments between 2013–14 and 2015–16
indicate a range of financial increases or reductions under SOR (Table 2.3).[28]
Of this list, three departments will experience an increase: Human Resources
and Social Development Canada (HRSDC), Finance and National Defence.
It is important to remember the annual Strategic Review process occurred
just before SOR so it is possible that prior to 2013-2014 some departments
experienced a reduction in financial resources that would not appear in this
table. Other departments, notably Industry (-23.5%) and Natural Resources
(-25.7%) are expected to experience significant reductions.

In terms of reductions in full-time equivalent (FTE) positions, every department listed in Table 2.3 will experience a reduction, although some more
than others. Industry Canada, for example, will experience a 0.1% reduction
in the number of FTE positions whereas Aboriginal Affairs and Northern
Development will experience the biggest reduction followed by Veterans
Affairs and HRSDC.

Under SOR, some departments will experience greater reductions than
others. The PR process was not proportional either and left many departments
significantly affected given the depth of the cuts. In 1995, the most affected
departments included: Agriculture and Agri-Food ($450 million), Industry
($900 million), Fisheries and Oceans ($200 million), HRDC ($900 million),

Table 2.2
Federal public sector employment figures

Year	Total population	Year-over-Year Change (%)
2006	249,932	-
2007	254,622	1.88%
2008	263,114	2.94%
2009	274,370	4.28%
2010	282,955	3.12%
2011	282,352	-0.21%
2012	278,092	-1.51%

Source: Office of the Chief Human Resources Officer, Treasury Board of Canada Secretariat, http://www.tbs-sct.gc.ca/res/stats/ssen-ane-eng.asp

Natural Resources ($600 million), and Transport ($1.4 billion).[29] Scale matters here as P R instituted much deeper cuts than S O R (Table 2.5). Two departments that took the most severe cuts under P R are the same two departments that experienced the biggest reduction in spending under S O R: Industry and Natural Resources.

Geographically, job losses are not evenly distributed either under S O R. Some jurisdictions (notably P E I and Nunavut) experienced a slight increase in the population of public servants in their jurisdiction between 2011 and 2012 (Table 2.4). The majority, however, experienced a decline, notably N W T, New Brunswick, Yukon, and Alberta.

Regionally, the North experienced the greatest reduction between 2011–12, followed by Atlantic Canada, the West and Central Canada (Table 2.6). As a caveat, S O R is still 'in process' and thus it may be possible that these percentages change in the next fiscal year. Given that public sector jobs constitute 'good' jobs with benefits and pensions, these figures give rise to discussions as to the degree that 'equity' plays in public sector cuts especially in historically economically disadvantaged regions.

The types of employee and employment categories impacted seem to differ between P R and S O R, although this observation may change as more data on S O R becomes available. P R showed that "Blue collar, technical, and semi-skilled people with lower levels of education opt[ed] disproportionately for E D I [Early Departure Incentive] or similar incentives to leave their jobs, while professionals have lower propensities to leave."[30] It is unclear whether or not this trend will be seen in S O R.

Assessing Transparency

In both P R and S O R, governments have been challenged to provide greater transparency. While Paquet and Shepherd noted that during P R the O A G was

Table 2.3
Changes in financial and human resources of key departments

Department	Financial Resources ($ millions in planned spending)				Human Resources (FTEs) reductions			
	2013–2014	2014–2015	2015–2016	Change (%)	2013–2014	2013–2014	2014–2015	Change (%)
Aboriginal Affairs and Northern Development	7,905.0	6,909.5	6,753.9	-14.5	4,997	4,456	4,259	-14.8
Agriculture and Agri-Food Canada	2,450.5	2,282.8	2,278.6	-7.0	5,721	5,439	5,425	-5.2
Justice	748.2	626.6	617.5	-17.5	4,719	4,643	4,643	-1.6
National Defence	18,312	19,220	18,978	3.6	94,008	93,414	93,414	-0.6
Public Safety	443	404	383	-13.5	1,070	1,023	1,015	-5.1
HRSDC	110,293.8	114,355.2	119,404.7	8.3	20,532	18,516	18,239	-11.2
Public Works and Government Services	6,078.9	5,626.9	5,245.2	-13.7	12,498	12,524	12,261	-1.9
DFAIT	2,285.6	2,115.6	2,031.8	-11.1	12,413	12,353	11,733	-5.5
TBS	242	230	229	-5.4	1,847	1,746	1,738	-5.9
Finance	87,611.8	89,624.3	93,261.3	6.5	757	746	743	-1.9
Citizenship, Immigration and Multiculturalism	1,655.4	1,493.0	1,465.2	-11.5	4,689	4,499	4,304	-8.2
Industry	1,219.6	1,012.9	933.3	-23.5	4,873	4,867	4,867	-0.1
Canadian Heritage	1,317.2	1,367.9	1,087.1	-17.5	1,493	1,485	1,391	-6.8
Transport Canada	1,523	1,450	1,336	-12.3	5,276	5,137	5,093	-3.5
Health	3,301.1	3,222.2	3,128.3	-5.2	9,375	9,037	8,915	-4.9
Fisheries and Oceans	1,674.9	1,581.5	1,534.8	-8.4	10,409	10,072	9,999	-3.9
Environment	951.6	991.1	846.0	-11.1	6,518	6,349	6,221	-4.6
Veterans Affairs	3,643.6	3,538.4	3,511.2	-3.6	3,115	2,796	2,755	-11.6
Natural Resources	2,767	2,316	2,056	-25.7	4,156	4,117	4,006	-3.6

*operating expenditures only

Source: 2013–2014 Report on Plans and Priorities

Table 2.4

Public sector employment by province / territory

	NU	NWT	YK	BC	AB	SK	MB	NCR	ON	QC	NB	NS	PEI	NL	Outside CDA
2011	277	746	441	25,650	16,228	6,597	11,614	116,357	40,764	33,043	8,672	11,844	3,257	5,222	1,640
2012	287	680	423	25,377	15,651	6,476	11,518	114,656	40,767	32,421	8,173	11,630	3,289	5,162	1,582
Change (%)	3.6	-8.8	-4.0	-1.0	-3.6	-1.8	-0.8	-1.5	0.0	-1.9	-5.8	-1.8	1.0	-1.1	-3.5

Note: NCR is the National Capital Region. Data for Ontario and Québec excludes data form the NCR.

Source: Office of the Chief Human Resources Officer, Treasury Board of Canada Secretariat, http://www.tbs-sct.gc.ca/res/stats/sneg-aneg-eng.asp

Table 2.5
Change in spending levels under PR and SOR

Most affected department	Change in spending levels under PR	Change in spending levels under SOR
Agriculture	-21.5%	-7%
Industry	-43%	-23.5%
Fisheries and Oceans	-27.2%	-8.4%
HRDC/HRSDC	-34.8%	8.3%
Natural Resources	-49.4%	-25.7%
Transport	-50.8%	-12.3%
Justice	-8.4%	-17.5%
Aboriginal Affairs and Northern Development	11.9%	-14.5%

Data from 1995 Budget, Table 4.2 on page 36; and 2013-2014 Report on Plans and Priorities.

unable to audit the PR process due to the limited amount of information recorded and much information was classified as advice to Cabinet,[31] it is also clear that the OAG had much to say about PR as the decade wore on: "In the 1998 April Report of the Auditor General of Canada, Chapter 1 focused on Expenditure and Work Force Reductions in the Public Services. The OAG reported that, despite the apparent success of PR, government still had work to do regarding transparency and accountability."[32] Information was held tightly within government for both processes. One of the challenges with assessing SOR has been the difficulty in gathering information about the proposed and actual cuts to programming as well as the public servants supporting that programming. Problems accessing this information has resulted in questions about process and outcomes from media, opposition, unions, and the parliamentary budget officer (PBO).

The PBO's report of October 3, 2012 concluded that while quarterly reporting had improved since 2011, "gaps persist in the disclosure of federal restraint measures as less than one-third of organizations affected by the 2012 Budget reduction initiative explain the operational impacts."[33] Within a week of releasing this report, Parliamentary Budget Officer Kevin Page issued an ultimatum to 56 departments and agencies, saying that if they did not provide fundamental information on cuts and savings he would go to court to get the information.[34]

Clerk of the Privy Council Wayne Wouters says, "in his view, federal organizations should not respond to the PBO."[35] In a May 15 letter to Page, Wouters argued that the departments had to provide information first to affected employees and then to their unions, as required under the collective agreements.[36] At this point, unions were also asking for this same information.

Table 2.6
Public sector employment by region

	North	West	Central	Atlantic
Change in public sector employment from 2011 to 2012	-5.1%	-1.8%	-1.2%	-2.6%

Source: Percentages calculated by authors based on data from Office of the Chief Human Resources Officer, Treasury Board of Canada Secretariat, http://www.tbs-sct.gc.ca/res/stats/sneg-aneg-eng.asp

While the first rounds of cuts to the public service have been implemented, they will be ongoing. Cuts were announced in April 2013 to the Department of Fisheries and Oceans and Agriculture and Agri-Food Canada and further cuts are anticipated. What is unclear is whether these cuts are SOR cuts or the result of SR recommendations. It is also unclear exactly how many public servants have been affected or have left the public service altogether as of May 2013. Minister Clement pointed observers to the department plans for more detailed understandings of how cuts would be achieved.[37] However, as the 2012–13 plans were released in May 2013, more detailed information is only now being made available. David Macdonald's study for the Centre for Policy Alternatives has argued that this is much too late for MPs to make budgetary decisions: if they cannot determine the impact of cuts at the time of approving the budget, then that is problematic.[38]

Concerns around transparency in SOR focus primarily on what cuts have been made, are being made, and how public servants are learning about these cuts. It is not always clear who is making the recommendations related to the SOR cuts and whether or not SOR recommendations can be fully separated from the other reform processes. Questions about transparency are also linked to concerns about political ideology and purpose. The Harper government has also made an effort to address the power of public sector unions. Pierre Pollievre (MP, Nepean–Carleton) launched a campaign in fall 2012 designed to garner support for making union dues optional for public sector workers and potentially for those in federally-regulated industries. This proposed bill would "force unions to further open their books, including what they spend on political activities."[39] Additionally, Budget 2013 suggests that government would be addressing sick leave and other benefits while working to bring public sector salaries in line with the private sector. The recent decision to have the Treasury Board finalize any bargaining agreements with crown corporations reinforces the government's focus on managing the perceived power of public sector unions. This element of public sector reform speaks to the approach being taken by the Harper government and their attitude toward public servants – which may be linked to how they have approached public sector reform overall.

CONCLUSIONS

It is challenging to compare two reform processes, particularly when one is ongoing and the other is historically complete. However, the experience and analysis of P R allows us to ask different questions and conduct a more thorough analysis of S O R. It is clear that P R and S O R have distinctive characteristics as well as being similar in a number of ways.

While both rounds of public sector reform were paired with governance and administrative reform, the Liberal government highlighted governance reform much more than the Harper government. The Harper government is clearly revisiting the role of government, but in an arguably less transparent way. Both governments emphasized the importance of economic stability, but the crisis facing the Liberal government was many years in the making and required the government to act quickly.

The Liberal public service reform was an expansion of existing reform processes established under the previous Conservative government. They were able to capitalize on the difficult decisions made by a previous government without having to take full responsibility for the actions. The Harper reform to the public service came after an upswing in the size of the public service, related in part to the increased government activity in its E A P. What is perhaps most intriguing about both processes is the vulnerability of two departments – Industry and Natural Resources – that experienced the biggest reductions under P R and S O R. While crucial to the maintenance of the capitalist system overall (Industry Canada) and the development of a key sector within the capitalist system (Natural Resources), both experienced significant reductions under governments of different political stripes. Perception matters here: Industry Canada and Natural Resources may have been perceived as hindering the ability of the market to grow and thus, in turn, delay economic recovery. If this perception was in place, it is easy to understand why funding was reduced to these departments under both processes.[40]

Both processes of reform were managed centrally. While both processes involved a deputy minister committee, the role of Treasury Board could not be underemphasized. While under the Liberals, a Minister was appointed to oversee Public Sector Reform, the Harper Government saw the President of Treasury Board taking on that role. Some say the Harper government's approach has been "more 'hard-nosed' and 'mean-spirited' compared to the downsizing of the 1990s when the Liberals shed 50,000 jobs in the public service."[41] This may be a reflection of the differences in attitudes toward the value of the public service and / or the role of government; it may also reflect the chronological distance between P R and the ongoing implementation of S O R. It may also be a reflection of decisions not being thought out fully in advance.

Transparency has been a key issue in any discussion of SOR. While there certainly were issues with PR – including how decisions were made and implemented – in SOR there are fundamental questions surrounding the number of people affected, how they will be impacted, and how government will ensure a solid public service to meet the needs of Canadians going forward. This highlights not only the central control and decision-making at play in SOR, but also the limited role of parliamentarians in being able to fully assess financial information within the context of budgetary planning and approval.

NOTES

1 The authors thank Dr Evelyn Nimmo for her editing assistance. They also thank the editors and reviewers for helpful comments. An earlier draft was presented to the second annual Canadian Association of Programs in Public Administration (CAP-PA) Conference at Ryerson University, Toronto, Ontario on May 27, 2013.

2 Ian Lee and Clem Hobbs, "Pink Slips and Running Shoes: The Liberal Government's Downsizing of the Public Service." In *How Ottawa Spends, 1996–1997: Life under the Knife*, ed. G. Swimmer (Ottawa: Carleton University Press, 1996), 341.

3 Canada, Department of Finance, *Canada: A New Framework for Economic Policy* (October 1994), 82

4 Gilles Paquet and Robert Shepherd, "The Program Review Process: A Deconstruction." In *How Ottawa Spends, 1996–1997: Life under the Knife*, ed. G. Swimmer (Ottawa: Carleton University Press, 1996), 39.

5 Ibid., 40.

6 Canada, Treasury Board of Canada Secretariat, "Getting Government Right" (1997), 5.

7 Canada, *Budget Speech 1994*, 14.

8 Lee and Hobbs, "Pink Slips and Running Shoes," 355.

9 Canada, *Budget Speech 1995*, 9.

10 Paquet and Shepherd, "The Program Review Process," 61.

11 Ibid., 51.

12 Canada, Office of the Auditor General, "April Report of the Auditor General of Canada, 1997." See Chapter 1, "Maintaining a Competent and Efficient Public Service."

13 Jessica Bruno, "A Primer: Feds' Strategic Review, Strategic Operating Review, Administrative Services Review and Red Tape Commission." *The Hill Times, July 4, 2011*.

14 Canada, Budget 2012: Annex 1, http://www.budget.gc.ca/2012/plan/anx1-eng.html Accessed March 8, 2013.

15 Bruce Doern and Christopher Stoney, "The Harper Majority, Budget Cuts, and the New Opposition." In *How Ottawa Spends: The Harper Majority, Budget Cuts*

and the New Opposition, eds. Bruce Doern and Christopher Stoney (Montreal and Kingston: McGill-Queen's University Press, 2012), 12.

16 This committee is actually a subcommittee of the Cabinet Priorities and Planning Committee.
17 Jessica Bruno, "A Primer: Feds' Strategic Review, Strategic Operating Review" (2012), 2.
18 Canada, Clerk of the Privy Council, *2013 Report*, 12.
19 Canada, *Report of the Parliamentary Budget Officer* (October 3, 2012), 1
20 Budget Plan 2008, 8. http://www.budget.gc.ca/2008/pdf/plan-eng.pdf Budget Speech http://www.budget.gc.ca/2008/pdf/speech-discours-eng.pdf
21 Canada, Department of Finance. *Budget Speech 2008,* 3.
22 Canada, Department of Finance. *Budget Speech 2009,* 4.
23 Canada, Department of Finance. *Budget Speech 2010,* 14
24 Kathryn May, "Tony Clement Questioned on Toll on Public Service from Cuts, Lawyer's Suicide." *Ottawa Citizen* (September 21, 2012).
25 Canada, Clerk of the Privy Council, *Annual Report to the Prime Minister on the Public Service of Canada: Twentieth Annual Report* (2013–14).
26 Ibid., Annex B, 3.
27 Ian Lee, as cited in Jessica Bruno, "Public Service Reforms 'Step One' in Conservatives 2015 Re-election Plan: Lee." *The Hill Times* (March 25, 2013).
28 We use 2013–14 as a starting point for the analysis because a significant portion of the reductions under SOR are expected to start in this fiscal year.
29 Lee and Hobbs, "Pink Slips and Running Shoes," 362.
30 Ibid., 371.
31 Paquet and Shepherd, "The Program Review Process."
32 Canada, Office of the Auditor General. *1998 Report of the Auditor General of Canada.* See Chapter 1, "Expenditure and Work Force Reductions in the Public Service." Accessed May 10, 2013. http://www.oag-bvg.gc.ca/internet/English/parl_oag_199804_01_e_9307.html
33 Canada, Parliamentary Budget Officer. "Monitoring Implementation of the Government's Expense Plan" (Ottawa, ON: Office of the Parliamentary Budget Officer, October 3, 2012), i.
34 *The Globe and Mail,* "Budget Watchdog Says He Is Willing to Go to Court to Get Information on Federal Cuts" (October 7, 2012).
35 As cited in *The Hill Times* (September 10, 2012), 8.
36 Letter from Wayne Wouters, clerk of the Privy Council to PBO (May 15, 2013).
37 Jessica Bruno, "MPs Missed Chance to Make Informed Decision of 29,000 PS Job Cuts: Canadian Centre for Policy Alternatives." *The Hill Times* (April 15, 2013).
38 David Macdonald, *The Fog Finally Clears: The Job and Services Impact of Federal Austerity* (Ottawa, ON: Canadian Centre for Policy Alternatives 2013). http://www.policyalternatives.ca/publications/reports/fog-finally-clears
39 Kathryn May, "Public Service Unions Worry whether They Can Survive Government Campaigns," *Ottawa Citizen* (October 9, 2012). http://www.ottawacitizen.com/

business/Public+service+unions+worry+whether+they+survive+government /7364888/story.html Accessed October 10, 2012.
40   The authors thank Patrice Dutil for raising this point.
41   Kathryn May, "Tony Clement Questioned on Toll on Public Service from Cuts, Lawyer's Suicide." *Ottawa Citizen* (September 21, 2012).

3 The Parliamentary Budget Officer: The First Five Years

IAN LEE AND PHILIP CROSS

INTRODUCTION

Now that five years has passed since the establishment of the Parliamentary Budget Office (PBO) and the recent exit of Canada's first parliamentary budget officer, Kevin Page, it is timely to evaluate the role of both the office and the first incumbent. During the past five years, it is not hyperbole to suggest that the relationship between the parliamentary budget officer and the Government of Canada was confrontational on both sides degenerating, at times, into name calling by both sides. The obvious question to dispassionate and non-partisan observers is why? The auditor general of Canada and other parliamentary watchdogs such as the privacy commissioner or the access commissioner have never experienced such a negative relationship with the government and in such a short period of time.[1]

Supporters of the Harper government have argued that Kevin Page crossed the line into advocacy and partisanship while supporters of Kevin Page argued that the government simply revealed its mean spiritedness and hyper partisanship. Prophetically, T.S. Eliot anticipated this in his post-World War I masterpiece, "The Hollow Men," when he wrote, "Between the conception / And the creation / Between the emotion / And the response / Falls the shadow." We first look at the creation of the PBO and its mandate. This is followed by a brief review of the PBO in the 2008 to 2013 period. A summary analysis of the PBO is offered regarding what went right, what went wrong and what reforms are needed. Conclusions then follow.

THE CREATION OF THE PBO

The Canadian election of 2006 was fought over the enduring question of accountability in the context of the Abscam scandal and the subsequent Gomery Inquiry that revealed fundamental failures of accountability by the Liberal government of the day. The Harper conservatives were elected – albeit with a minority – on a platform of enhanced accountability. And, true to his word, on April 11, 2006, after assuming power, Harper's first major Bill, C-2, provided for conflict of interest rules, restrictions on election financing and measures respecting administrative transparency, oversight and accountability. This package was entitled The Federal Accountability Act and it included the creation of the PBO.

However, this provision by the Harper government did not allow for a truly independent parliamentary PBO. Rather, it placed the PBO under the auspices of the Library of Parliament. In the end, the legislation received Royal Assent on December 12, 2006 with the mandate of the PBO defined in Section 79.2 of the Parliament of Canada Act:

> 79.2 (a) provide independent analysis to the Senate and to the House of Commons about the state of the nation's finances, the estimates of the government and trends in the national economy;
> (b) when requested to do so by any of the following committees, undertake research for that committee into the nation's finances and economy:
>   (i) the Standing Committee on National Finance of the Senate or, in the event that there is not a Standing Committee on National Finance, the appropriate committee of the Senate,
>   (ii) the Standing Committee on Finance of the House of Commons or, in the event that there is not a Standing Committee on Finance, the appropriate committee of the House of Commons, or
>   (iii) the Standing Committee on Public Accounts of the House of Commons or, in the event that there is not a Standing Committee on Public Accounts, the appropriate committee of the House of Commons;
> (a) when requested to do so by a committee of the Senate or of the House of Commons, or a committee of both Houses, that is mandated to consider the estimates of the government, undertake research for that committee into those estimates; and
> (b) when requested to do so by a member of either House or by a committee of the Senate or of the House of Commons, or a committee of both Houses, estimate the financial cost of any proposal that relates to a matter over which Parliament has jurisdiction.

Section 79.3(1) provided for the PBO to have access to free and timely access to any financial or economic data in the possession of the department that are required for the performance of his or her mandate. However, exceptions were included in Section 79.2 of the Act:

(a) that are information the disclosure of which is restricted under section 19 of the Access to Information Act or any provision set out in Schedule II to that Act; or

(b) that are contained in a confidence of the Queens Privy Council for Canada described in subsection 69(1) of that Act, unless the data are also contained in any other record, within the meaning of section 3 of that Act, and are not information referred to in paragraph (a).

On April 27, 2006, Bill C-2 was referred to House of Commons Legislative Committee on Bill C-2 for review. The Act contained five complex sections on disparate issues. The Legislative Committee held nineteen meetings with witnesses concerning the contents of Bill C-2 and heard over seventy individuals and groups of witnesses. During those nineteen meetings, the creation of the PBO was only raised at three meetings. Of particular note, the PBO and the decision on its placement and role was never discussed with the sponsoring minister, the president of treasury board, John Baird, nor was it discussed with the chief librarian of Parliament.

When the bill was referred to the Senate Standing Committee on Constitutional and Legal Affairs for review on June 27, 2006, hearings included the testimony of Mr William Young, the parliamentary librarian, concerning the PBO's placement within the Library of Parliament, under his control. Mr Young had clear convictions that the PBO should be placed under his authority: "I believe it is essential to the effectiveness of this new function, especially from the perspective of Parliament as a whole, and from that of the government, that the parliamentary budget officer be clearly understood to be a specialized capability, fully integrated within the Library of Parliament and not a free-standing parliamentary officer or institution." Mr Young elaborated on the importance of this reporting structure:

> There must be one person accountable for its work to you people. Within that framework, however, I see this person as being akin to an associate parliamentary librarian with a special designated function. Because there will be a special designated function, obviously that person will need the ability to make decisions with regard to that function, to carry out the responsibilities associated with that function and to have the support required to do his or her job in an appropriate manner. The position would include an independent mandate to some extent within the library, but it

would definitely, for the purposes of accountability to Parliament and to the Speakers, who are my bosses, flow through me.

However, Mr Peter Dobell, the founding director of the Parliamentary Centre pointed out that this reporting structure could result in cultural clashes:

> It is proposed that this be part of the library, but I think, depending on who the head of PBO is and how much he or she takes up the mandate, it could be a tense relationship, because, as Bill Young pointed out, the library is neutral and is very careful to be neutral. It does not stick its neck out. This office will be expected to stick its neck out, and that, I think, is going to produce tension. I am happy that a man of Bill Young's ability is in that job and he has good personal relationships, because unless he is able to get hired someone who does not use the mandate and does not undertake an initiative, I think this is going to be difficult.

Mike McCracken, chair and chief executive officer of Informetrica Limited also testified during that same day and followed-up on the Librarian's concern about the PBO's access to data. Mr. McCracken's concern was not with the cost but rather that government data would be provided in a timely manner, if at all to the PBO. He stated: "There will be tension with central agencies. The Department of Finance has a long history of opposing anyone who criticizes their efforts, whether that be the Economic Council of Canada, which the department managed to kill in 1991–92; private sector agencies, who the department takes great umbrage with, or other agencies within government federally and provincially. There is no reason to believe that blissfulness will suddenly emerge in that area."

REVIEW OF THE PBO: 2008–2013

Despite the Accountability Act receiving royal assent on December 12, 2006, Canada's first parliamentary budget officer, Kevin Page, was not appointed until March 25, 2008 due to setbacks during the appointment process. One of the issues concerned the classification level of the PBO for the PBO Director had been set at a GCQ5 which was equivalent to a Director General in the Federal Public Service. As the Senate Standing Committee on Finance reported in May 2008, the Parliamentary Librarian noted that "no candidate was willing to accept the position at the then current level of classification and salary."[2]

The Standing Committee subsequently recommended the classification of the PBO be raised but Mark O'Sullivan, then assistant secretary to the cabinet for senior personnel and special appointments informed the committee that the "PCO decided to leave the classification unchanged but provide a higher salary to Mr. Page."[3]

With Mr Page installed as the parliamentary budget officer, different understandings over the meaning of "independent" soon became apparent. On August 15, 2008, Kevin Page reported that during his consultation process "parliamentarians were of near unanimous view that the PBO should employ a full transparent, open publishing model."[4] Page's belief was revealed five days before the federal election, on October 9, 2008, when he released the Afghan study stating that the "total projected mission cost of up to $18.1 billion over the 2001–02 to 2010–11 period, represents close to $1,500 dollars per Canadian household."[5]

It has been a long standing practice in federal politics that no member of the federal public service or watchdog agencies releases any report during the writ period because no public servant should influence in any way the outcome of an election. The Afghan Report was very controversial for it contradicted the government cost estimates and gained widespread media coverage. The beginning of a fractious relationship can be dated from this event. Life did not become easier for the Conservatives after the 2008 election. On November 20, 2008, the PBO released its Fiscal and Economic Assessment and predicted that: "modest deficits are projected in the near term of $3.9 billion in 2009–10."[6] On November 27, 2009, Finance Minister Flaherty, in his Economic and Fiscal Statement predicted "a small surplus."

Shortly thereafter, the PBO were informed that their budget was only going to be increased by 1.5% which meant that his budget would be nearly $1 million short of the proposed $2.7 million budget that he had been lead to believe that he would be receiving. Kevin Page reacted publicly, stating that "My budget was cut after we talked about a different economic scenario. It looked more like interference to me … It's asinine to be cutting oversight in a period of time when you're going into a deep recession, and adding a significant fiscal stimulus package. This is the time when you have to make sure there's proper oversight."[7]

Behind the scenes, things were not any more positive for the PBO. On February 25, 2009, the parliamentary librarian requested, through the speakers of the Senate and the House of Commons that co-chairs of the Standing Joint Committee on the Library of Parliament "undertake a review of the issues that have arisen with regard to the implementation of services of the Parliamentary Budget Office."[8]

The Standing Joint Committee decided to focus on "three main themes: governance and independence; the current approach taken by the PBO to providing services to clients and outside communications and the budget allocated to the PBO for the current fiscal year."[9] It strongly supported the parliamentary librarian and in its first recommendation stated that the "Speakers of the Senate and the House of Commons direct the Parliamentary Budget Officer to respect the provisions of the Act establishing his position within the Library of Parliament. The Parliamentary Budget Officer reports to the Parliamentary Librarian and, as a senior official of the Library, it is his responsibility to participate fully in management activities and to work closely with the Library's other service areas."[10] The committee report went on to say that the "Committee believes that the PBO's services are a natural extension of the services already provided by the Library of Parliament to parliamentarian and parliamentary committees."[11]

The release of the PBO's Afghanistan study was also reviewed by the Joint Committee and they were unequivocal in their seventh recommendation: "That the Speakers of the Senate and the House of Commons direct the Parliamentary Budget Officer not to release any report during a general election."[12] Debate was no less vigorous when it came to the third theme, the PBO's budget. The PBO's budget had remained at the 2008–09 levels. Once again, the Joint Committee did not agree with the PBO's position. Its report stated that: "any increase to the budget to the PBO must be approved and presented by the Parliamentary Librarian."[13] The Joint Committee, in its eighth recommendation linked any future increases to the PBO's budget to its compliance with the recommendations contained in the committee's report.

Over the first year of its operation, the PBO clashed repeatedly with the government, the parliamentary librarian, and the Standing Joint Committee on the Library of Parliament. In so doing, the PBO had become a "white knight" for the opposition as well as the media. However, many media questioned its future effectiveness given the controls that had been put in place in conjunction with the PBO budget reduction. On July 6, 2009, the PBO provided its five-year economic forecast to the House of Commons Finance Committee with the understanding that it would be released later that week to other Parliamentarians and the public. Contrary to the Government's forecast, he predicted $156-billion in cumulative budgetary deficits over the next five years and higher than predicted job losses. Kevin Page also stated that the "federal government now had a structural deficit that would not disappear once the recession ended, and that either spending would have to be cut or taxes raised if the budget was to be brought back into balance."[14]

But the confidentiality of the forecast was short-lived as the Liberal opposition leader leaked the document to media.[15] Again, there was Conservative furore and opposition glee, both over the contents of the forecast as well as the breach. Reaction from the prime minister was swift. He called "Page's conclusions 'dumb,' but he did concede that the government would not necessarily stick to the five-year timeline for naturally returning to a surplus position."[16] On the issue of the unauthorized release, Professor Sutherland of the University of Victoria said that "it was wrong of the OLO to break the embargo ... He should be allowed to make his own mistakes. He is in enough hot water, and if he is attempting to follow the rules of his appointment, the Liberals should allow him to do so as that is what they advocated as members of the Library Committee."[17]

On September 30, 2009, Kevin Page responded to the Joint Committee on the Library of Parliament recommendations to reform the PBO. His budget was still short $1 million. However on November 19, 2009, the parliamentary librarian appeared before the committee to advocate for $484,000 in supplementary estimates.[18] This request was supported by the Joint Committee. On March 3, 2010, the 2010–11 main estimates were tabled and included an allocation of $2.8 million for the PBO and, at last, the PBO's original budget was reinstated.[19]

However, controversy and the PBO did not go away. In June 2010, the PBO released one of his most contested reports, "The Funding Requirement and Impact of the 'Truth in Sentencing Act' on the Correctional System in Canada." This report forecast the cost of the government's Bill C-25, Truth in Sentencing Act. The bill was originally tabled in the House of Commons on March 27, 2009 and was intended to limit the credit a judge may allow for any time spent in pre-sentencing custody in order to reduce the punishment to be imposed at sentencing.[20]

Minister of Public Safety Vic Toews stated on April 28 that the implementation of Bill C-25 would cost $2 billion over five years.[21] The PBO figures were much higher. As reported on the CBC News on June 22, 2010: "It projected that annual costs of correctional services would more than double by 2015–16, from $4.4 billion to $9.5 billion, and responsibility for funding the majority of this would shift from the federal government to the provinces and territories."[22] Minister Toews was not willing to enter into the fiscal debate, stating: "If you indicate that he wasn't getting any information from Correctional Service Canada, he must be making this up."[23]

Before the end of 2010, Kevin Page was already telling media that he would not seek a second term as parliamentary budget officer.

It could be argued he finally understood the Conservative government would not reappoint him. Although they could hardly remove him without a major outcry, reappointment was highly unlikely. Others might argue that it freed Kevin Page from any vestiges that may have lingered in moderating his language in dealing with the government. As we see below, the last half of his mandate was no less controversial than the first.

In 2011, another major PBO report was released concerning the cost of acquiring a new fleet of fighter jets for Canada. On July 16, 2010 Minister of Defence Peter MacKay announced that the Government "has committed approximately $9 billion to the acquisition of 65 F-35 aircraft and associated weapons, infrastructure, initial spares, training simulators, contingency funds and project operating costs. Delivery of the new aircraft is expected to start in

2016."[24] Reaction from Parliament via the opposition parties was swift. They decried the lack of a competitive process, whether this was in fact the "right jet" and expressed skepticism concerning the cost.[25] They turned to the PBO to review the deal.

The PBO did not disappoint the opposition. The report, issued on March 10, 2011, maintained that the "PBO has estimated the total program cost – including acquisition and ongoing sustainment – to be US $29.3 billion. Divided over 65 aircraft, this results in a cost of approximately US $450 million per aircraft in FY 2009 dollars."[26] This was nearly three times as much as the original government estimate. The government rejected the PBO's estimate noting they had taken into account costs outside of the government estimates. The government argued the total costs would be about $16 billion over 20 years – nearly half what the PBO estimated, $29.3 billion, but over 30 years.[27]

However, on April 5, 2012, Auditor General Michael Ferguson stated the government would have known that the F-35 was estimated to cost $25 billion, not the $14.7-billion figure the public was told in the weeks before the last federal election. The AG said that the $25-billion figure: "would have been known throughout government."[28] In short, the AG backed the PBO.

Throughout 2012, the PBO continued to publicly clash with the Government and its slow release or refusal to release financial documents. In particular, the PBO had sought departmental financial information related to the 2012 Budget, specifically with respect to savings and reduction measures. Throughout the summer and fall, Kevin Page exchanged letters with the Clerk of the Privy Council and even sought a legal opinion as to his right to access that information.[29] On November 21, 2012, the PBO referred those questions to the federal court to confirm if the work requested by the Leader of the Opposition was within his mandate.[30] This action was unprecedented in the PBO's 5-year mandate. Although the Government and the PBO had disagreed many times during his mandate, the PBO had not appealed to the court previously.

By the end of 2012, no process had been started to replace the incumbent PBO. Speculation swirled as to whether the Government would even replace Kevin Page. His five-year mandate would come to an end on March 25, 2013. On March 7, 2013, the government published the job description and selection criteria for the Parliamentary Budget Officer. It also announced that Parliament's chief librarian Sonia L'Heureux would assume the role of interim budget officer. Interestingly, the court case to clarify the budget office's mandate was scheduled for March 21 and 22, 2013. In April 2013 the Federal Court of Canada ruled that it was within the mandate of the PBO to request this information.[31] Finally, on August 30, 2013, the government announced the appointment of a career public servant, Jean-Denis Fréchette, an economist with the Library of Parliament as the new permanent head of the PBO.

WHAT WENT RIGHT, WHAT WENT WRONG,
AND WHAT NEEDS TO BE REFORMED

The PBO provided a credible independent analysis of some major policy issues in the last five years that was absent previously. Indeed, the International
Monetary Fund found that the PBO "has built up a good reputation, both
domestically and internationally and gain(ed) credibility." The decision
of the PBO to release all its studies ensured a more fully informed debate
around costing (i.e. Afghanistan, F-35s, etc). However, the review of the first
five years of the PBO revealed three major issues regarding the accountability,
independence, and mandate of the PBO.

Accountability and Independence of the PBO

Unfortunately, there was a profound structural design flaw embedded in the
act that established the PBO from the very beginning that was perhaps not
fully understood by parliamentarians, the political parties and senior PCO
officials who advised on the construction of the PBO. Having said that, we
can surmise that the PMO fully understood the consequences of this decision. As discussed above, there was very little debate during parliamentary
committee reviews of the Federal Accountability Act and there was no experience in Canada with a parliamentary budget officer to draw on. With
Mr Page installed as the parliamentary budget officer, it quickly became obvious that views regarding to what degree he would be "independent" varied
greatly. The press release from the government house leader, Peter Van Loan,
on March 14, 2008 stated that the "Parliamentary Budget Officer is an independent officer of the Library of Parliament who reports to the Speakers
of both chambers."

Placing the PBO as a hierarchical subordinate within, and effectively accountable to, the Library of Parliament represented a profound structural
contradiction. As highlighted earlier, then parliamentary librarian Bill Young
pointed out, the library is neutral and is very careful to be neutral. It does
not stick its neck out. However, the PBO's mandate requires it to "provide
independent analysis to the Senate and to the House of Commons about the
state of the nation's finances, the estimates of the government and trends in
the national economy." This was captured succinctly by the International
Monetary Fund: "The Library of Parliament provides confidential services
to members of Parliament (MPs). This contrasts with the PBO's approach of
publishing all reports and correspondence and actively promoting its analysis
through the media."[32] How could the PBO then provide independent, potentially contradictory analysis through the parliamentary library? Inevitably,
these contrasting mandates pitted the Library of Parliament against the PBO
as evidenced by the library's attempts to suppress PBO reports.

In response, Kevin Page exercised the independence that he thought the PBO should have, not what the legislative mandate provided. Many have called him a hero for this but it has not resolved the debate surrounding the extent to which the PBO is independent. If the mandate of the PBO is to provide independent analysis that may not be palatable to the sitting government, then the enabling legislation should be amended to remove the PBO from the ambit of the Library of Parliament and be legislated as an independent officer of Parliament – similar to the Office of the Auditor General and other international fiscal councils.

Mandate of the PBO

The mandate assigned to the PBO unwittingly built conflict into the relationship for it was given responsibility to evaluate Finance Canada (and Treasury Board) economic forecasts and outlooks, notwithstanding that the Bank of Canada, IMF, OECD, and every major bank, pension fund, think tank and industry association already publish their own economic forecast and/or economic outlook. Not only was this a waste of very scarce PBO resources with a very small budget but it created inevitable hostility in duelling forecasts between Finance and PBO. However, as pointed out by the IMF, "In general the fiscal forecasts of the government and the PBO are close."[33]

Instead, the PBO should be refocused on what have historically been the most important lacunae in Ottawa – a horizontal evaluation of the financial cost of a policy across departments and ministries e.g. the Afghan costing study that analyzed costs of the multiple departments in Afghanistan and not just those of DND – rather than the vertical, silo-centric model of government, represented by the Main Estimates. Although the Afghan study was inappropriately released five days before an election, it was nonetheless a superb example of horizontal financial and costing analysis.

This raises a related issue. There must be a clear division of labour between the auditor general and the PBO. Auditors audit the past, not the future, because the future has not yet arrived. The AG should not be involved in evaluating procurement bids, such as the F-35s now that we have a PBO which is responsible for evaluation of prospective spending.

CONCLUSIONS

Properly understood, the establishment of the PBO needs to be seen in the context of earlier examples of macro economy advisory bodies and in relation to the nature of working parliamentary – cabinet government and accountability.

It is highly unlikely that Canada will abolish the PBO. Therefore, the focus should be on reforming the PBO to eliminate the structural contradictions. In summary, the PBO's mandate, independence and accountability were determined in haste and not fully debated during House of Commons' committee hearings. Much of what was proposed during the senate committee hearings emanated from either the Library of Parliament or public servants, both of whom clearly were looking to limit the independence of the PBO and insert the PBO into existing structures. From the library's perspective, it was to ensure the new PBO was under its jurisdiction. From the perspective of the public service, it was to demonstrate that this was not an additional layer of bureaucracy.

However, the government touted that it was the first to create an independent PBO. As noted earlier, Kevin Page commenced his mandate with a higher salary than what the position provided for and placed him as an equal to his putative superior, the parliamentary librarian. On equal footing and with the government through its house leader, Peter Van Loan, insisting that the PBO was an "independent officer," the stage was set for confrontation, both inside the Parliamentary Library and outside with the Government.

The opposition parties learned quickly that requesting the PBO to review controversial policy issues such as Afghanistan, F-35 jets and the costs of justice reforms would be done in a sophisticated quantitative manner that would be publicly released upon completion and lend credence to their criticisms of government policy and costing proposals.

In sum, the PBO was fighting battles on many fronts with the Library of Parliament concerning the release of its studies; to the battles for appropriate budgetary funding; to the Standing Joint Committee concerning the mandate of the PBO to the government concerning the provision of information he required. These controversies ensured that the government could not abolish the PBO without a major outcry yet equally ensured the government's intransigence concerning further necessary reforms. What will change with the appointment of a new PBO? Not much because the mandate, legislation, reporting relationship to the Parliamentary Librarian, the Opposition demand for review of controversial issues, all have remained unchanged. Is the Government counting on the new PBO to be more compliant? Was the discordant relationship simply a clash of personalities or evidence of deeper structural issues?

A review of the evidence in this chapter suggests the issues were much deeper than a clash of personalities. While there are clearly mandate and accountability issues surrounding any watchdog agency, the PBO (and the OAG) address the most fundamental responsibility of Parliament – the approval of budgetary supply - and the spending of supply by the government. Supply and spending are necessarily and always controversial for they are the quintessential policy choices.

Removing the PBO from the Library of Parliament and its concomitant establishment as an independent officer of Parliament with a revised mandate focused on the relative costs of competing policy choices is crucial. In conjunction with a revised appointment policy mandating recruitment from outside the public service of Canada such steps will go a long way to addressing the problems addressed in this chapter in the relationship of the past five years between the government and the P B O.

NOTES

1 For a more comprehensive analysis of watchdog agencies see Bruce Doern, Michael J. Prince and Richard J. Schultz, *Rules and Unruliness: Canadian Regulatory Democracy, Governance, Capitalism and Welfarism* (McGill-Queen's University Press, 2014), 271–300.

2 Standing Senate Committee on National Finance, *Report on the Officers and Agents of Parliament Created or Modified by the Federal Accountability Act* (Thirteenth Report, May 2008).

3 Ibid., 14.

4 Office of the Parliamentary Budget Officer, *Stakeholder Consultation Summary* (August 15, 2008).

5 Office of the Parliamentary Budget Officer, *The Fiscal Impact of the Canadian Mission in Afghanistan* (October 9, 2008).

6 Office of the Parliamentary Budget Officer, *Economic and Fiscal Assessment* (November 20, 2008).

7 Kathryn May, "I Am Being Undermined, Budget Officer Says." Canwest News Service (January 19, 2009).

8 Report of the Standing Joint Committee on the Library of Parliament (Hon. Sharon Carstairs, Senator), 1.

9 Ibid., 2.

10 Ibid., 9.

11 Ibid., 11.

12 Ibid., 18.

13 Ibid., 22.

14 John Ibbitson, "The Man Who Knows Too Much." *Globe and Mail* (October 5, 2009).

15 Cynthis Munster, "Liberals Broke Embargo on P B O's Five-Year Forecast." *The Hill Times* (July 13, 2009).

16 David Akin, "Economists Call on M P s to Safeguard Budget Office," *CanWest News* (July 18, 2009).

17 Quoted in Cynthia Master, "Liberals Broke Embargo on P B O's 5 Year Forecast," *The Hill Times* (July 9, 2013).

18 Evidence from the 40th Parliament, 2nd Session, Standing Joint Committee on the Library of Parliament (November 19, 2009).

19 Bea Vongdouangchanh, "Parliamentary Budget Officer Kevin Page Will get $2.8 million Budget after High-Profile Fight," *The Hill Times* (March 8, 2010).

20 Parliament of Canada website, Legislative Summary of Bill C-25, accessed on March 31, 2013 http://www.parl.gc.ca/About/Parliament/LegislativeSummaries/bills_ls. asp?source=library_prb&ls=C25&Parl=40&Ses=2&Language=E&Mode=1# purpose

21   c b c News, "Sentencing Act to Cost Billions: Report" (June 22, 2010).

22   Ibid.

23   Ibid.

24   National Defence and the Canadian Forces News Release, *Government of Canada Strengthens Sovereignty While Generating Significant Economic Benefits* (July 16, 2010).

25   c b c News, July 16, 2010, "Canada to spend $9 B on F-35 fighter jets", July 16, 2010.

26   The Parliamentary Budget Office, *An Estimate of the Fiscal Impact of Canada's Proposed Acquisition of the F-35 Lightning II Joint Strike Fighter* (March 10, 2011).

27   Allan Woods, "Budget Watchdog Doubles Price Estimate for F-35 Jets," *Toronto Star* (March 10, 2011).

28   Michael Den Tandt, "Tories' Failure to Reveal F-35's True $25B Cost before Election 'Political Fraud': n d p," *National Post* (April 5, 2012).

29   Letter from p b o Kevin Page to Wayne Wouters (June 18, 2012).

30   Communique on p b o website (November 21, 2012).

31   p b o statement regarding Federal Court of Canada's Decision, http://www.pbo-dpb. gc.ca/en/news? news_id=102&myID=1.

32   The International Monetary Fund, *Case Studies of Fiscal Councils – Functions and Impact* (July 16, 2013).

33   Ibid.

4 Crime or Punishment: What Is the Harper Justice Agenda?

CRAIG JONES

Ottawa's current sentencing agenda is an almost incomprehensible departure from the theory of penal justice that has prevailed in Canada for the past 40 years. A policy of punishment, incapacitation and stigmatization has replaced one premised on the prospect of rehabilitation, restoration and reform. Bill C-10 and its sister amendments seem primarily driven by an ideology of unabashed Puritanism, marketed through fearmongering and the invidious exploitation of communal differences.

Justice Melvyn Green[1]

INTRODUCTION

This chapter argues that the Harper government views justice policy through a Hobbesian lens with little regard for the downstream consequences of its policy choices.[2] The justice agenda is an exercise in wedge politics that panders to short-term electoral outcomes while transferring the costs to provincial treasuries. This government's policy stance toward justice and corrections represents a philosophical rupture with the trajectory of post-war Canadian – and most European – practice, which largely concedes the limited efficacy of the criminal justice system to prevent, deter or suppress crime. Contradicting experience, evidence and expertise across a spectrum of domains and playing to the retributive sentiments of its electoral base,[3] the government has enacted a suite of legislation that exacerbates existing problems in sentencing, incarceration and safe reintegration.

The government is harshening the conditions of penal confinement in a context of declining rates of crime and crime severity. Sentencing principles of restraint and proportionality, which have enabled Canada to maintain a moderate rate of incarceration while reaping the benefit of declining crime rates, have been displaced by an approach that prioritizes optics over outcomes. Ministers have expressed antagonism toward evidence and expertise that questions justice policy.[4] Ironically, these long-term consequences – i.e., a larger and more marginalized underclass – may ultimately redound to the advantage of future Hobbesian policy makers.

The chapter's first section seeks to clarify the nature of the justice legislation to discern its true intent. I then explore the ideological and political contexts from which this legislation emerged. The next sections discuss the magical thinking and symbolic content of the agenda before turning to how Ottawa spends on – and who pays for – the legislation. I close with some observations on Aboriginal corrections and a note of optimism about how future governments may undo this justice agenda.

WHAT EXACTLY IS THE JUSTICE AGENDA?

Building on foundations laid by the Reform and Alliance parties, including the Progressive Conservative Party's critique of the Corrections and Conditional Release Act (CCRA), the Conservatives came to office convinced that the correctional system was insufficiently punitive; that victims were ill-treated; that offenders took inadequate responsibility for their offenses; that the deterrent value of a prison sentence ought to be augmented; that judges exercised too much discretion; and that correctional managers needed more authority to incentivize appropriate inmate conduct.[5] Drawing from a populist script, the thrust of the Reform/Alliance and Conservative Party recommendations was to restore public confidence in the justice system by enhancing the role of denunciation in sentencing, increasing the quanta of punishment and introducing measures to hold offenders accountable for their actions while simultaneously enhancing the rights of victims.

Experts inside, or retired from, the justice system, criminologists and correctional psychologists, attentive newspaper columnists and community-based NGOs argued that simply increasing levels of punishment would produce little to no effect on the rate or severity of crime; that it did nothing to address the antecedents of crime; that harshness of punishment bore no relation to the level or severity of crime; and that there were opportunity costs to incarceration. As the government began rolling out legislation, it rapidly became clear that it was using the legitimate desire for "public safety" and "victim's rights" not to reduce rates or severity of crime so much as to torque up levels of punishment, tacitly inviting Canadians to conflate crime reduction with punishment enhancement. Simultaneously, the government signaled that it would not engage with informed criticism or evidence that did not support its punishment agenda. Take this example from the October 2007 launch of the National Anti-Drug Strategy: "If drugs do get hold of you – there's help to get you off them. And if you sell or produce drugs – you'll pay with jail time."[6] To ordinary Canadians this formulation may have seemed banal. But to the community of public health practitioners it was a dog-whistle: your expertise is not welcome.

As punishment is not the same as crime, so a punishment agenda is not the same as a crime agenda.[7] That most citizens may not be aware of this distinction certainly works to the government's advantage. Few citizens asked "how does increasing punishment reduce crime?" Even fewer asked, "what does it cost to increase punishment *vs.* implementing crime reduction policies?"[8] And no one asked, "how much crime reduction can be bought – at any price – in a context of already declining crime rates?" As Figure 4.1 shows, when the Conservatives came to power in 2006, crime rates had been in decline for several years already – making it hard to evaluate the effectiveness of a "crime agenda" against the background of decade-long decline in crime.

THE IDEOLOGICAL CONTEXT
OF THE PUNISHMENT AGENDA

The Canadian Alliance dissent to the CCRA, the spirit of which pervades justice legislation, is infused with price theory and methodological individualist epistemology. This perspective holds that punishment is a price for crime.[9] Like other social phenomena, crime rates respond to market signals: when the price goes down, crime rates trend upward and down again when the price for crime increases because criminals calculate the costs / benefit of one crime versus another just as all rational actors seek to maximize utility. This view resonated with elements of the Conservative coalition and is present in their response to the CCRA review. Considerations of information asymmetry or impairment of rationality – to say nothing of the social determinants of crime – are displaced by "do the crime, do the time" simplicities.[10] That it doesn't work that way, even in jurisdictions where penalties are severe by the standards that democratic societies will tolerate, had no effect on this belief. Scholars of crime and deviance have largely concluded that the literature does not support a relationship between severity of sentencing and general deterrence,[11] but this evidence was disparaged or ignored.

In the early 1990s a House of Commons committee summarized the efficacy of the criminal justice system to prevent or reduce crime: "If locking up those who violate the law contributed to safer societies then the United States should be the safest country in the world. In fact the United States affords a glaring example of the limited impact that criminal justice responses may have on crime."[12] This finding echoed the conclusions of comparable studies in the United States and the United Kingdom. "Prison," concluded a report from the British Home Office, "is an expensive way to make bad people worse." Indeed, experience showed that high rates of incarceration could produce higher rates of re-offending and that longer sentences made prisoners harder to reintegrate. Certainty of apprehension and prosecution was a greater deterrent to crime than harsher sentencing – and *prevention* was the optimal investment.

But "science, statistics, reason, and rational compromise are barriers to swinging the [ideological] pendulum back to where [the Conservatives] be-

Figure 4.1
Police-reported crime rate, Canada, 1962 to 2011˙

rate per 100,000 population

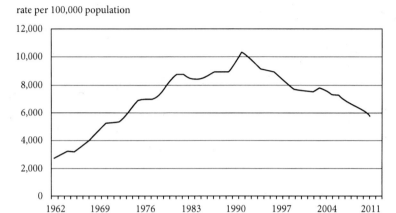

Source: Statistics Canada, Canadian Centre for Justice Statistics, Uniform Crime Reporting Survey.
* Information presented in this graph represents data from the Uniform Crime Reporting Aggregate Survey, and allow for historical comparisons to be made back to 1962. New definitions of crime categories were introduced in 2009 and are only available in the new format back to 1998. As a result, numbers in this graph will not match data released in the new Incident-based Uniform Crime Reporting Survey format.

lieve it belongs."[13] Ideology trumps science, which requires that policy makers ignore dissenters – even suppress them.[14] Speaking to a conference at McGill University, former principal secretary Ian Brodie, explained that "politically, it helped us tremendously to be attacked by [sociologists, criminologists, and defence lawyers] ... we never really had to engage in the question of what the evidence actually shows about various approaches to crime."[15] This, then, forms the ideological backdrop of the punishment agenda: an amalgam of neo-conservative price theory grounded in populist belief in the efficacy of punishment wedded to a conviction that the state must, in Hobbesian terms, assert its sovereign power to act against deviants in the larger context of anti-elitist backlash toward justice policy informed by evidence or experience.[16]

THE POLITICAL CONTEXT
OF THE PUNISHMENT AGENDA

For reasons no one fully understands, crime rates peaked in the early 1990s then either flattened or declined with the United States leading the trend.[17] But the murder of Jane Creba on Boxing Day 2006, weeks before the Conservatives formed their first minority government, energized all parties to be seen to be tough on crime. Her death, at the hands of a black gang-member, gave immediacy to the "get tough" voices in the Conservative

Figure 4.2
Police-reported crime severity index, Canada, 1998 to 2011[*]

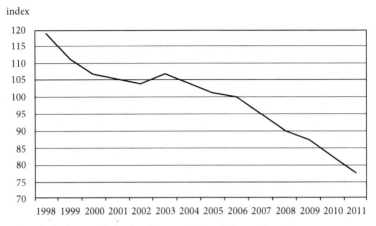

index

Note: The Index has been standardized to a base year of 2006 which is equal to 100.
Source: Statistics Canada, Canadian Centre for Justice Statistics, Uniform Crime Reporting Survey.
[*] The CSI, which measures the seriousness of crime, was 77.6 in 2011, its lowest point since 1998 when the CSI began. Since that time, the severity of police-reported crime has decreased in all but one year (2003).

coalition. The persistence of high crime rates in Canada's western cities – Winnipeg, Regina, Edmonton, and Vancouver, where Conservative support was strongest – seemed to validate the claims of the fear-mongering tabloid press that crime rates were actually rising rather than, as Statistics Canada claimed, declining.[18]

The context of urban violent crime was not open for debate, so Ms Creba's murder assumed a political salience that enabled the Conservatives to ignore its meaning by abstracting it out of its context: paradoxically drug prohibition drives much urban violent crime – particularly in the inner cities – yet supporters of harsher justice measures support this engine of violent crime. The political context for the punishment agenda, then, was a confluence of ideology, resentment, distrust of elites, populist wedge politics, and adventitious events. But what emerged in legislation was not directed toward reducing either crime rates or severity.

The justice agenda is not about reducing crime, improving the conditions of victims or creating safer communities. Reflecting on the government's justice legislation, recently retired director general of corrections and criminal justice Mary Campbell told a conference that "the deeply embedded nastiness of the current governing party is constantly displayed in their actions, whether it be creating even more punitive carceral conditions, erecting barriers to reintegration, never letting the offender be more than the worst thing they have ever done, using victims for political ends – the list is truly endless."[19]

CRIME CAUSES PUNISHMENT
AND OTHER MAGICAL THINKING

At the heart of the punishment agenda is the belief that crime and punishment are connected: the presumption that severity of punishment relates to rates or severity of crime.[20] Crime, in this view, is a commodity for which there is a demand and supply. Following this logic leads one to posit that a higher rate of crime is reflective of the sentencing practices of the presiding judiciary. A higher rate of crime, therefore, is indicative of "soft-on-crime" judges. Crime rates, accordingly, vary with sentencing practices through a magical process of social learning whereby potential first-time or chronic long-term criminals calculate the utility of one crime versus another on the basis of what they know about sentencing for similar convictions. Impulse and opportunity, impairment or criminal associates may play a role, but these are subordinate to considerations of utility.

Such magical thinking infuses the punishment agenda: Canada's justice and correctional systems are insufficiently retributive to effectively deter potential criminals (through general deterrence) or previously convicted criminals (through specific deterrence). Mandatory minimum sentences, then, because they are so obviously a disutility to the rational policy maker, must deter. This belief in deterrence through severity of sentencing is an article of faith. Lost in the doctrine of deterrence is the comparative evidence on the efficacy, which evidence is as conclusive as any finding in criminal justice is likely to be: deterrence does not work as its champions claim. Severity of punishment cannot be made to work as effectively as certainty of apprehension.

THE APPEAL OF POLITICAL SYMBOLISM:
MANDATORY MINIMUM SENTENCES

Political theatre and symbolic ritual are the instruments of choice when governments contemplate how to appear effective on issues that are resistant to easy amelioration.[21] For the government, crime offers a menu of symbolic quick-wins that simultaneously (a) keep the spectre of fear and disorder in the public imagination; and (b) burnish the government's reputation for toughness and compassion for victims; without (c) exposing it to a long-term commitment in crime's root causes; while also (d) kicking the can of sentencing, penal and legal reform down the road. It's a win-win-win because there is limited advocacy for the rights of the marginalized and dispossessed while academic critics of the punishment agenda can be dismissed as "ivory tower elite statisticians" or "on the side of the child pornographers." These tropes are reliably recycled by moral entrepreneurs reinforcing the myth that there exists a disconnect between the populist "common sense" of ordinary Canadians and the "reality-based community" of career professionals in the justice system.[22] In short, little political risk is coupled with good prospective electoral payoff.

Much attention was focused on the expanded use of mandatory minimum sentences, which infringe on judicial discretion by sentencing a *class* of crime rather than the *actions* of an individual. Rather than introducing more transparency and predictability, these often have the opposite effect in practice – one of the many reasons that American jurisdictions are backing away from them. The ease with which mandatory sentences can be introduced relieves policy makers of the much harder work of bringing rationality to a justice system increasingly pushed into incoherence.[23]

Ironically, more research has been conducted into mandatory minimum sentences than almost any other issue in criminological history. But "there is no evidence for the claim that mandatory/minimum sentencing has any impact on consistency of sentencing or levels of crime. The primary function of such sentences is for governments to symbolically say 'we are doing something about crime.' This does not seem to fool anybody. The percentage of people who say they are fearful to go out at night before and after the imposition of mandatory sentencing does not seem to change."[24]

HOW OTTAWA SPENDS: OFF-LOADING THE COSTS OF PUNISHMENT TO THE PROVINCES

The federal government has jurisdiction over the criminal code and the provinces administer its application. Only the federal government is able to determine criminal procedure – i.e., prosecution – and to appoint judges for those courts. Provinces administer their systems of justice and the level of enforcement. Amendments to the federal criminal code change the rules that provincial justice systems have to enforce.

The government has still not costed out its punishment agenda – or provided estimates on how the costs will be distributed between federal and provincial governments. Various projections have appeared but have been dismissed or disparaged by the justice or public safety ministers.

The parliamentary budget officer (PBO) attempted to estimate the cost of one component of the Omnibus Crime Bill of 2012: the changes to eligibility for conditional sentences of imprisonment (CSI). The PBO modeled what might have been the fiscal impact of these changes if the amendments proposed in Bill C-10 had been in force in 2008-2009. Assuming no behavioral changes, and employing conservative assumptions about rates of conviction, the PBO calculated that the average cost would have risen from approximately $2,600 to approximately $41,000 per offender – an increase of almost 16 fold – while the average time spent under judicial supervision per offender would have fallen from 348 to 225 days and the average number of offenders would have fallen from 4,468 to 3,818. Had this amendment been enacted in 2008–09, it would have cost an average of $38,431 more to punish 650 *fewer* offenders for 123 fewer days.[25]

The most recent P B O analysis estimated that of $20.3 billion for criminal justice expenditures nationally, 27% ($5.5 billion) was assumed by the federal government with the balance downloaded to provinces.[26] As a percentage of G D P, justice expenditures have increased since 2006 from .99% to 1.11% while the crime rate has fallen steadily. Correctional expenditures – driven by changes to federal laws – as a percentage of G D P increased by 0.15% through 2011–12 while the provinces have seen an increase of 0.109% to 2011–12.[27] Whatever the merit of the estimates produced by the P B O, they have consistently presented their methodology for outside examination. The government has yet to reveal either its methodology or its estimates for its punishment agenda.

DOUBLE BUNKING: SHORT TERM PUNISHMENT FOR LONG-TERM PAIN

As part of its overall target of increasing the quanta of punishment – and contending with the cost of increasing the rate of incarceration – within the correctional system, the government revised its accommodation norms to permit double bunking up to 20% of all beds in a given region. This marks a dramatic departure in Canada's adherence to United Nations norms – one person per cell – and our history of progressive correctional practice. The theory behind single occupancy is that because prisons are harsh places under the best of circumstances where, for security reasons, some persons are locked in their cells for 23 of 24 hours, single occupancy was a means of lowering tension and preventing violence. Double bunking has always been an acknowledged reality imposed by short-term necessity. "As double-bunking goes up," warns the Correctional Investigator, "you see increased incidents of institutional violence."[28] Howard Sapers observes that double-bunking has increased 50% in the past five years, so that prisons have approval to let 1,300 prisoners, or 10% of the population, share cells – some sleeping in bunk beds and others in cots or mattresses on the floor. Only a decade ago the goal of the Correctional Service of Canada was to abolish cell sharing.[29]

The biggest crisis is in remand, or pre-trial detention. Legislation since 2006 has exacerbated a problem that precedes the punishment agenda. Currently, there are more people behind bars in remand facilities – i.e., not yet found guilty – than are serving sentences of custody in provincial facilities. This points to problems with the speed of justice and interim release provisions. Conditions in some facilities are so crowded that dangerous triple bunking is common. Because they have not been sentenced, there are no correctional programs, giving rise to the appellation "dead time." Worst of all, remand mixes sentenced with un-sentenced – a violation of widely accepted best practices.[30]

ABORIGINAL CANADIANS

The punishment agenda comes to its sharpest point with our most marginalized and politically powerless citizens. While crime rates have been in steady decline since the early 1990s, the ratio of incarcerated Aboriginal Canadians is approaching 1 in 4 federally sentenced offenders.[31] The disproportion would be serious enough[32] were they being released and returned to the community with similar alacrity. But as successive correctional investigator reports warn, Aboriginal persons

- serve disproportionately more of their sentence behind bars before first release;
- are under-represented in community supervision and over-represented in maximum security;
- are more likely to return to prison on revocation of parole; and,
- are disproportionately involved in institutional security incidents, use of force interventions, segregation placements and self-injury.[33]

These problems are most acute where Aboriginals are a higher percentage of the general population. In the Prairie region, Aboriginals comprise more than 55% of the total inmate population – and more than 60% at Stony Mountain outside Winnipeg. In Saskatchewan's provincial institutions – for sentences of two years less a day – Aboriginals comprise 81% of those admitted to custody, and 76% of those admitted to youth custody in a province where they comprise 14.9% of the general population. This translates into a rate of adult incarceration – both federally and provincially – of 910 per 100,000 compared to 109 per 100,000 for non-Aboriginals.[34]

What explains this worsening disproportionality? One theory points to the nervousness that has infected the Correctional Service and Parole Board of Canada.[35] These two institutions regulate the rate at which prisoners return to the community according to a matrix of criteria including how offenders hit their correctional milestones. In a study for the Aboriginal Initiatives Directorate of Correctional Services Canada, this writer interviewed individuals working in various aspects of Aboriginal corrections and return to the community in different parts of Canada.[36] Serving public servants were, naturally, reluctant to share their insights, but those near retirement – or recently retired – reported the pervasiveness of institutional fear, risk aversion, blame avoidance and unwillingness to take chances even when protected by the provisions of the Corrections and Custodial Release Act. They described a "systemic sclerosis" in correctional practice that, in combination with staff shortages and other job-design dysfunctions, keep inmates incarcerated longer than necessary, impose more stringent release requirements than previously and return offenders to prison at higher rates than prior to 2006 for the assessed level of risk. An analysis of internal Correctional Service audits revealed

- a lack of clarity in the policies staff are expected to enact;
- systemic shortfalls in training of front line staff;
- turnover of Parole Officer staff along the continuum of care;
- excessive work burden coupled to poor work design resulting in burnout; and,
- poor communication between members of the case management team resulting in many offenders failing to meet their correctional milestones.[37]

The system is operating at the limits of its capacity and in an environment in which best practices are hard to effect. Interviewees told this writer that morale in the Correctional Service mirrors that across the federal public service as a whole and has worsened with the ongoing politicization of justice policy.[38]

CONCLUSIONS: SWINGING THE PENDULUM BACK TOWARD EFFECTIVE JUSTICE POLICY

The future of Canada's justice regime is contingent on a political environment committed to effective, evidence-based, practices in sentencing and corrections. Fortunately, the philosophical and practical groundwork is established in several documents.[39] Canadians actually know how to do effective sentencing and correctional policy premised on safe return to the community. There will always be pressure to tweak and refine but it is likely that, with the departure of the Harper government, the fever for retributive justice policy will pass. Future governments would be well served to return to the deliberations and findings of the *Correctional Law Review*. In the interim, however, Canadians face the real prospect of harshened penal conditions producing persons less able to be safely reintegrated – and of sentencing practices growing steadily more incoherent as the government formulates policy on the basis of exceptional and particularistic cases like Graham James and Clifford Olson. Ironically, future Canadian governments may take direction from our American neighbors who – at incredible human and social cost – have tested the limits of 'tough on crime' and turned their attention to their northern neighbors to see what works.

Although demographics suggest that crime rates and severity will probably continue to decline, the punishment agenda may sow the seeds of future criminality by enlarging the pool of persons seriously damaged by harsh conditions of incarceration and limited resources for safe reintegration. When the cohort of offenders enlarged by the punishment regime begins to return to their communities, policy makers may find themselves dealing with an increase in the kinds of crimes that contemporary critics of the justice agenda warned were likely to arise from a punishment agenda enacted for political purposes.

NOTES

1 Justice Melvyn Green, "Exercising Restraint in a Punitive Age," http://www. criminallawyers.ca/For_the_Defence_Melvin_Green_web.pdf
2 Michael Prince, "A Hobbesian Prime Minister and the Night Watchman State: Social Policy under the Harper Conservatives," in G. Bruce Doern and Christopher Stoney, eds., *How Ottawa Spends, 2012–2013: The Harper Majority, Budget Cuts and the New Opposition*, (McGill-Queen's University Press, 2012), 53–70.
3 "The Conservative Base is hard to precisely define. But among its elements are: a high degree of religiosity, a moralistic view of foreign policy, a populist dislike of government, a loathing of the media (except Sun News Network, Sun newspapers and a few very right-wing columnists), a distaste of anything that smacks of high culture, a reverence for the military, an abhorrence of abortion, a suspicion of "intellectuals" and their reasoning, a belief (against all evidence) that crime is out of control, a generalized sense that honest, God-fearing people like themselves have been marginalized and patronized by secular "elites," a sense that produces bursts of resentment and anger about the state of the country." Jeffrey Simpson, "Don't Forget the Base – You Can Bet Harper Won't," *Globe and Mail* (8 June 2013).
4 See Greg Millard, "Stephen Harper and the Politics of the Bully," *The Dalhousie Review* 89, 3 (2009).
5 Jim Gouk, "Official Opposition Minority Report on the Corrections and Conditional Release Act" (Canadian Alliance, 2000). See also "Dissenting Report of the Progressive Conservative Party on the CCRA," in Paul DeVillers, "A Work In Progress: The Corrections and Conditional Release Act," Sub-committee on Corrections and Conditional Release Act of the Standing Committee on Justice and Human Rights (May 2000).
6 Speech for The Right Honourable Stephen Harper, Prime Minister, "The National Anti-Drug Strategy" (Winnipeg, October 4, 2007).
7 This distinction that has been lost on some observers. See Ian Lee, "Righting Wrongs: Locking Them Up without Losing the Key – Tory Reforms to Crime and Punishment," in Bruce Doern, ed., *How Ottawa Spends, 2007–2008* (Montreal and Kingston: McGill-Queen's University Press 2007), 220–53.
8 Tom Flanagan, "It's No Time to Be Complacent about Doing Time," *Globe and Mail* (May 15, 2010).
9 John Donohue III, "Economic Models of Crime and Punishment," *Social Research: An International Quarterly of the Social Sciences* 74, 2 (Summer 2007): 379–412.
10 See Timothy F. Hartnagel and Laura J. Templeton, "Emotions about Crime and Attitudes to Punishment," *Punishment & Society* 14, 4 (2012): 452–74.
11 Anthony Doob and Cheryl Marie Webster, "Sentence Severity and Crime: Accepting the Null Hypothesis," in Michael Tonry, ed., *Crime and Justice: A Review of Research* vol. 30 (University of Chicago Press, 2003), 143–95; and Cheryl Marie Webster and Anthony N. Doob, "Searching for Sasquatch: Deterrence of Crime through Sentence Severity," *Oxford Handbook on Sentencing and Corrections*, Joan Petersilia and Kevin Reitz, eds. (Oxford University Press, 2010).

12 Bob Horner, *Crime Prevention in Canada: Toward a National Strategy* (Ottawa: House of Commons, 1993).

13 Allan Gregg: http://rabble.ca/blogs/bloggers/djclimenhaga/2013/04/former-tory-strategist-allan-gregg-rips-harper-cons-systematic-a

14 "It's like an Iron Curtain has been drawn across the communication of science in this country," Jeff Hutchings, former DFO biologist, now a Killam chair at Dalhousie University quoted in Jonathon Gatehouse, "When Science Goes Silent: Harper's Obsession with Controlling the Message Verges on the Orwellian," *Maclean's* (May 3, 2013).

15 John Geddes, "Ian Brodie Offers a Candid Case Study in Politics and Policy," *Maclean's* (March 27, 2009).

16 David Garland, *The Culture of Control: Crime and Social Order in Contemporary Society* (University of Chicago Press, 2001), Chapter 5.

17 Jan van Dijk, John van Kesteren and Paul Smit, "Criminal Victimisation in International Perspective: Key findings from the 2004–2005 International Crime Victims Survey and the European Survey on Crime and Safety" (WODC, 2007) at http://rechten.uvt.nl/icvs/pdffiles/ICVS2004_05.pdf.

18 Lorne Gunter, "Crime Stats Are All Just a Mirage," *QMI Agency* (February 24, 2013).

19 Mary Campbell quoted in Douglas Quan. "Federal Policy on Crime Just Plain Nasty, Says Retired Senior Public Safety Official," Postmedia News (October 3, 2013); and David Daubney, "Harper Government Misguided in Its Tough-on-Crime Approach," *The Globe and Mail* (December 11, 2011). While an MP, Mr. Daubney chaired the Standing Committee on Justice, which produced a review of sentencing that was well-received by criminologists, the judiciary, and much of the legal community.

20 Michael Tonry, "Crime Does Not Cause Punishment: The Impact of Sentencing Policy on Levels of Crime," *South African Crime Quarterly* 20 (June 2007): 13–20.

21 Murray Edelman, *Constructing the Political Spectacle* (University of Chicago, 1988).

22 The expression "reality-based community" was coined by Karl Rove as a term of derision for people who "believe that solutions emerge from your judicious study of discernible reality." See Ron Suskind, "Faith, Certainty and the Presidency of George W. Bush," *New York Times Magazine* (October 17, 2004).

23 Allan Manson, "Bill C-25: The Truth in Sentencing Act, or Let's Be Truthful about Sentencing," Evidence: Senate Committee on Justice and Legal Affairs (September 17, 2009).

24 Tonry, "Crime Does Not Cause Punishment," 20.

25 Parliamentary Budget Office, "The Fiscal Impact of Changes to Eligibility for Conditional Sentences of Imprisonment in Canada" (Ottawa, February 28, 2012), 1.

26 Parliamentary Budget Office, "Expenditure Analysis of Criminal Justice in Canada," (Ottawa, March 2013).

27 Parliamentary Budget Office, http://www.pbo-dpb.gc.ca/files/files/Crime_Cost_EN.pdf

28 Janice Tibbets, "Minister Downplays Prison Double-Bunking," *National Post* (4 May 2010).

29 Ibid.

30 http://www.johnhowardbc.ca/images/jhsbc-factsheet-remand-overcrowding.pdf
31 Aboriginals – Métis, First Nations, and Inuit – comprise less than 5% of Canada's total population.
32 In 2010–11, Aboriginal women accounted for over 31.9% of all federally incarcerated women, representing an increase of 85.7% over the last decade.
33 Office of the Correctional Investigator, *Spirit Matters: Aboriginal People and the Corrections and Conditional Release Act* (October 22, 2012), 5.
34 Ibid., 44.
35 Stephen Maher, "Stephen Harper's PR Obsession Is Fostering Paranoia and Paralysis in Public Service," *The Province* (December 2, 2011); Kathryn May, "Kevin Page Blames 'Weak' Public Service for Not Serving Parliament, Canadians," *Ottawa Citizen* (March 15, 2013); and Frances Russell, "Harperites Undermine Democracy," *Winnipeg Free Press* (April 4, 2013).
36 These interviews were conducted on the understanding that identities would be protected.
37 Craig Jones, "Systemic Sclerosis, Risk Aversion and the Aboriginal/Non-Aboriginal Outcomes Gap" (Ottawa: National Headquarters, Correctional Service Canada, June 2011).
38 Greg Weston, "What's Behind Rising Public Service Absenteeism? Downsizing Stress, Low Morale and Demographics Help Explain High Levels," CBC *National News* (June 20, 2012), online at http://www.cbc.ca/news/canada/story/2012/06/20/pol-weston-absenteeism-public-service-why.html
39 To see how far Canada has drifted from its commitment to evidence-based and best practices justice policy, compare *Influences on Canadian Correctional Reform between 1986 and 1988* (Ottawa: Department of the Solicitor General) with *Roadmap to Strengthening Public Safety* (Ottawa: Report of the Correctional Service of Canada Review Panel, October 2007).

5 Justin Trudeau and Leadership Idolization: The Centralization of Power in Canadian Politics and Political Parties

CRAIG MacNAUGHTON
AND CHRISTOPHER STONEY

> Justin Trudeau does not shake your hand; he inhabits it.
>
> Micheal Den Tandt[1]

> He's got more charisma than the royal family and Lady Gaga combined.
>
> Warren Kinsella[2]

> Under his suit jacket, the sleeve buttons on his dress shirt were undone. His necktie was knotted, but left loose over an open top button. His mane of black hair was tousled. Even in genteel disarray, even dressed more or less like a couple hundred of his parliamentary colleagues, the 40-year-old Liberal M P for the Montreal riding of Papineau looked like a million bucks.
>
> Paul Wells[3]

INTRODUCTION

While the 2012–13 Liberal leadership campaign was portrayed as a competitive race, by March 24, 2013 it was clear what the outcome would be. The Trudeau campaign financial statements submitted to Elections Canada on that day reported that in the first six months of the campaign the Trudeau camp had raised just over $1 million, double that of all the other candidates combined and more than five times that of the second place fundraiser Martha Hall Findlay.[4] This massive financial advantage was later reflected in the final leadership vote; more coronation than election, Justin Trudeau won on the first ballot with 77.8% of the votes cast.[5] While some viewed a Trudeau victory as another predictable step on route to fulfilling his destiny, we argue that Trudeau's victory and overwhelming popularity both reflects and is consistent with broader structural shifts in the Canadian political landscape. Specifically, an increasing centralization of political power combined with diminishing checks and balances has magnified the focus on party leaders generating changes in our political system that are not yet fully appreciated or understood.

A heightened focus on the individual as chief executive, talisman, voice and face of the party has strengthened the leader's position and made followers, including MPs and party members, increasingly dependent upon them for electoral success not to mention their own careers in the case of the latter. Rather than creating conditions within which open debate and differences of opinion over issues can flourish we argue these changes have helped create the conditions that encourage an unquestioning loyalty and deference to party leaders that borders on "leadership idolization."

Idolization (*1. To regard with blind admiration or devotion. 2. To worship as an idol.*) in this context may involve loyalty to genuinely charismatic leaders such as Justin Trudeau or can also relate to more manufactured and controlled forms leadership such as under Harper or Chrétien and Martin. Idolization is used because it both captures and expresses our contention that as the framing and projection of party leaders continues to grow in importance, substantive issues such as ideology, policy and debate are increasingly secondary to the leader's personal image and appeal. As Harold Clarke et al. observed presciently over two decades ago:

> Candidates have no choice but to organize around leaders rather than
> political principles and ideologies and expect the leader to work out
> the multitude of compromises required for the party to enjoy electoral
> success. This process is a sign of things to come if his or her party should
> form the government. The party's lack of firm political principles and
> ideologies and of a clear understanding of what it wants to accomplish also
> affects the work of career officials. It also means that policy making, to the
> extent that it takes place at the political level, centres around leaders"[6]

We believe this trend has continued in the decades since Clarke made these comments and this growing dependency on the leader has serious consequences for political debate and the democratic process.

This chapter will examine the "idolization" of political party leaders, with the aim of mapping the political landscape that provided Justin Trudeau his definitive victory and consider the implications for him, the party and for the future of federal politics in Canada. Importantly, it also examines leadership by analyzing "followers" in the context of centralizing political trends and reforms that have continued apace during the Harper and previous Chrétien-Martin prime ministerial eras.[7] In the first section of the chapter we examine this context of political leadership idolization. We then look at party leaders in the current era of such leadership dynamics. A brief discussion is then presented of how this increasingly results in leadership trumping policy. Conclusions then follow.

THE POLITICS OF LEADERSHIP IDOLIZATION: CONTEXT, TRENDS, AND CAUSES

The conditions that facilitate and promote leadership idolization have been ushered into the Canadian system by a series of incremental but significant changes in the political landscape that have simultaneously empowered leaders and disempowered the party rank and file. We begin by briefly examining the growing centralisation of political power and the declining influence and voice of individual MPs both in parliament and within their own party. We then focus on the implication of these changes for political leadership and focus on the "coronation" of Justin Trudeau as leader of the Liberal party.

Centralization and Changing Power Dynamics

After several decades of centralisation the Canadian parliamentary system grants more power to its political leaders than virtually any other modern democracy. This trend has been well documented by Donald Savoie: "What we've witnessed over the past 30 or 40 years is slowly but surely a movement toward where the party leader and those around him dominate the whole process of politics … [t]hey not only define what the party stands for and its policies, but also dominate government. It's a party-leader centred process and MPs have become less and less relevant."[8] Most contemporary democratic systems of governance include checks on the power of the executive branch, a classic example being the American political system where the legislative, judicial, and executive branches were designed explicitly as checks on the power of the other two. In parliamentary democracies, the power of the leader of the governing party is supposedly checked by parliament. This challenge function is significantly reduced when the governing party enjoys a majority of seats. However, even in the case of a majority government there can be a climate of intense policy debate among individual members and factions within the majority party. In the UK for example, the Conservative party's fundamental divisions over closer ties with EU have endured for decades and help explain why today the UK remains outside of the EU's exchange rate mechanism and have negotiated several significant EU opt outs.

In Canada, party dissention is rare as MPs have largely failed to resist incremental but ultimately transformational changes in their power and roles.[9] While holding government to account is historically a parliamentarians most critical function, only a few Canadian MPs mentioned this role when questioned in a recent survey.[10] Question Period and private members' business were traditionally the main venue through which accountability could be pursued but, based on the survey findings, Loat suggests this is no longer the case and notes there is barely any time in the House when MP's words are not scripted:

Long gone are the days where Question Period involved a genuine exchange of questions and answers. Today, as any observer will tell you, it's 45 minutes of scripted statements, feigned outrage and repetitive talking points. Private members' business, where individual M P s were once free to vote as they wished, is now increasingly used by all parties to test prospective legislation. Votes are increasingly whipped, and seen as yet another test of party discipline – with the media pointing to differing opinions as leadership failures.[11]

In practice this means that the public persona or image of the leader of a party has become increasingly important to political campaigns and electoral success. An important consequence of this shift is that instead of the leader representing the views of the party, and being accountable to it, the party is increasingly beholden to the leader for attracting party funds, establishing policy direction, campaign strategy and ultimately electoral success.[12] As Savoie has highlighted;

> Local candidates are often at the mercy of their leader's performance and of the party's spin doctors and pollsters. Modern campaigns are such that leaders try to pave the way to success by scoring political points in the national media and by avoiding political gaffes. Decades ago, things were different. Leaders played a major role, but regional ministers … or local party bosses were also crucial. Today, the local candidate is expected to campaign hard, to keep his or her name out of the limelight, to avoid getting the party into trouble, and to leave the campaign decisions to the professionals in Ottawa- who, they are told, are always in a position to see regional trade-offs, understand the national interest, and protect the party leader.[13]

Recent evidence of these shifts can be seen in the Conservative government's 2010 decision to replace the term "Government of Canada" with "Harper Government" in federal communications material.[14] In doing so, the prime minister has branded himself as the personal representative of Conservatives in their governing capacity. This approach is an interesting political gambit, because it intimately links government policy with the leader rather than the party or the country.

The Declining Influence of M P s

The relevance of M P s in Parliament has been eroding over many decades. The problem they face is that they are simultaneously becoming less valuable to their party, while also losing their leverage to resist the will of the party. With the growing focus on the party leaders, individual M P s now have few avenues through which they can influence policy.

Declining M P power is not a new trend and Pierre Trudeau's description of them as "nobodies" when they depart the parliamentary precinct was both telling and ironic. As critics point out "[i]t was under [Trudeau's] watch that members of parliament began to see their role trivialized as more and more decision-making power was concentrated in the grasping claws of the prime minister's office."[15]

Traditionally M P s had been able to make significant contributions at the riding level, ensuring their re-election by representing the will of the riding in caucus and parliament, building connections within their riding in order to secure a broad base of support for the party and expressing their views in the party decision-making process. Today, the ability of individual M P s to get elected in their riding is based largely on the nomination by the party. There have been numerous justifications given for implementing these reforms, including protecting the local candidate or M P from interest group capture, but the vetting of the nominations process combined with the increased visibility and communications capabilities of the federal parties have played a major role in increasing the dependence of local M P s on the party and the leadership in particular. The November 2013 by-election in Brandon–Souris, Manitoba, was a case in point. After disqualifying the two preferred local candidates (Isleifson and Kennedy), the Conservative party's preferred candidate (Maguire) was left to contest the relatively safe seat; a decision that was controversial and unpopular with local party activists. "Whatever the answer, a large number of Brandon–Souris Conservatives are angered by the way Isleifson and Kennedy have been treated by the party, and the party's denial of their right to choose their candidate. Many have decided to sit on the sidelines during the by-election campaign, refusing to work for a party that treats its own this way."[16]

Although the system in the U K is also undergoing reform, British M P s have maintained more power than their Canadian counterparts, largely because of their power to select the party leader. Labour M P s, for example, are entitled to vote three times in the leadership selection process; once as an M P, again as a party member, and once again as a member of a union. In Canada, "M P s have been displaced by party members, many of whom are little more than 'instant members,' when it comes to selecting the party leader, while policy decisions are made by the prime minister and his advisers."[17] Savoie suggests this has given party leaders complete say (over party members) while M P s have been effectively sidelined."[18]

Signing up new or "instant members" is a tactic used to secure votes for favoured party candidates and was used extensively in the Liberal party leadership race to help secure victory for Trudeau "Justin Trudeau won the leadership by selling party memberships and signing up thousands of 'supporters.' Liberal M P s had little say in who their new leader would be. But then Liberal officials are more concerned about filling party coffers than they are in anything the M P s might contribute."[19] In addition to seeing their organising and communication roles diminish M P s now have fewer opportunities to establish reputations by excelling in their positions. The avenues for expressing dissent from the party leadership's position on the issues of the day or promoting their own issues and agendas have also been severely curtailed through the imposition of strict communications strategies and rigid party discipline in the legislature.

Even on matters of conscience M P s have been silenced. In March 2013 the speaker of the House determined that Conservative M P Mark Warawa's parliamentary privileges were not violated when his party prevented him from addressing the House of Commons on the issue of sex-selection abortion. Although the Speaker ruled that there was no evidence that Warawa had been "systematically prevented" from speaking in the chamber he did acknowledge that Warawa's concerns about whether M P s receive "equitable distribution" on speaking in the House may be "legitimate." He later told M P s that if they wished to speak in the future, they didn't necessarily need to follow the current convention and obtain approval from the party whip,[20] but this course of action would clearly still carry significant risk.

If M P s resist towing the party line, they can be removed in the next election by revocation of the party nomination, forcing them to run as an independent. An M P challenging party restrictions is a rare occurrence but recently former Conservative M P Brent Rathgeber did so. Before his resignation from the Conservative Party, Rathgeber detailed his views on party loyalty in a blog post on his personal website: "One can occasionally be critical of the Government without being disloyal. I proudly serve in the Conservative (Government) Caucus but do not leave the viewpoints of my constituents behind every time I board a plane to Ottawa."[21] Rathgeber saw his principles put to the test when the government amended key provisions in his private member's bill which sought to make public the salaries of public servants who were paid more than $188,000 per year. In response, Rathgeber resigned, telling reporters "I don't think that I can continue to represent them when I am told how to vote, told what to speak."[22]

More recently, Bloc Québécois M P Maria Mourani was expelled from the party caucus after she spoke publicly about plans by the provincial wing of the Bloc Québécois to institute a secular charter in Quebec saying, "Whether they like it or not, they are discriminating against minorities."[23] Her expulsion from the caucus is particularly significant since Mourani was one of only five Bloc M P s, hence her expulsion reduced the presence of the party by 20 per cent in the House of Commons. The fact that the federal wing of the Bloc Québécois felt they could and should eject M P Mourani for her statements is illuminating with regards to the status of M P s in the House of Commons. In previous eras the Bloc might have balked at eliminating one fifth of their seats in the House and alienating the voters who elected Mourani. Instead party leadership appears to have calculated that presenting a consistent and unified message to the public is more important in the modern context.

The experiences of Mourani and Rathgeber are consistent with the declining importance and independence of MPs and their removal from caucus, is indicative of their disposability when challenging party supremacy or threatening the all-important image of firm leadership. To add insult to injury, MPs are routinely described as party "bobbleheads and bootlickers"[24] and "plant pots and trained seals"[25] by an increasingly cynical media and public.

Public concern and derision has prompted some MPs to try and redefine their roles in an effort to restore some credibility with the public and reinvigorate the democratic process. In December of 2013, Michael Chong, a backbench Conservative MP, introduced the Reform Act, "an effort to strengthen Canada's democratic institutions by restoring the role of elected [MPs]."[26] The primary reforms presented in the act include: restoring local control over party nominations; giving the parliamentary caucus the ability to reinstate expelled party members and providing MPs with powers to initiate reviews of the party leadership with a motion supported by at least 15% of caucus members.[27] When initially proposed, the act received mixed support from other MPs. While many agreed that the power of individual MPs was in need of enhancement there were also concerns from Conservative MPs in particular that the Act could be interpreted as an attempt to undermine Stephen Harper's leadership coming as it did in the midst of the Senate-PMO scandal.[28] While the act had not come to a vote at the time of writing, given its controversial nature and the low success rate of private member's bills (1.4% from 2004 to 2011[29]), the Act seems unlikely to be adopted.

Even if full passage of the Reform Bill through Parliament is unrealistic at the present time, private member bills can serve as a focal point for an issue not previously discussed in public by MPs[30] and provide a platform for disaffected backbench MPs to speak publicly about the issue. In addition to several Liberal and NDP MPs, Conservative MPs James Rajotte, Stella Ambler, and Larry Miller as well as Tory senator Hugh Segal have already expressed support for the bill. Rajotte, the chair of the finance committee, said Chong's bill fixes a "longstanding issue that needs to be addressed."[31] How the party leadership responds to this initiative and, specifically, whether they are prepared to allow a free vote on the bill, will reveal much about the longer term prospects for reform.

PARTY LEADERS IN THE ERA OF LEADERSHIP IDOLIZATION

To this point the chapter has focused on the power of MPs and parties relative to their leaders. Here we shift the focus to look at how the era of idolization has changed what is required and expected of party leaders. Under conditions of *primus inter pares* the leader needed to focus on maintaining the goodwill and support of party members and especially those colleagues in the cabinet, including those two or three cabinet members who saw themselves as future party leaders. In the current climate, that support is all but assured provided the leader is seen as an electoral asset and can demonstrate and maintain popular appeal through opinion polls and elections. Consequently MPs are less inclined to undermine the image of the leader especially as perceived disloyalty does not sit well with local party supporters in their own riding, or the broader electorate, and can generate unwelcome media interest and speculation.

The image a leader projects will obviously be shaped by their personal characteristics and strengths but also attaches greater importance to the party's communications strategy. Framing, branding, and marketing become increasingly potent in the battle to define and project a leader's image. As recent Liberal leaders have found, if they are unable to define and establish their own image, the opposition, the media and the public will do it for them. Paul Martin's perceived indecision and pursuance of multiple priorities earned him the unfortunate moniker of "Mr Dithers," which certainly damaged his and his party's electoral chances. In the case of Michael Ignatieff, many political observers believe that his unsuccessful tenure as Liberal party leader was all but assured by Conservative attack ads that painted him as "just visiting" because of his time spent outside the country. By May 2010, one year prior to the 2011 election, only 26% of Canadians had a favourable view of Ignatieff, with 52% saying that they had an unfavourable view of the leader.[32] The undermining of Stéphane Dion via Tory attack ads saying that "He is not a leader" and later Michael Ignatieff through similar sustained negative attack ads provided strong evidence that the political framing techniques successfully deployed in US elections have taken root in Canada.

Fearful of the ability and demonstrated willingness of a well-funded Conservative party to frame, define and exploit weaknesses in opposition leaders, the Liberal and NDP parties have had to place greater emphasis on the personalities of their respective leaders. The election of Thomas Mulcair and Justin Trudeau is in part a reflection of the opposition parties' realization that the leader's image must be sufficiently robust and well defined to withstand the negative attacks they will have to endure before, during and after campaigns. Mulcair was chosen in large part because he was seen as a strong abrasive leader capable of debating Stephen Harper in the House and during the increasingly pivotal leader debates.

In addition to a formidable Liberal heritage, Justin Trudeau's youth, charm, and charisma were seen as qualities that would contrast favourably with the popular characterization of Harper and Mulcair as middle-aged, dour and at times ruthless political combatants. As Warren Kinsella writes of Trudeau, "[o]n the election hustings, when measured against Trudeau, Stephen Harper and Thomas Mulcair will look like Angry Old Guys, because, er, they are."[33] Cohen makes a similar point: "In Trudeau, they may have found a cultural phenomenon. After all, who else in Canadian politics answers to his first name alone? No one calls the bloodless Stephen Harper 'Stephen' nor the dark Thomas Mulcair 'Thomas' (or, is it Tom?). In charm, the sunny Justin bests Harper, the accountant, and Mulcair, the undertaker."[34]

Trudeau's statements on his past use of marijuana and his support for legalization are part of a carefully orchestrated strategy to gain national attention on an issue that will illustrate many of the key generational and personality differences between the leaders. The Liberal Party decided to support the legalization of marijuana at the party convention in January of 2012,[35] a move which stirred some interest among the public, but had a relatively short media cycle. Trudeau, however, did not introduce the issue as a matter of Liberal policy, decided upon more than a year in advance of his public statements, but as a personal matter which had led him to his current views on legalization. Using an interview with the *Huffington Post* in August of 2013 Trudeau framed the issue as a matter of personal conviction sparking weeks of intense media coverage and placing the new Liberal leader firmly in the spotlight as a progressive reformer. In the interview, he told an anecdote, making sure to set a scene that Canadians could identify with. "We had a few good friends over for a dinner party, our kids were at their grandmother's for the night, and one of our friends lit a joint and passed it around. I had a puff."[36] By introducing the public to his stance on marijuana by making it about his choice to partake responsibly, Trudeau personalized the debate and attempted to highlight clear lines between his own "enlightened" and empathetic thinking on the issue and, by comparison, the relatively Draconian views of the prime minister.

The media's reaction to Trudeau's admission of past use was notable in that it focused almost entirely on individual reactions to Trudeau's revelations rather than the established party platforms and talking points on the matter. This involved questions being posed to virtually every other Canadian political personality about whether or not they had smoked marijuana in the past. Prime Minister Harper's reply to this question "Do I look like a person who would smoke pot" was also personal and deliberate in reassuring his base but also avoiding the trap of appearing too serious or sanctimonious on the issue, particularly in the eyes of younger voters.

LEADERSHIP TRUMPS POLICY

Trudeau's victory in the leadership race can be seen as a triumph of faith and hope over policy, competing ideologies or visions formulated and debated through the leadership campaign. As Cohen writes, "Having rejected Bob Rae, their seasoned interim leader, they are placing their hopes on a meteoric wunderkind with the right name, the right looks, the right age, the right words and the right instincts. The rest – policy, money, organization, candidates – will fall into place later, they hope."[37] Prior to the election of Justin Trudeau, the Liberal Party had generated lively policy debates during their recent leadership campaigns, with candidates like Stéphane Dion, Sheila Copps, Gerard Kennedy, and Bob Rae representing different ideological wings of the party.[38]

In Justin Trudeau's campaign for the Liberal leadership however, there was very little debate over the substance of policies, even though the party scheduled an unprecedented six debates occurring over a three month period.[39] Unfortunately, the debates were poorly organized and the questions posed and format used did little to reveal ideological or policy differences between the candidates. Candidates like Marc Garneau and Martha Hall-Findlay who did attempt to debate with Trudeau and push him to adopt a position were themselves criticized for challenging the heir apparent. "It has got so that two weeks ago, when the leadership contender Martha Hall Findlay hinted at Trudeau's obvious unsuitability to the task of championing the 'middle class' he claims to be uniquely qualified to champion, she was jeered at and shouted at and hounded until she apologized. *Maclean's* magazine called her question a 'jarring outburst.'"[40] Glavin attributes this deference to a "pathetic and distinctly Canadian variety of Canadian celebrity-worship,"[41] but this ignores the fact that party strategists were no doubt concerned that criticism from fellow liberals during the debates would be used in Conservative attack-ads, as happened to both Ignatieff and Dion. In the era of leadership idolization a leader is chosen largely based on his image and marketing potential and cannot be seen to be undermined by attacks from his own party. Conceding "own goals" in this way could unravel the entire continuous campaign strategy and hand priceless ammunition to political opponents.

When parties expected more substantive policy platforms and debate from their leaders, Trudeau would have had a much more trying time in a Liberal leadership contest. If nothing else this would have allowed MPs and party members to assess how potential leaders performed under pressure before being thrust into the spotlight of a federal election campaign. Instead, his lack of leadership experience or demonstrated interest in policymaking did nothing to dampen "Trudeaumania." In our view, his "coronation" as Liberal leader is a clear acknowledgement of the politics of leadership idolization, whereby party members line up behind the leader because it is seen to in the best interest of the party to do so.

Whether or not this type of symbolic and ceremonial "contest" is in the public interest is another matter. Cohen argues that it would have been better had the Liberal party leadership race "forced the party to reinvent itself with a coherent vision and a set of bold, evidence-based proposals."[42] Whether or not this is wise for the party in the current political climate is debatable, but surely it is in the public interest for parties to define themselves and their policies so that voters can assess and choose between coherent alternatives. This is after all the basis of a democratic parliamentary system.

CONCLUSIONS

The politics of leadership idolization as defined in this chapter will be difficult to change given the Canadian system's emphasis on the power of the party leader. Since we cannot look to leaders to voluntarily diminish their own power, party memberships appear to be the only viable solution. Unfortunately, party members appear to be acting rationally when they put the personal attributes of the leader ahead of political acumen and espoused policy platforms. In a political climate characterized by sound bites, attack ads and wedge issues, party manifestoes have all but disappeared with policies now construed as hostages to political fortune that may not resonate with focus groups and could offend interest groups and alienate potential voters.

With policy platforms seen as high risk and unnecessary political strategies, image management, advertising and branding become more attractive and serve to further conflate the party with its leader in the minds of the electorate. Moreover, while it is difficult to run a 30 second advertisement outlining a policy platform it is relatively simple to ridicule and demonise an opposing leader's character through short repetitive messaging. Attack-ads are supposedly unpopular with Canadians but that does not mean that they are not effective and we should expect to see further usage as elections are increasingly centred on image and personality.

It is difficult to determine the precise causes for Canadians' declining trust and engagement in the political process, but it is hard to imagine that shallow, negative campaigning of this type does anything to inspire increased participation in the democratic process. Worryingly, it is more likely to produce a largely uninformed and disengaged electorate who become more susceptible to branding, marketing and personality driven campaigns and increasingly base voting decisions on emotion rather than evidence or careful policy analysis of the major issues. Those looking to engage in more substantive, policy driven political debate will instead become increasingly cynical and disillusioned which may also result in further disengagement.

In spite of continuing disenchantment and disengagement with the politics of leadership idolization, particularly amongst younger voters, the focus on leadership will continue unabated so long as parties continue to consolidate power at the top of their political structures and the public fails to demand more from political leaders, parties and democratic institutions, especially Parliament. With growing signs of restlessness amongst back benchers, proposals for reform being tabled and public outrage over the Senate, the PMO and the contempt shown during question period, the upcoming 2015 federal election could be a significant turning point or simply further confirmation of this style of political campaign. Justin Trudeau will provide an excellent test case for how influential the power of leadership idolization has become in Canadian politics. He embodies many of the qualities required of a modern party political leader and, if successful could serve as a prototype for future leaders. Young, charismatic, confident, and unencumbered by policy "baggage," Trudeau is blessed with celebrity status and appears ideally equipped to revel in and excel at the politics of leadership idolization.

Nevertheless his political skills and judgement remain untested and he appears to have a knack for making comments that his opponents can easily exploit and use against him as they work to undermine his image and create doubts in the minds of voters about his stature, judgement and experience. If Trudeau were to win the next election, or even return the Liberal Party to opposition after being written off by many four years earlier, the lesson for all the political parties will be that modern campaign politics are first and foremost about the image and the control by and marketing of the leader. If, on the other hand, Trudeau and the Liberals perform badly in the next election, this may instigate a rethink about how and on what basis leaders are assessed.

Alternatively it may simply confirm the views of political strategists that negative campaigning and character assassination are an effective way of combating iconic leaders. Neither scenario bodes well for those hoping to see reinvigorated political debate, informed by policies, evidence and competing visions, concerning the environmental, economic, demographic and social challenges that loom large on the political horizon.

NOTES

1 Quoted in M. Bolen, "The 11 Most Ridiculously Flattering Things The Media Has Said About Justin Trudeau," *The Huffington Post Canada* (August 17, 2012). http://www.huffingtonpost.ca/2012/08/17/justin-trudeau-media-canada_n_1798871.html

2 Ibid.

3 Ibid.

4 Elections Canada, *Contestant's Weekly Leadership Campaign Return* (March 23, 2013). http://www.elections.ca/WPAPPS/WPF/EN/LC/SummaryReport?act=C2&eventid=7073&returntype=1&option=1&period=2&queryid=180abec4d5a34b3587bb6b5cdc9f3667

5 Jane Taber and Daniel Leblanc, "Justin Trudeau Elected Liberal Leader in a Landslide," *The Globe and Mail* (April 14, 2013).

6 Harold D. Clarke et al., *Absent Mandate: Interpreting Change in Canadian Elections*, 2nd ed. (Toronto: Gage Educational Publishing Co., 1991), quoted in Donald Savoie, *Breaking the Bargain: Public Servants, Ministers and Parliament* (University of Toronto Press, 2003), 176–7.

7 See Savoie, *Breaking the Bargain*; Donald Savoie, *Governing from the Centre: The Concentration of Power in Canadian Politics* (University of Toronto Press, 1999); Donald Savoie, *Power: Where Is It?* (Montreal and Kingston McGill-Queen's

University Press, 2010); and Peter Aucoin, Mark D. Jarvis, and Lori Turnbull, *Democratizing the Constitution: Reforming Responsible Government* (Edmond Montgomery, 2011).

8   "Speaking Up in Parliament," *Ottawa Citizen* editorial (April 24, 2013).
9   See Aucoin, Jarvis, and Turnbull, *Democratizing the Constitution.*
10   Samara exit poll cited in Alison Loat, "Why Are MPs Here? Good Question," *Ottawa Citizen* (April 13, 2013).
11   Loat, "Why are MPs here? Good question."
12   See Savoie, *Governing from the Centre*; and Aucoin, Jarvis, and Turnbull, *Democratizing the Constitution.*
13   Savoie, *Breaking the Bargain*, 176.
14   Bruce Cheadle, "Tories Re-brand Government in Stephen Harper's Name," *Globe and Mail* (March 3, 2011).
15   "Speaking Up in Parliament," *Ottawa Citizen* editorial (April 24, 2013).
16   D. Ross, "Nomination Process Will Cost Tories Votes," *Westman Journal* (September 27, 2013).
17   "Speaking Up in Parliament," *Ottawa Citizen* editorial (April 24, 2013).
18   Ibid.
19   Ibid.
20   Ibid.
21   B. Curry, "Harper May Have to Watch His Back(bench)," *The Globe and Mail* (September 17, 2012), http://www.theglobeandmail.com/news/politics/ottawa-notebook/harper-may-have-to-watch-his-backbench/article4548668/
22   CBC News, "MP Rathgeber Refuses to Be 'Cheerleader' and Quits Tory Caucus," CBC.ca, (June 5, 2013), http://www.cbc.ca/news/canada/edmonton/mp-rathgeber-refuses-to-be-cheerleader-and-quits-tory-caucus-1.1330541
23   Maria Mourani, "Quebec MP, Kicked Out of Bloc Quebecois for Denouncing Charter of Values," *Huffington Post Canada* (September 12, 2013), http://www.huffingtonpost.ca/2013/09/12/maria-mourani-bloc-quebec-values-charter_n_3913967.html
24   Dan Gardner, "Power Makes Politicians Stupid," *The Ottawa Citizen* (June 21, 2012).
25   Loat, "Why Are MPs Here? Good Question."
26   http://www.reformact2013.ca/Backgrounder.pdf.
27   Ibid.
28   Tonda MacCharles, "MP's reform bill would strike 'a blow for democracy'" *Toronto Star* (December 3, 2013), http://www.thestar.com/news/canada/2013/12/03/mps_reform_bill_would_strike_a_blow_for_democracy.html
29   Evan Sotiropoulos, "Private Members' Bills in Recent Minority and Majority Parliaments" *Canadian Parliamentary Review* 34, 3 (2011), http://www.revparl.ca/english/issue.asp?param=205&art=1446
30   Ibid., 3.
31   A. Raj, "Pierre Poilievre Suggests Tories Don't Need Reform Act," *The Huffington Post* (December 12, 2013), http://www.huffingtonpost.ca/2013/12/03/pierre-poilievre-michael-chong-reform-act_n_4379581.html.

32 Canadian Press, "Ignatieff Far and Away the Least Popular
    Leader: Poll," C T V News (May 18, 2010), http://www.ctvnews.ca/
    ignatieff-far-and-away-the-least-popular-leader-poll-1.513789
33 M. Bolen, "The 11 Most Ridiculously Flattering Things."
34 Andrew Cohen, "The Liberals' Rebuilding Is Still to Come," *Ottawa Citizen* (April 14, 2013).
35 Liberal Party of Canada, "Ottawa 2012 – Liberal Biennial Convention: Priority Policy
    Resolutions" (January 15, 2012), https://www.liberal.ca/files/2013/01/Ottawa-2012_
    Adopted-Policy-Resolutions.pdf
36 Liberal Party of Canada, "Ottawa 2012 – Liberal Biennial Convention: Priority Policy
    Resolutions."
37 Cohen, "The Liberals' Rebuilding Is Still to Come."
38 The N D P had only one leadership race between 1995 and 2011, making it difficult to
    judge any variety in ideology.
39 John Ibbitson, "Liberal Leadership Debate Stays on Script," *The Globe and Mail*
    (January 21, 2013).
40 Terry Glavin, "The Trudeau Effect," *Ottawa Citizen* (February 28, 2013).
41 Ibid.
42 C. Mikula, "Liberals Aren't Free of Ideas," *Ottawa Citizen* (February 22, 2013).

6 Coming Full Circle? Ottawa's Search for Parsimonious Cost and Efficiency Reporting

EVERT LINDQUIST

INTRODUCTION[1]

Even countries that had strong budgetary and financial regulatory systems, which allowed them to respond well to the global financial crisis of the late 2000s, find their economies and public finances on precarious footing, reflecting slow growth and exposure to the vicissitudes of key trade partners. Governments of all ideological dispositions are seeking to control costs and to moderate, reduce or reallocate spending. In September 2012, the Government of Canada announced that, in addition to previous and ongoing expenditure reviews, it would seek more cost efficiencies and establish a sub-committee of the Planning and Priorities Cabinet Committee for this purpose. In November 2012 the Treasury Board of Canada required departments to develop "program efficiency indicators" to "realize operational efficiencies and increase internal productivity,"[2] with the first submissions due in October 2013.

Drives for more efficient and effective government, of course, are not new.[3] Nor is the interest in systematic measurement new: for example, the Canadian government began focusing on service quality standards in the early 1990s, later adopting the common measurement tool,[4] developed a framework for measuring results and outcomes as part of the policy on management, resources, and results structures (MRRS), and instituted monitoring the quality of departmental management systems with the management accountability framework (MAF).[5] Indeed, recent focus on costs and efficiency reporting has an antecedent in the operational performance measurement system (OPMS) of the early 1970s.[6] Connecting these two initiatives might induce heart palpitations of many who lived through and critiqued the rise and fall of OPMS and other initiatives of TBS's former planning branch,[7] and qualify as the latest example of "surreal" management reform,[8] even if driven by the government and not TBS. This initiative is nevertheless worth monitoring because governments everywhere are getting hard-nosed about lowering costs and increasing efficiency, the costs of collecting and analyzing data have dropped, and many citizens would be surprised if ministers and central agencies were not monitoring costs. Central agencies and departments, however, must find new ways to present data to ministers and tools for real-time data-diving.

This chapter has four parts. The first provides background on the Treasury Board Secretariat (TBS) guidance on developing cost and efficiency indicators as part of departmental reporting for the 2013–14 fiscal year and considers the implications of emergent and parsimonious reporting. The second part identifies the cost dimensions of programs, and suggests that departments and central agencies should compare similar classes of organizations, but observing that considerably more background data and documentation is needed to meet this reporting request, which will require data-mining and visualization techniques. The third part identifies broader issues arising from these new reporting requirements, while the conclusion considers why we might be more sanguine about the potential of this latest reporting initiative.

THE CHALLENGE: MEASURING AND REPORTING ON PROGRAM COSTS AND EFFICIENCY

The general goal driving TBS's call for efficiency indicators is to "gain insight in the cost of delivering a program relative to the work performed."[9] In addition to finding savings, TBS notes that a "key function of successful management is to continually look for ways to deliver programs more efficiently. As experience is gained in a particular program, it is reasonable to expect the efficiency of a program to improve."[10] Departments were asked to identify one efficiency indicator (perhaps a second one under exceptional circumstances) to best show the costs of work or outputs of a given program, which might be the cost per transaction, major output, client population, or other proxy units. The guidance states that efficiency is "concerned with the cost of producing something, usually a specific output" or "the cost of completing a certain unit of work."[11]

Interestingly, departments are *not* to measure the benefits, public value, or effectiveness of programs. However, the indicators should be aligned with the expected results and strategic outcome indicators for the programs defined in a department's program activity architecture (PAA) under the MRRS. Developing single efficiency indicators for programs is meant to capture more detailed MRRS information, but TBS guidance notes that doing so "is not an exercise in absolute precision, but rather one that shows a year-over-year trend that allows for insights and facilitates management decision making" and goes on to note that "In some cases, efficiency may decrease for a host of valid reasons, and it is important to establish those reasons."[12] Reasons for a decline in efficiency may include public or government demands for increased reliability in delivering programs, better or more tailored ways to deliver them, the price of certain inputs may increase, or the government may insist that a program get delivered by a certain time regardless of the cost.

Ottawa has typically relied on a "vanguard" approach with willing departments and agencies to roll-out management improvement initiatives, but this one requires all departments to engage early on, which is daunting for several reasons. First, initial efforts may under-state or over-state real costs in comparison to other programs, leading to ill-informed decisions about funding levels for programs based on imperfect or misleading cost or efficiency data. Second, although TBS guidance situates cost and efficiency indicators as part of the broader expenditure management framework, the request de-couples them from assessing the value and benefits of activities. For many public servants and observers, to simply "cost" is not to fully assess programs. Finally, departments typically oversee diverse programs with different cost structures, and may count and apportion overhead costs in different ways. These differences across departments might not be easily accounted for if reporting is too parsimonious. In short, departments might worry that providing incomplete and emergent information on program costs and efficiency might have real consequences in review and decision-making processes.

Many Treasury Board management improvement initiatives started as formative practices, which were later institutionalized or systematically monitored after iterative learning. In this case the guidance for efficiency indicators explicitly notes: "it is expected that efficiency measures will be used in expenditure proposals."[13] The indicators might also inform program reviews, decisions about investing in new technology and service delivery systems, market-testing of internal and program services possibly leading to alternative delivery arrangements, and MAF reporting. This initiative was announced just after the subcommittee on government administration was established under the aegis of the Cabinet Policy and Planning Committee (chaired by the president of the Treasury Board). It signals that the government will take an interest in this reporting, even if it is only one stream of information on programs and departments. Ministers will review the efficiency data, which is why TBS guidance emphasized parsimony in indicators.

TBS's guidance observes that developing efficiency indicators "is not an exercise in absolute precision, but rather one that shows a year-over-year trend that allows for insights and facilitates management decision-making."[14] While some departments may have robust systems for monitoring program costs,[15] the new focus on costs represents a significant shift from the new public management (NPM) emphasis on measuring outputs, outcomes, and perceptions of citizens and clients receiving services.[16] That said, the focus on results and outcomes has not been relinquished; indeed, requiring more careful measurement of inputs and activities in connection to outputs suggests that the government could be moving departments towards a more well-rounded total quality management approach for collecting and analyzing data.

DIFFERENTIATION: FROM ASCERTAINING COSTS TO DISPLAYING EFFICENCY INFORMATION

Unlike M A F, which seeks indicators on the performance of department-wide management systems, the level of analysis for developing program efficiency measures is specific programs or activities, but departments often have diverse programs. An important test of cost-related reporting will involve how similar and different programs get compared and interpreted within and across departments.[17] It raises the crucial matter of how best to present information in a context when T B S seeks reporting parsimony in the face of program complexity and diversity.

Cost Dimensions of Programs

Although T B S seeks parsimony in efficiency reporting, cost structures will vary considerably across programs. These differences should be identified and understood in order to analyze and assess the data at higher levels. Table 6.1 sets out different aspects of cost for identified outputs and activities, a basis for arriving at a small group of indicators for reporting on department programs. This list of cost data may seem daunting, flying in the face of Treasury Board guidelines about departments developing only a handful of efficiency indicators for consideration by T B S officials and ministers. However, producing good indicators requires that departments develop a deeper understanding of the drivers of costs.

During 2013, then, the challenge for departments was to identify reliable, robust and suitably parsimonious efficiency and costing information on programs as quickly as possible, often working with external consultants. Corralling and reporting such information had to anticipate the need to differentiate across programs and to link to program goals and outputs to increase the likelihood of productive comparisons and conclusions. Such parsimonious efficiency and cost reporting must be informed and supported by vertically integrated reporting systems and a hierarchy of data, including parallel indicators which may not have made the cut into the final group, requiring good dashboard and other visualization techniques.

The drive for parsimony in reporting up the line will not rule out collecting a great deal of cost-related data and developing multiple indicators for programs. Program cost and efficiency data need to be understood and interpreted as the information moves from specific program areas to department executive teams to central agencies and eventually to ministers for the

Table 6.1
Cost dimensions of programs

A. *Program: Work and Client.* Here the focus is on ascertaining the nature of program in terms of the kind of work or tasks undertaken, clients served, and whether intermediaries are involved:

- PROGRAM ACTIVITIES: does the program focus on service delivery, regulation, funding, policy, communications, internal services, etc?

- PROGRAM OUTPUTS AND CLIENTS: What does the program "produce"? What clients does it serve? Does the program provide direct or indirect delivery? Are intermediaries involved in delivering services?

- QUICKNESS OF SERVICE DELIVERY: Do the tasks of the program require immediate service responses or interactions over months or years?

B. *Program Factor Inputs.* The cost structure of programs may vary according to the nature of inputs and where transforming activities take place. Some input dimensions to consider are:

- POINT OF SERVICE: What is the extent of reliance on headquarters vs. regional operations?

- RELIANCE ON INFORMATION TECHNOLOGY: What is the extent of reliance on information technology and other systems (IT vs. non-IT costs)?

- STAFFING COSTS: What is the extent of reliance on staff or human resource capabilities (ratio of HR to non-HR costs)? Have the costs of benefits and training been factored in?

- SERVICE CHANNELS: How many channels are used to deliver the services associated with a program? Do they have different cost structures? Has the mix and volumes changed?

C. *Program Infrastructure Cost Cycle.* Programs vary with respect to their newness and the lifecycle of technologies they need to carry out work (technological and social). Such costs may vary with respect to:

- MATURITY. Is the program old or new? Does the program have sunset provisions?

- INFRASTRUCTURE COSTS: Do costs need to be amortized over the length of the program?

- EXPECTED SPIKES AND DIPS: Does the program have cycles within and across years?

- PHASES: Will the program have phases when fixed as opposed to variable costs are completed, partners engage, putative benefits are anticipated to come on stream, etc.

D. *Department Cost Allocation.* Departments have distinct corporate practices for assigning costs to support programs and corporate services (HR, FM, IT, accounting, contracting, real property, communications, etc.), which will affect how efficient programs appear to be. These may vary with respect to:

- COSTING INTERNAL SERVICES: Does the department assign costs as a central corporate program or assign these costs to programs on a distributed basis? A mixed model?

- COSTING PROGRAM SERVICES: Do all of the costs of programs rest with a given programs or are they shouldered by program clusters or corporate services? A mixed model?

- COSTING OVERHEAD: What constitutes overhead? Are there different levels? How are overhead costs calculated, allocated, and amortized?

E. *Accounting for scale.* Programs vary with respect to scale, creating difficulty in comparing programs across departments and affecting the robustness of cost and efficiency indicators used to describe programs.

- CONSIDERING SCALE: What are the number of clients are served? The amount of staff resources used? What amount of funding is moved to clients or intermediaries?

- LEVEL FOR COMPARISON: Should a program, distinct activities, or even sub-activities be compared with each other?

review or decision purposes at hand. Productively comparing cost and efficiency indicators requires understanding that programs vary considerably and evolve over time.

Comparing Programs

Cost and efficiency indicators will not mean much on their own; even with year-over-year information. Executives and ministers need to appreciate the essential differences across programs and activities to properly interpret the data and indicators, and this requires identifying and categorizing, at a high level, different kinds of programs. Many dimensions that have been identified for comparing organizations, but the most promising comes from the James Q. Wilson's seminal work on how public bureaus work and differ from each other, which led a two-sided typology based on the extent to which the outputs of organizations were observable, and the extent to which the process of producing those outputs were readily observable.[18] Figure 6.1 shows the resulting typology, with four broad categories based on the nature of organizational work – production, procedural, craft, and coping – which can lead to finer-grained distinctions about different program types: direct service-delivery, funding other governments or entities, science (in-house or externally), regulation, policy, communications, internal services, etc.

Identifying different program types will allow for more subtle comparison of cost and efficiency indicators within and across departments and agencies, controlling for differences in the nature of work and clients served (e.g., we might expect higher costs for science-based programs, as opposed to funding programs, as well as different time horizons). Whether these proposed categories are appropriate is a matter for debate, but there cannot be too many categories, nor too few. Once the categories are determined, this could provide the basis for data analytics and colour-coded tables and charts containing cost and efficiency information.

Comparing Costs

One challenge for departments and agencies will be to display year-over-year cost and efficiency indicators for multiple programs as part of high-level reporting to ministers and executives. In 1974 Treasury Board of Canada performance reporting displayed a mock-up chart (see Figure 6.2) for actual versus forecast data for input, output, and efficiency data for three distinct program activities over several years (base year, then four subsequent years).[19] This is the kind of parsimony that T B S is currently seeking to encourage (but only *one* cost or efficiency index for a program!), useful for scanning and high-level pattern recognition. But, given the request for single indicators, T B S might prefer *only* the efficiency indicators for each program knowing that departments have input and output "back-up" data on programs at hand.

Figure 6.1
Wilson Typology applied to programs

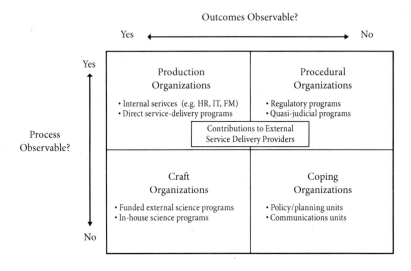

Displaying Cost Drivers

Cost and efficiency dashboards are great for showing and comparing indicators, but they only display summary information, distilled from a broader set of data on programs, activities and sub-activities. Ministers and central agency analysts will likely ask about trends, anomalies, and differences across programs and departments. Finer-grained information will need to be on tap (along with other indicators not chosen as the summary indicators). The challenge will be to analyze and display the potentially relevant cost information identified in Table 6.1. Figure 6.3 shows a parallel-coordinates graph (which can display data on five variables), one technique used in information visualization and data analytics,[20] which could be adapted to address this need. Such graphs are flexible and can compare indicators on different costs, activities and outputs associated with diverse programs in a department or similar types of programs from across departments. They can filter and highlight different cost components and show data year-over-year by isolating different categories of data using brushing (or colouring) techniques or showing finer-grained data (component elements).

The same information visualization and data analytic techniques can be used for *upstream* analysis: to review cost and efficiency data, to identify key trends and issues, to explore and explain anomalies, and to select indicators. There are also myriad possibilities for linking cost and efficiency data and indicators to MRRS and PAA information using these techniques.

Figure 6.2
Example: "Performance Reporting to Senior Management"

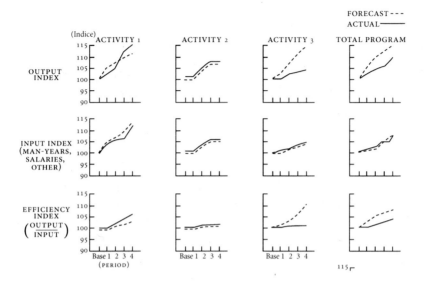

Figure 6.3
Example of parallel coordinate plots

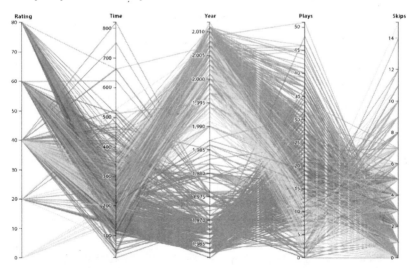

From Max Curran's May 2, 2012 blog posting at the Rensselaer Polytechnic Institute's "Tetherless World Constellation" website at http://twcmaxcurran.blogspot.ca/.

REPPORTING ON PROGRAM EFFICIENCY:
CAUTIONARY NOTES

In responding to TB guidelines, departments will rightly focus attention on developing cost and efficiency indicators. However, there are broader institutional and system issues to consider, such as the use of the indicators by decision-makers, the allocation and displacement of resources, recruitment of expertise, and potential impact on other streams of reporting.

Some Costing Issues and Challenges to Consider

TBS guidance suggests that, if cost changes are significant enough to draw attention in central reviews, then departments can explain what is driving those changes. However, some changes might be policy-induced or externally driven, respectively arising from ministers or citizens demanding more reliability when delivering certain programs, or due to increase in market prices for inputs. In other words, departments may not have been able to control costs. The parsimony in cost indicators might mask interesting cost shifts due to data aggregated at a high-level *and* trends moving in opposite directions across programs at a lower level, netting out. Department officials would have access to the lower-level information, but central analysts and ministers might not. Central analysts might seek out and compare more detailed cost data and indicators for similar programs across departments.

Many years ago Hartle pointed out that, while year-over-year cost and efficiency indicators are undoubtedly useful, the "base" or overhead costs may not be easily understood and compared: "Fat operations can appear to have remarkable reductions in unit costs with little effort, while lean ones have to struggle for improvements."[21] This suggests that Treasury Board carefully analyze overhead cost components, since the initial costing will likely function as *de facto* benchmarks for comparison with other departments, providers, and other governments. It is critical to fully understand how different programs and departmental costing systems work, particularly program-base outlays (including overhead costs), before exploring alternative service delivery, contracting out, or adopting public-service-wide systems.

Assessing Costs and Outcomes: Bifurcated or Integrated, and Realistic?

TBS guidance suggests that costing and efficiency indicators could be linked to and leaven deliberations using the MRRS and strategic objectives. But it is only one strand of reporting in a much broader ecology of the reporting, planning, review, and decision-making of the Canadian government. However, a greater focus on costs and efficiency requires non-trivial reallocation and investments by department corporate staff for upstream planning and reporting, and downstream response to central decisions. Limited resources may lead to crowding-out of focus and effort, prioritizing central reporting demands, diverting resources from other internal services or programs, or creatively striking new more productive balances.

The hope that cost/efficiency indicators might be used alongside MRRS strategic outcomes and indicators is interesting, but begs the question of how and by whom. Connecting cost and efficiency indicators with program goals and strategic outcome indicators introduces a level of complexity and, presumably, additional reporting. One possibility is that departments supply the indicators, and responsibility for integration falls to central agencies, which might produce conclusions independent of departments. Another is that departments are charged with better connecting cost and efficiency information with progress on strategic outcome indicators.

In this context, as departments match cost and efficiency indicators with strategic outcome indicators, a variant of the "attribution challenge"[22] might become a practical concern: if more accurate and accessible cost-reporting reveals a trend of increasing costs, and if the original aspirations for changing outcomes were unrealistic, then questions may be raised about the worth of those investments. There will be considerable incentive to revisit the realism and feasibility of strategic MRRS goals with limited resources. Program goals and objectives may have been approved based on insufficiently nuanced and realistic claims about how such interventions might single-handedly alter the trajectory of outcomes or difficult problems.

Trade-offs and Costs in Reporting?

Producing new reporting for central agencies is not cost-less: it requires accessing and analyzing new streams of data and diverting scarce staff and executive time to handle this work. As French and others have asked,[23] will the increased costs and diverted resources be worth the ostensible benefits in improved decision-making? Who will monitor the costs of measuring and monitoring costs, as well as the putative benefits? Similar objections arose with the more stringent reporting on grants and contributions for accountability, and reporting costs heaped on recipients.[24] The key question is whether the costs of cost and efficiency indicators will be kept proportional to their use and value. As with MAF, TBS might consider an independent review after five years.[25] Exploring the cost of reporting on costs and efficiency should stimulate thinking on how it can inform and lever other reporting.

Another concern rests with shifting expertise to handle cost and efficiency data and analysis. When the Australian government adopted full accrual accounting methodology for estimates and budget reporting, the then Department of Finance and Administration (equivalent to TBS) dispensed with its more generalist program analysts, hiring more narrowly-trained analysts with expertise in cost accounting.[26] However, despite the shift to accrual budgetary reporting, ministers still wanted to understand programs and budget decisions in broader terms – eventually more traditional expertise had to be re-built. A similar temptation could arise in Ottawa, particularly if the government aggressively uses cost and efficiency information as part of internal or external market-testing of program and corporate services.

Will Cost and Efficiency Reporting Affect the Use of Other Reporting?

The Treasury Board guidance presumes that ministers will have limited time to digest cost and efficiency information from departments – hence the call for one indicator. Not only has the use of evaluations by governments long been low, so too the use of performance reports by legislators,[27] and presumably this holds for ministers and deputy ministers. Arguably, in the late 1990s and early 2000s, the drive for performance reporting crowded out the appetite for funding and reviewing evaluations, since the latter took too long to produce and could not be summarized with a few indicators.

Given Canada's economic circumstances, ministers will focus more on lowering or containing costs in the medium term, and less on measuring the benefits and value of programs, which suggests less demand for evaluation studies on program effectiveness and outcomes. Ministers will be interested in meeting global performance targets, and making their own judgments on the worth and value of existing and new programs.

A related challenge concerns what departments learn, formally or informally, about how the cost and efficiency indicators are used by ministers and central agencies. In a different context, Hartle commented on his experience with cost and efficiency reporting:

> Unless the dollar and manpower budgets arrived at for those activities to which OPMS has been applied in fact reflect the results, the incentive for agencies to maintain, much less extend, OPMS is, to say the least, minimal. There has been a tendency, I am afraid, to have the Planning Branch of the Treasury Board out flogging OPMS to departments while the Program Branch of the Treasury Board has found it expedient to make its recommendations to ministers as though the information were not available … The Treasury Board Secretariat has the obligation, it seems to me, to explain why its recommendations are inconsistent with the OPMS numbers.[28]

Departments stopped making necessary investments in building OPMS repertoires because they had little incentive. That said, the producers of MAF reports, department performance reports, audits, evaluations, etc., should recognize that most research and other studies are rarely directly used in decision-making, but serve important symbolic and readiness-building functions.[29] It may matter less that cost and efficiency indicators inform decisions (although they might be used episodically in reviews), and more that the reports were *seen* to be requested and departments *could* produce them.[30] We should anticipate that evidence of the ability to produce costing and efficiency indicators will be required for departmental M A F submissions.

CONCLUSIONS: IS THERE CAUSE FOR OPTIMISM?

Forty years ago Hartle and Treasury Board's Planning Branch produced a broad, coherent approach to analysis and decision-making for government encompassing priority-setting, budgeting, evaluation, cost-benefit analysis, and more. That ambitious effort has been well- chronicled, particularly with respect to the low level of interest of ministers in using such information. Such reminders inject much-needed realism when introducing management improvement initiatives. While we should be realistic about what the extent to which cost and efficiency reporting will be used by policy-makers and central-agency analysts, and aware of potential displacement effects in terms of work and absorbing other information and analysis, we should also consider what has changed.

What new capabilities and dispositions might make it more likely to realize improved cost and efficiency monitoring and reporting, and utilization? These might include the following: vast increases in computational power, significantly lowering the costs of assembling, linking, and analyzing data; significant improvements in visualization techniques for analyzing and presenting data; improvements in information technology and financial management systems, and movement towards common platforms across the government; increasing interest of governments and the public in containing costs and productive use of resources; considerable experience rolling out multi-year corporate initiatives such as Modern Comptrollership, Results for Canadians, Management Accountability Framework, and M R R S /P A A reporting; successfully responded to the Government Accountability Act which mandated new reporting repertoires; and most of the data for developing cost and efficiency indicators are already in systems, and some departments and agencies already pay close attention to costing and efficiency reporting.

In short, there is potential to produce the indicators requested by the Harper government, and to better link them to other reporting vehicles. Despite the focus on parsimonious reporting to ministers, at the very least this initiative promises to motivate executives and senior managers of departments to become even more cost-conscious and conversant about cost-drivers. More fundamentally, citizens would expect that our government is concerned about least-cost and most-efficient ways to delivering programs, as would for-profit and non-profit organizations.

The candidates for cost and efficiency indicators were submitted by departments in mid-fall 2013. They will be reviewed by T B S analysts and T B ministers, with efficiency measures to be included in the departments' 2014–15

Performance Management Frameworks. Data in support of the indicators are to be collected during 2014, followed by refinement and adjustment of the measures in the years to follow. It will be interesting to learn about the extent to which cost and efficiency reporting has influence government understanding and decision-making about programs. However, our expectations should be in order: in addition to the predilections of the government, many decisions revealed in the 2014 and 2015 budgets will have been informed by a host of representations by experts and interest groups earlier in their respective budget cycles as well as a succession of strategic and operating reviews, evaluations, and internal and external audits. Perhaps the most important clue about the views of ministers and top advisors will arise from the next round of T B guidance to departments on reporting.

NOTES

1 This chapter emerged from presentations to the PPX Workshop on Developing Effective Efficiency Indicators (22 January 2013) and the 17th Annual PPX Symposium (15 May 2013), both intended to stimulate dialogue among central agency and department representatives. Special thanks to the leadership of the Performance Planning Exchange (PPX) in Ottawa and to Bruce Doern and Chris Stoney for editorial advice.

2 D. Ovsey, "Ottawa Wants Better Productivity, so Why Not Measure Its Own?" *Financial Post* (20 November 2012); and Canada, "PM Announces the Establishment of the Priorities and Planning Sub-Committee on Government Administration" (Ottawa, 13 September 2012). Accessed at: http://pm.gc.ca/eng/media.asp?id=5027.

3 E. Lindquist, "How Ottawa Reviews Spending: Moving Beyond Adhocracy?" in *How Ottawa Spends, 2006–2007: In from the Cold – The Tory Rise and the Liberal Demise*, ed. Bruce Doern (Montreal and Kingston: McGill-Queen's University Press, 2006), 185–207.

4 F. Schmidt and T. Strickland, *Client Satisfaction Surveying: Common Measurements Tool* (Ottawa: Citizen-Centric Service Network and Canadian Centre for Management Development, December 1998).

5 E. Lindquist, "How Ottawa Assesses Department/Agency Performance: Treasury Board's Management Accountability Framework," in *How Ottawa Spends, 2009–2010: Economic Upheaval and Political Dysfunction*, ed. Allan Maslove (McGill-Queen's University Press, 2009), 47–88.

6 D.G. Hartle, "Operational Performance Measurement in the Federal Government." *Optimum: The Journal of Public Sector Management* (Winter 1972): 5–17; Treasury Board of Canada, *Operational Performance Measurement: A Managerial Overview, Vol. 1* (Ottawa: Information Canada, 1974a); and Treasury Board of Canada, *Operational Performance Measurement: Techniques, Vol. 2* (Ottawa: Information Canada, 1974b).

7   R. French, *How Ottawa Decides: Planning and Industrial Policy Making 1968–1984*, 2nd ed. (Toronto: Lorimer, 1984); D.G. Hartle, "A Proposed System of Program and Policy Evaluation." *Canadian Public Administration* 16, 2 (June 1973): 243–66; and D.G. Hartle, "Techniques for Improving Effectiveness," in *The Expenditure Budget Process in the Government of Canada* (Toronto: Canadian Tax Foundation, 1978): 57–93.

8   I.D. Clark and H. Swain, "Distinguishing the Real from the Surreal in Management Reform: Suggestions for Beleaguered Administrators in the Government of Canada." *Canadian Public Administration* 48, 4 (December 2005): 453–76.

9   Treasury Board of Canada, "TBS Guidance on Developing Efficiency Indicators for PMF 2013–14" (September 2012).

10 Ibid.

11 Ibid.

12 Ibid.

13 Ibid.

14 Ibid.

15 Some activities are more conducive to such reporting, and some organizations such as the Canada Revenue Agency, have had incentives to do so, such as keeping savings from lower costs.

16 G. Dinsdale and D.B. Marson, *Citizen/Client Surveys: Dispelling Myths and Redrawing Maps.* (Ottawa: Canadian Centre for Management Development), 199; and B. Marson and R. Heintzman, *From Research to Results: A Decade of Results-Based Service Improvement in Canada. Toronto: Institute of Public Administration of Canada* (Toronto: Institute of Public Administration of Canada, 2009).

17 M. Brulot and M. Hale, "Comparable Program Efficiency Indicators." *Canadian Government Executive* 19 (May 2013), 4.

18 J.Q. Wilson, *Bureaucracy* (New York: Basic Books, 1989).

19 See Treasury Board of Canada, *Operational Performance Measurement, Vol. 1*, Fig. 10, p. 45.

20 For an introduction to the diverse practice fields of visualization, see E. Lindquist, "Surveying the World(s) of Visualization," Background Paper for the Australian National University's HC Coombs Policy Forum Roundtables on Policy Visualization (6 May 2011). Accessible at http://publicpolicy.anu.edu.au/coombs/research/visualization.

21 D. Hartle, "Techniques and Processes of Administration." *Canadian Public Administration* 19, 1 (March 1976): 26.

22 On attribution, See J. Mayne, "Addressing Attribution through Contribution Analysis: Using Performance Measures Sensibly." Ottawa: Office of the Auditor General of Canada, 1999. This discussion paper accessed at http://www.oag-bvg.gc.ca/internet/docs/99dp1_e.pdf.

23 French, *How Ottawa Decides.*

24 Canada, *From Red Tape to Clear Results: The Report of the Independent Blue Ribbon Panel on Grants and Contributions Programs* (Ottawa: Treasury Board of Canada Secretariat, 2006).

25 See Lindquist, "How Ottawa Assesses." However, if the goal is only to "find savings," it might be better to rely on Australia's annual efficiency dividends, notwithstanding concerns about whether it equitably treats different programs. See Parliament of the Commonwealth of Australia, Joint Committee of Public Accounts and Audit, *The Efficiency Dividend and Small Agencies: Size Does Matter* (Canberra: Commonwealth of Australia, December 2008).

26 J. Kelly and J. Wanna, "Crashing through with Accrual-Output Price Budgeting in Australia: Technical Adjustment or a New Way of Doing Business?" *American Review of Public Administration* 34, 1 (2004): 94–111.

27 J.C. McDavid and I. Huse, "Legislator Uses of Public Performance Reports: Findings from a Five Year Study." *American Journal of Evaluation* (2011).

28 Hartle, "Techniques and Processes of Administration," 26–7.

29 M.S. Feldman and J.G. March, "Information in Organizations as Signal and Symbol." *Administrative Science Quarterly* 26 (1981): 171–86.

30 See March and Feldman, "Information in Organizations"; and J.W. Meyer and B. Rowan, "Institutionalized Organizations: Formal Structure as Myth and Ceremony," *American Journal of Sociology* 83 (September 1977): 340–63.

7 Tax Expenditures and Government Program Spending: Reforming the Two "Spending" Worlds for Better Expenditure Management

JOHN LESTER

INTRODUCTION

The federal government has set up an expenditure management system with considerable potential for improving the efficiency and effectiveness of its spending. A key innovation of the system implemented in 2007 is the use of ongoing strategic reviews to ensure that programs are aligned with federal responsibilities and priorities, and that they are efficiently delivered and performing effectively. These strategic reviews are expected to be underpinned by formal evaluations of program performance undertaken by departments.

In order to maximize the system's potential, however, I argue that two changes should be made. First, spending programs delivered through the tax system, also known as tax expenditures, should be integrated into the expenditure management system. Failure to integrate tax expenditures means that about $35 billion in spending escapes the discipline imposed by strategic reviews and systematic evaluation of program performance. Second, federal evaluation policy should be reformed so that program effectiveness is evaluated by an independent entity making use of the benefit-cost framework, which is now used to evaluate *regulatory* policies. Program evaluation is not fulfilling its intended role in the expenditure management process or its role in promoting accountability to Parliament and Canadians generally. The main shortcoming of the current approach is that most published evaluations focus on administrative efficiency of programs and do not often deal with their effectiveness and relevance.

Reform of the expenditure management system along the lines proposed in this chapter cannot proceed unless responsibility for tax expenditures that are substitutes for program spending is transferred from the minister of finance to program ministers. Further, the finance minister would have to relinquish his power, exercised jointly with the prime minister, to introduce, modify, or eliminate tax measures related to the mandate of a program minister without the consent of the minister.

THE FEDERAL GOVERNMENT'S EXPENDITURE MANAGEMENT SYSTEM

The federal government introduced a new expenditure management system in 2007. Under the new system program spending by every department and agency must be reviewed on a four-year cycle. More specifically, these strategic reviews cover "direct" program spending, defined as program spending less major transfers to other levels of government and individuals. Strategic reviews are intended to identify programs, or program elements, that are no longer aligned with government priorities or are not achieving expected results, and to generate savings by reducing program delivery costs. Departments are typically required to identify five per cent of their direct program spending that could be reallocated to other priorities, including deficit reduction.

Federal departments must also undertake formal evaluations of direct program spending on a five-year cycle.[1] These evaluations are expected to provide evidence for use in strategic reviews as well as to support accountability to Parliament and Canadians generally, in particular by requiring the evaluations to be made public. There is also a formal obligation to evaluate the major transfers,[2] but unlike direct program spending there is no predetermined cycle and there is no requirement to make the results public.

Public reporting and parliamentary oversight of government spending is an important element of an effective expenditure management system. Most federal spending is governed by specific legislation that does not require annual approval by Parliament; but non-statutory spending, most of which is direct program spending, must be "voted" each year by Parliament. The details of planned spending are tabled in the House of Commons no later than March 1 each year in the *Estimates*.[3] Departments must prepare reports on their spending plans (reports on plans and priorities) and table them before Parliament shortly after the *Estimates*. They are also required to table reports on spending outcomes (Departmental Performance Reports) in the fall. These two reports, which are considered part of the *Estimates*, present detailed, multi-year information on spending by strategic outcome and program activity. The audited financial statements of the federal government are presented in the public accounts. The accounts also contain details of revenues and expenditures by department.

Tax expenditures are not included in the expenditure management system, nor are they covered by the government's evaluation policy. Estimates of the tax revenue forgone through tax expenditures are presented in *Tax Expenditures and Evaluations*, published by the Department of Finance. Following a recommendation by the Public Sector Accounting Board in 2011, refundable tax credits, which are payable even if the taxpayer has no tax liabilities, are recorded as spending in the government's financial accounts and revenues are reported gross of refundable tax credits. Non-refundable tax credits continue to be netted against revenue.

Parliament reviews expenditures through various standing committees, which have broad powers to examine spending, including the right to question ministers and public servants. There is, however, widespread concern that Parliament does not fulfill its role in scrutinizing government spending and "standing committees are at best giving perfunctory attention to the government's spending plans."[4] The committee system was substantially strengthened by the creation of the Standing Committee on Government Operations and Estimates in 2002. The mandate of this committee, which is chaired by a member of the opposition, includes the review of statutory programs and tax expenditures, although the Committee has not been active in these new areas of responsibility.

INTEGRATION OF TAX EXPENDITURES IN EXPENDITURE MANAGEMENT

The Case for Integration

The term "tax expenditure" was coined in the 1960s by Stanley Surrey[5] in order to draw attention to the fact that the tax system can be used to achieve economic and social objectives in the same way as spending programs. This can be seen most clearly in the case of refundable tax credits, which are identical to spending programs with no funding cap. While a non-refundable tax credit cannot exactly duplicate the impact of a spending program because benefiting from the credit is conditional on having tax liabilities, the need for transparency, accountability and assessment of performance does not change if a program is delivered through the tax system instead of as a direct spending program. There are strong arguments for including tax expenditures within the purview of strategic reviews, the government's evaluation policy and financial reports to Parliament.

The integration of tax expenditures into the expenditure management system requires that tax expenditures be allocated to the budgets of spending departments. This change would encourage a "whole-of-government" approach to program delivery: lead departments would see, and be responsible for, all government programming on a particular issue, which should lead to better decision making. For example, including tax expenditures in an expenditure reduction or containment exercise would pay dividends in terms of equity, effectiveness, and efficiency

- by considering both tax and spending initiatives, the burden of controlling spending or achieving deficit reduction targets would be spread more fairly across the beneficiaries of government spending;
- by the perceived fairness of the exercise, which would make it easier to implement the required changes;
- by identifying the least effective spending and tax measures, the economic cost of expenditure reduction can be minimized.

The integration of tax expenditures into the expenditure management system would impose some discipline on the use of the tax system to deliver programs. With integration, implementing a new tax expenditure would cause program spending to rise, which would create an additional constraint on their use. Further, if spending departments were responsible for both direct and tax-based spending programs, they would have an incentive to choose the most efficient way to achieve program objectives.

Previous Experience

Tax expenditures were included in the Policy and Expenditure Management System in effect from 1979 to 1989,[6] but the experiment was not successful and was abandoned in the mid-1980s. Integration applied only to new tax measures; existing tax expenditures were not allocated to departments, apparently because there was no consensus on how they should be distributed.[7] Tax expenditures proposed by program departments were submitted to the minister of finance for assessment of technical and administrative feasibility. A curious feature of the integrated system was that the cost of measures proposed by departments were automatically debited against the appropriate funding envelope, but allocating savings from scaling back existing measures required approval of the minister of finance and the relevant cabinet committee because they involved tax increases.

In principle, the minister of finance could only implement measures in specific program areas with the concurrence of the relevant minister and cabinet committee, but this constraint was not always respected.[8] In addition, the minister of finance had considerable discretion in the allocation of costs and savings to spending envelopes. In his assessment of why the integration of tax and spending programs was not successful, Poddar emphasizes the over-use of the discretion provided to the minister of finance. Poddar also mentions the exclusion of existing tax measures as a reason for the failure of integration, which made the system appear to be arbitrary. In addition, Poddar cites the lack of systematic accounting for tax expenditures as a contributing factor to the demise of the system.

A PROPOSAL FOR AN INTEGRATED SYSTEM

This section provides the broad outline for a reformed expenditure management system, drawing on Canada's past experience and an assessment of potential pitfalls. In order to maximize the benefits from integration, existing tax expenditures would have to be allocated to the budget of the relevant spending department, which would then absorb the cost or savings arising from any modifications to the measures. Program ministers proposing to shift delivery from the tax system to program spending, or vice versa, would have to demonstrate the existence of a net benefit from the change, either from lower costs or from improved effectiveness. In order to provide the right incentive for departments to choose the most efficient delivery method, program delivery costs of the Canada Revenue Agency should be attributed to spending departments.

Allocating existing tax expenditures to spending departments means that tax expenditures as reported by Finance Canada have to be carefully reviewed to determine which are substitutes for program spending; this issue is discussed in more detail below. As an illustration of how the allocation of existing tax expenditures would be carried out, consider the following:

- funding for the Scientific Research and Experimental Development (SR&ED) investment tax credit would become part of the Industry Canada portfolio, which now includes most spending programs that provide support for business R&D and innovation, including venture capital financing;
- all tax measures providing benefits to older Canadians (e.g. the age credit, the pension income credit, pension income splitting and the non-taxation of the guaranteed income supplement and allowances) would become part of Human Resources and Skills Development Canada's portfolio, which includes expenditure programs such as old age security, the guaranteed income supplement and allowances; and,
- tax expenditures supporting arts and culture (e.g. the children's arts tax credit, donations of cultural property and the Canadian film or video production tax credit) would become part of the Canadian Heritage portfolio.

A reformed expenditure management system would include improved accounting for tax expenditures. Some progress has already been made as a result of adopting in 2012 the Public Sector Accounting Board standard requiring that the cost of refundable tax credits be added to program spending and budgetary revenues. Prior to this change, most refundable tax credits were netted against tax revenues, which caused both program spending and tax revenue to be understated.[9] While this is a substantive change, all tax-based spending programs should be presented in the *Estimates,* which includes departmental performance reports and reports on plans and priorities, so that Parliament has a complete picture of spending. Over the longer term, the government should develop options for revising the public accounts to report tax revenue gross of non-refundable credits and to include the cost of these credits in program spending.

This change to financial reporting would help offset the perception, noted above, that elimination of tax expenditures amounts to sustaining existing levels of spending with higher taxes. Under the existing financial reporting system, elimination of a non-refundable tax credit would raise tax revenue but would not show up in lower program spending. With the proposed presentation of financial results, elimination of a non-refundable credit would result in lower program spending, but there would be no change in tax revenue.

The role of the minister of finance has to be carefully considered to promote successful integration of tax expenditures into the expenditure management system. The minister of finance has the prerogative, exercised jointly with the prime minister, to introduce, modify or eliminate tax measures related to the mandate of a program department without the concurrence of the relevant minister. This power would be lost if tax-delivered programs were the responsibility of spending departments. In contrast, the minister of finance should continue to have the power to propose new tax-based spending programs, but implementation would require the consent of the affected minister and the relevant cabinet committee. Further, proposals to implement new tax expenditures would only be accepted if the minister of finance deems them to be administratively and technically feasible.

In addition, the reform proposals would not eliminate Finance Canada's role in developing policy for measures "transferred" to other departments. As a central agency responsible for providing economic and fiscal advice on the government's policy agenda, Finance Canada plays a key role in many issues without having responsibility for program delivery – examples include areas such as justice and public safety, labour markets, income security and aboriginal issues. To take a specific example, if the SR&ED were to become part of the Industry Canada portfolio, Finance Canada would continue to offer advice on the government's innovation agenda, the amount of resources that should be allocated to the agenda, and how the budget allocation for innovation should be distributed. But the decision to change the policy parameters of the SR&ED investment tax credit would no longer be made by the minister of finance and the prime minister independently of the rest of the cabinet.

The government response to the recommendations of the standing committee on government operations and the estimates[10] gives a very clear idea of how the current government would react to a more explicit proposal to integrate tax expenditures into the expenditure management system. The government rejected the committee's recommendation to include tax expenditures in the appropriate departmental reports on plans and priorities, on the grounds that the "tax system, including all tax expenditures, is the responsibility of the Minister of Finance."[11] The general reason advanced for supporting the status quo is that other departments would not be capable of incorporating broad tax considerations into assessments of tax expenditures.

This argument is not convincing. The measures transferred to other departments would be close substitutes for program spending, so tax policy concerns would be limited to the administrative and technical feasibility of the measures, over which the finance minister would continue to exercise a veto.

WHICH TAX MEASURES SHOULD BE INCLUDED?

The federal government identifies 200 tax expenditures in the 2012 edition of *Tax Expenditures and Evaluations*; these measures result in tax revenue forgone well in excess of $125 billion. *Tax Expenditures and Evaluations* explicitly takes a broad view of what constitutes a tax expenditure, with the result that many measures that could be considered part of a fair and efficient tax system are included as tax expenditures. The intention is to provide information on a full range of measures that can be used by analysts and parliamentarians to address a variety of issues. The interest in this study is to determine which measures reported in *Tax Expenditures and Evaluations* are close substitutes for spending programs and should therefore be integrated into the expenditure management system. This exercise is similar to the U.S. approach of preparing tax-expenditure estimates for two different "baselines" or benchmarks: normal tax law and reference tax law.[12] The normal tax-law baseline is similar to the benchmark used in *Tax Expenditures and Evaluations*, although it is not as broad. In contrast, "[r]eference law tax expenditures are limited to special exemptions from a generally provided tax rule that serve programmatic functions in a way that is analogous to spending programs."[13]

Applying this approach to Canadian tax expenditures results in the identification of 115 tax-based spending programs.[14] Cost estimates are available for 89 of these measures, which had an aggregate value of about $37 billion[15] in 2012. This cost represented 19.5 per cent of federal revenues from personal income, corporate income and goods and services taxes, 31 per cent of direct program spending and almost 18 per cent of overall program spending in 2012. The tax revenue forgone from the top ten tax expenditures was approximately $28 billion, or about 75 per cent of the aggregate tax revenue forgone in 2012 (Table 7.1).

Table 7.1
Largest Tax Expenditures in 2012 ($millions)

Canada child tax benefit	10,266
Non-taxation of business-paid health and dental benefits	3,390
Low tax rate for small businesses	2,935
Age credit	2,605
Charitable donations tax credit	2,490
Regular S R & E D tax credit	1,895
Enhanced S R & E D tax credit	1,745
Working income tax benefit	1,105
Pension income credit	1,055
Pension income splitting	1,005
Total	28,491

Source: Finance Canada Tax Expenditures and Evaluations 2012

REFORMING EVALUATION POLICY

Federal Evaluation Policy

As discussed above, federal direct spending must be evaluated on a five-year cycle. These evaluations have to be undertaken by an independent group in departments and the results must be made public, along with a response from management.

The evaluation policy does not impose a specific evaluation methodology on departments but does require that all evaluations address program relevance, efficiency and effectiveness.[16] In assessing program effectiveness evaluators are to consider immediate, intermediate and ultimate outcomes. No definitions of the various outcome measures are provided, but with respect to a business subsidy program, the immediate outcome could be the receipt of the subsidy within the time frames envisaged by the policy, the intermediate outcome could be the impact of the subsidy on employment and output of the subsidized firms and the ultimate outcome could be the net economic benefit of the subsidy.

Departmental evaluations of program effectiveness are not considered satisfactory by the auditor general (A G) or by the Treasury Board Secretariat (T B S). In a 2009 report, the A G concluded that "departments were not able to demonstrate that they are fully meeting needs for effectiveness evaluation."[17] This conclusion is based on a review of evaluations in six departments over the four years ending in 2007–08. These departments prepared a total of 152 evaluations over the period reviewed, but only about a sixth of these evaluations addressed program effectiveness. In the 2010 annual review of the evaluation function, the TBS stated that "the use of evaluations has not reached its potential for informing expenditure decisions and policy development"[18] due to weaknesses in effectiveness evaluation.

Both agencies attribute this state of affairs to a lack of the data required to measure program effectiveness and to a limited supply of program evaluators. These are clearly important factors, but in previous reports, the auditor general drew attention to the political context of evaluations and to consequences of giving departments the responsibility for performing evaluations of their own programs.[19] The current approach gets full marks for transparency, but evaluation managers reporting on program relevance and effectiveness may end up providing information that could be used to embarrass their minister or to set the political agenda. The natural reaction of evaluation managers in this situation is to do effectiveness evaluations of programs that are known to be functioning well; to release effectiveness evaluations after a decision to change program parameters has been made and announced by the minister; and to undertake evaluations that are focused on program efficiency rather than effectiveness.

Who Should Perform the Evaluations?

The government of Canada has been trying to integrate program evaluation into expenditure decisions and policy development since the evaluation policy was first formulated. Various approaches have been tried to improve the usefulness of evaluations, but giving departments the responsibility for undertaking evaluations has been a feature of evaluation policy since the late 1970s. Enough time has passed to conclude that the structural resistance to undertaking effectiveness evaluations will not be overcome as long as departments play the lead role. A better approach would be to have an independent entity evaluate program effectiveness while departments focus on evaluating program efficiency. This recommendation applies with equal force to the tax expenditures identified in this chapter. Finance Canada should continue to have responsibility for designing a fair and efficient tax system and assessing the results, but the effectiveness of tax-based spending programs should be evaluated by a separate agency.

Who should undertake the effectiveness evaluations? There is a strong case for expanding the Parliamentary Budget Officer's (PBO) mandate to explicitly include the evaluation of tax expenditures. Centralizing effectiveness evaluation with the PBO would have other advantages in addition to overcoming the structural resistance to undertaking such evaluations in departments. First, effectiveness evaluation requires specialized data-analysis skills that are independent of the program being evaluated, so some duplication of effort will be reduced through centralization. Second, a centralized approach makes it easier to undertake a whole-of-government approach to evaluations. Third, given the P B O's direct linkage to Parliament, an expanded role for the P B O in evaluation would encourage Parliament to take more interest in effectiveness reporting and to reclaim some of the power of the purse that has been allowed, in the words of former senator Lowell Murray, to "become a dead letter, their Supply and Estimates process an empty ritual."[20]

There is also a good case for governments to pay private sector analysts and organizations to undertake evaluations to complement efforts in the public sector. This approach could be a cost-effective way of increasing the supply of evaluators while providing useful diversity in methodological frameworks. Given the confidentiality requirements of the Income Tax Act, private sector researchers would have to access the tax data through existing research centres maintained by Statistics Canada.

An Alternative Evaluation Framework: Benefit-Cost Analysis

The core issues identified in the federal evaluation policy are sensible and the flexibility allowed in undertaking evaluations is appropriate given the range of activities subject to the evaluation policy: departmental operating budgets, statutory program delivery costs, economic development programs and transfers to individuals. The absence of an explicit definition of ultimate program outcomes against which the effectiveness of economic development programs and transfers to individuals would be assessed is, however, an important gap. Without a well-defined common ultimate objective, it is more difficult to assess relative program effectiveness and hence to use evaluations to support spending reallocation decisions.

This lack of precision also allows departments to assess program effectiveness against intermediate outcomes, which can be misleading indicators of the benefits realized from the program. For example, the ultimate objective of economic development programs is to improve economic performance leading to higher living standards, so evaluators should be required to assess effectiveness of these programs in terms of the net economic benefit to society.[21] In contrast, additional output or job growth in the subsidized industry is not an adequate measure of success for an economic development program: over a complete business cycle, taxing one group of firms and giving the proceeds to another group cannot do any more than change the composition of output and employment.

The approach to effectiveness evaluation of program spending is surprising given the federal government's approach to regulatory policy, which requires departments and agencies to apply a benefit-cost analysis when assessing proposed regulations. The Treasury Board Secretariat has prepared a guide to help federal departments and agencies perform the required benefit-cost analysis.[22] In a nutshell, benefit-cost analysis requires quantifying in monetary terms the benefits of an initiative and deducting all of the costs incurred.

The guide emphasizes the costs incurred by private sector entities in order to comply with the regulation and the costs incurred by the government to administer, monitor and enforce the regulation, but it also states that it may be necessary to include "indirect costs" in the analysis. An example of an indirect cost is the loss in economic efficiency as capital and labour are shifted from their market-determined use as a result of the regulation.[23] Since the benefits and costs occur over time, it is important to determine their present value using an appropriate discount rate.

The guide discusses the situations in which attributing a monetary value to the benefits cannot be done with sufficient precision. In these cases, the guide recommends preparing a cost-effectiveness indicator, defined as the total cost of the initiative (expressed in present value terms) divided by a relevant intermediate outcome measure; in the case of a health-related initiative, the denominator could be the impact of the measure on quality-adjusted years of life. This approach allows options to be ranked in terms of the cost incurred to achieve a specific outcome, although differences in program scale are not captured.

The benefit-cost framework is perfectly suitable for evaluating economic development programs such as the SR&ED tax credit since their ultimate objective is to provide a net economic benefit to society.[24] On the other hand, measures implemented to change the distribution of income would have to be assessed using the guide's cost-effectiveness measure. While generally-accepted methodologies exist for estimating the economic cost of reducing income inequality through a specific program, there is no consensus on how to monetize the benefits of reduced inequality.[25] Calculating the economic cost of achieving a given reduction in some measure of inequality would provide policy makers with useful information that would help assess the performance of a program both in an absolute sense and relative to other income distribution programs. However, as emphasized in the regulation directive, a cost-effectiveness measure would have to be supplemented with other information, such as a detailed assessment of winners and losers, which would allow policy makers to perform their own subjective benefit-cost analysis and ranking of alternatives.

CONCLUSIONS

The federal government's expenditure management system has the potential to substantially improve the effectiveness of government spending. In order to maximize the new system's potential, however, two changes should be made. First, tax-based spending programs should be integrated into the expenditure management system. Integration involves transferring responsibility for tax-based spending programs to the relevant spending department from the Finance Department and making them subject to strategic reviews and the government's evaluation policy. Second, responsibility for effectiveness evaluations of tax and spending programs should be transferred from departments to an independent agency such as the parliamentary budget officer. Effectiveness evaluations should be carried out using a variant of the benefit-cost framework that is now applied to government regulatory initiatives.

What are the prospects for reform? The current finance minister and prime minister have made it clear that they are not willing to relinquish their power over tax-based spending programs, so transferring responsibility for these programs to spending ministers will not occur unless there is a change of government. Refundable tax credits are now included in program spending, so they are in principle included in strategic reviews and subject to the government's evaluation policy. These changes would pave the way for a similar treatment of non-refundable tax credits. The changes to evaluation policy proposed in this chapter are less contentious because they do not challenge the power of the prime minister and the minister of finance. Nevertheless, making progress would require action by Parliamentary committees, political party activists and public policy analysts.

NOTES

1   Treasury Board Secretariat, "Policy on Evaluation" (2009). http://www.tbs-sct.gc.ca/pol/doc-eng.aspx?id=15024

2   Treasury Board Secretariat, "Policy on Transfer Payments" (April 2012). http://www.tbs-sct.gc.ca/pol/doc-eng.aspx?id=13525&section=text

3   See the *2011–12 Estimates Parts I and II: The Government Expenditure Plan and The Main Estimates*, www.tbs-sct.gc.ca/est-pre/20112012/me-bpd/docs/me-bpd-eng.pdf; and *A Guide to the Estimates*, http://www.parl.gc.ca/Content/LOP/ResearchPublications/prb0925-e.htm#a11

4   House of Commons Standing Committee on Government Operations and Estimates, *Strengthening Parliamentary Scrutiny of Estimates and Supply* (June 2012), (http://www.parl.gc.ca/HousePublications/Publication.aspx?DocId=5690996&Language=E&Mode=1&Parl=41&Ses=1&File=18).

5   See Jonathan Barry Forman, "Origins of the Tax Expenditure Budget," *Tax Notes* 30, 6 (February 10, 1986), 538.

6   For a discussion see Satya Poddar, "Integration of Tax Expenditures into the Expenditure Management System: The Canadian Experience," in *Tax Expenditures and Government Policy*, ed. Neil Bruce (Kingston: John Deutsch Institute for the Study of Economic Policy, 1988): 259–68.

7   Ibid., 263.

8   Ibid., 264.

9   An important exception was the Canada child tax benefit (CCTB), which delivered $10.3 billion in benefits in 2012. In 2006 the government removed the CCTB from the tax expenditure accounts, started reporting it as program spending and began

reporting tax revenues gross of the CCTB. The CCTB is included in the 2012 edition of Tax Expenditures and Evaluations.

10 House of Commons Standing Committee on Government Operations and Estimates, *Strengthening Parliamentary Scrutiny of Estimates and Supply* (June 2012).

11 House of Commons Standing Committee on Government Operations and Estimates, "Government Response."

12 See Office of Management and Budget, *Analytical Perspectives: Budget of the U.S. Government, Fiscal Year 2011* (Washington: Office of Management and Budget).

13 Ibid., 208.

14 Measures relating to the taxation of investment income, housing, and foreign-source income are considered to be structural provisions addressing the equity and efficiency of the tax system rather than substitutes for program spending.

15 This is the sum of the individual cost estimates presented in *Tax Expenditures and Evaluations*. The sum of the individual costs understates the true cost of maintaining all of the measures due to interactions among the measures.

16 This is a summary of the five core issues listed in the Treasury Board Secretariat publication "Directive on the Evaluation Function" (2009), http://www.tbs-sct.gc.ca/pol/doc-eng.aspx?id=15681&section=text#appA.

17 Auditor General of Canada, *2009 Fall Report of the Auditor General of Canada*, paragraph 1.15. http://www.oag-bvg.gc.ca/internet/English /parl_oag_200911_e_33252.html.

18 Treasury Board Secretariat, "Report on the Health of the Evaluation Function" (2010), 36.

19 See, for example, Auditor General of Canada, *Report of the Auditor General of Canada* (November 2000), paragraphs 19.122–3; and Auditor General of Canada, *Report of the Auditor General of Canada* (1993), paragraphs 1.55–7.

20 Speech by Senator Lowell Murray in Bouctouche, NB (October 13, 2011), http://www.ipolitics.ca/2011/10/13/lowell-murray-you-do-not-govern-you-hold-to-account-those-who-do/.

21 Given the flexibility permitted in evaluation methods, program effectiveness is sometimes assessed in terms of the net economic benefit to society. See, for example, *Impact Evaluation of the NRC Industrial Research Assistance Program – Final Report*, which is available on request from NRC-IRAP.

22 Treasury Board of Canada Secretariat, *The Canadian Cost-Benefit Analysis Guide: Regulatory Proposals* (2007).

23 Ibid., 26.

24 For an example of how to apply the benefit-cost framework to economic development programs see John Lester "Benefit-Cost Analysis of R&D Support Programs" *Canadian Tax Journal* 60, 4 (2012): 793–836.

25 There is evidence that reducing income inequality results in better health and other social outcomes. See Richard Wilkinson and Kate Pickett, *The Spirit Level* (Penguin Books, 2010).

8 Harper's Partisan Wedge Politics: Bad Environmental Policy and Bad Energy Policy

GLEN TONER AND JENNIFER MCKEE

INTRODUCTION

This chapter argues that the combination of a majority government, global economic challenges, and deficit finances set the stage for two radical budgets in which the Harper Conservative government dropped federal commitments to sustainable development (s D) by embracing an approach called responsible resource development (R R D). R R D emphasizes the rapid extraction of resources from the earth's crust and the construction of transportation infrastructure to ship these largely unprocessed commodities to world markets while reducing the influence of environmental considerations on decision making. The Conservatives justify this approach by arguing that Canada is teetering on the edge of economic decline and only the frenetic extraction of resources and the furious construction of transportation infrastructure can save Canada.[1] While crafting this atmosphere of fear, the Conservatives slid environmental reforms into omnibus budget bills C-38 (2012) and C-45 (2013), rather than debating amendments through regular parliamentary processes. This unconventional approach to wholesale environmental regulatory reform was devious, cowardly, and largely recognized as an abuse of Parliament, even by commentators normally supportive of the Conservatives.[2]

Transforming Canada into a global quarry required "correcting" legislation and governance processes introduced by the Brian Mulroney Conservative and Jean Chrétien Liberal governments. While the omnibus budget bills were portrayed as part of the government's austerity plan designed to shrink the federal government's presence across Canada, they provided cover to roll back environmental regulations and eliminate key s D agencies. The National

Round Table of the Environment and Economy (NRTEE) was killed for publishing independent research the government did not like, and arm's length regulatory agencies such as the Canadian Environmental Assessment Agency and the National Energy Board (NEB) saw their mandates and autonomy reduced in the interests of "efficiency and timeliness" (of resource projects).

Gutting troublesome legislation was just one element of the Conservative's arsenal in its partisan zeal to reverse the incipient sd efforts launched by previous governments.[3] At various points in Canada's past, energy/environmental policies have become highly politicized spheres of crisis because of federal policies. Canadians have been intentionally led into another period of conflict – inflamed by the polarizing rhetoric of Harper and his ministers. The Harper government's demonization of scientists, aboriginals, environmentalists, opposition parties, and anyone else who questions their vision is part of a larger strategy of wedge politics. The intentional elevation of energy/environment policy to a crisis level is not without serious risks for the government, nor is it a mature way to govern this critically important field of Canadian public policy. The next section explores the wedge politics approach, followed by a section detailing the sweeping legislative changes. The final section will assess the consequences to date.

WEDGE POLITICS: POLARIZE, PATRONIZE, AND DEMONIZE ... THEN ADVERTISE LIKE CRAZY

The Harper government's strategy is to polarize energy/environment issues, patronize the public, and demonize any group that disagrees with them in the service of wedge politics; a strategy that divides Canadians into friends and enemies in order to undermine opponent's legitimacy and enrage the Conservative base who can then be tapped for donations. Their plan to re-ignite energy as a sphere of conflict and drive a wedge between different groups of Canadians follows a pattern of wedge politics employed in the crime, justice, terrorism, and foreign affairs policy spheres.[4] Gutting environmental laws, demonizing scientists, and rabidly championing rapid oilsands growth is meant to appeal to the Conservative base and curry favour with the most conservative elements of the Calgary oil patch and the Bay Street financial markets. Multimillion dollar taxpayer funded advertising campaigns were deployed to "re-educate" Canadians to believe that bitumen exports from the Alberta oilsands are the only hope for future prosperity and the ability to fund health, education, and social programs.

Polarize

Harper's strategy is to frighten Canadians about their employment opportunities and social security, and then offer the Conservative agenda as the only reasonable solution. This strategy associates job creation and economic growth with rapid resource development while portraying environmental regulations as "job killers." This partisan good-versus-evil, them-versus-us mentality drives the Conservative's never-ending election campaign, replete with on-going attack ads on opposition leaders. Conservative operatives realize that given a divided opposition and Canada's electoral system, they need only about 38 percent of voters in order to win a majority. Picking friends and isolating enemies was one of the key strategies learned from the American Republican party during the Reform party's years in opposition.[5] It also leads to a policy approach designed to please a minority of 40% of Canadian voters.

In 2011–12 the Conservatives began characterizing their approach as responsible resource development. This framework finds its roots in the Alberta oil patch since the term was introduced by industry with the goal of privileging economic growth over environmental protection.[6] In 2012 natural resources minister Joe Oliver referenced RRD at industry events, before parliamentary committees, and ultimately it became a section title in the 2012 budget. While in a minority government, Harper spoke about the need to "balance" resource development and environmental protection, making many speeches referencing climate change and renewable energy while placing value on environmental protection.[7] The core message of RRD is that environmental protection practices were excessively strong and needed to be rolled back to avoid slowing resource development. Since the 2011 majority victory, any pretence of "balance" has disappeared.

Oliver argued that "to promote long-term economic growth, jobs and prosperity," the government would "take action to streamline the review process for major economic projects through RRD." This reveals a sense of desperation that these opportunities are fleeting, that the world will soon lose interest in oilsands bitumen. "We have to compete with other resource-rich countries for fast-growing markets and scarce capital. And we must do it now."[8] The SD paradigm has a long-term perspective designed to integrate economic, environmental and social values in development decisions and therefore clashes fundamentally with the RRD approach that privileges economic goals. SD, in the ideological lens of the Harper Conservatives, is associated with Maurice Strong, the United Nations, the Chrétien/Martin Liberals, and is viewed as part of the legacy that must be purged. Ironically, much of the environmental legislation being "streamlined" was introduced or strengthened by the Mulroney Conservatives; however, that was a different conservative party that was reviled by the hard right rebels like Harper who left the Progressive Conservatives to form the Reform Party. Some of the harshest critics of Harper's reforms are former ministers who wrote an open letter to Harper addressing their "serious concern" for C-38. They critique the lack of clarity and transparency in the amendments being pushed through, and are alarmed that it will "weaken the habitat protection provisions" particularly because "the responsible ministers have provided no plausible, let alone convincing, rationale for proceeding with the process that has been adopted." The former ministers observed that the amendments were created by industry interest groups to further the development agenda.[9] Even friendly sources criticized the Conservatives for being dishonest with "one sentence outlining the controversial proposal to hand the federal Cabinet the authority to overrule the National Energy Board on projects like Northern Gateway."[10]

Patronize

It was impossible to watch television in 2012–14 without being subjected to a steady dose of Economic Action Plan RRD propaganda, followed by advertisements from Canadian Association of Petroleum Producers (CAPP), the Canadian Energy Pipeline Association (CEPA), and individual oilsands companies as part of a coordinated multi-million dollar propaganda campaign to "re-educate" sceptical Canadians on the correctness of the government's vision. Harper's instinct to isolate and undercut his opposition extends to aboriginal organizations. Former Conservative minister Jim Prentice warned Harper to improve relations with First Nations arguing that

> the constitutional obligation to consult with first nations is not a corporate obligation. It is the federal government's responsibility. Second, the obligation to define an ocean management regime for terminals and shipping on the west coast is not a corporate responsibility. It is the federal government's responsibility. Finally, these issues cannot be resolved by regulatory fiat – they require negotiation. The real risk is not regulatory rejection but regulatory approval, undermined by subsequent legal challenges and the absence of "social licence" to operate.[11]

The Conservative's assumption is that some short-term construction jobs and minor project equity will win over First Nations. Terry Glavin described how the Northern Gateway pipeline shifted from the glittering light of Canada's future, to a complete embarrassment. "Every time there's some minor oil pipeline fracture ... Oliver look(s) directly into the camera and explains why, miraculously, bad things just can't happen in Canada ... the great national energy superpower journey that ... Harper shanghaied everyone into embarking upon two years ago has turned into a voyage of the damned." Glavin pointed to the gaping holes emerging in the RRD strategy. Double-hulled ships were not new but part of earlier 1993 reforms to the Canada Shipping Act requiring double-hulls by 2015. Glavin dismissed Oliver as Calamity Joe, and characterized Harper's last minute attempts at "consultation" using a "Special Federal Representative on West Coast Energy Infrastructure," or "Indian Whisperer" as laughable.[12] The Conservatives' approach to First Nations is fraught with danger, especially in B C where both interior and coastal First Nations, in the pathways of the pipelines and tankers, retain authority over their lands and have a significant capacity for political action. It is also problematic for oil-sands expansion in Alberta.[13] Re-educating Canadians and patronizing First Nations is an expensive and dubious strategy.

Demonize

Demonizing your opponents is a central principle of wedge politics designed to mobilize the partisan base. The Conservatives hard-core base is around 30 percent of the electorate. The focus on job creation and economic growth in the Economic Action Plan advertisements is meant to appeal to the "striv-er" class in the suburbs of Toronto and Vancouver and to the prairie base. Demonizing scientists and environmentalists who care about the environ-ment as "radicals" who want to "stop any major project no matter what the cost to Canadian families in lost jobs and economic growth" as Oliver did in his infamous Open Letter[14] plays well to the base but distorts Canadian policy processes in which environmental organizations have become central players over the past twenty-five years. The campaign against the environ-mental community was designed to generate ill will towards environmental N G O s to justify legislative changes that would limit their ability to raise funds. Environment Minister Peter Kent went even further than Oliver and accused Canadian environmental groups of "money laundering" foreign donations mimicking charges made by the pro-Conservative group Ethical Oil.

In what verges on abuse of power, the 2012 budget earmarked $8 million to have the Canada Revenue Agency target audits at N G O s. A year later after the expenditure of $5 million tax dollars and the audit of nearly 900 N G O s only 1 had its charitable tax status revoked (and this was a nuclear disarma-ment group of physicians).[15] The only environmental group in the top ten of foreign donations was the hunter/conservation group Ducks Unlimited.[16] Around this same period reports began to emerge that Cabinet has instructed the Canadian Security Intelligence Service (C S I S) to turn its attentions to environmental groups critical of oilsands expansion and pipeline construc-tion.[17] Changes to the project review process designed to reduce participa-tion to those with a "local interest" and changes to the tax code to reduce fund raising opportunities are patently transparent attempts to stifle critical Canadian voices.

Oliver was a rookie minister with limited political experience outside of Conservative circles and naively assumed these changes would unfold with-out challenge. This ideological and ahistorical approach lacks understanding of the environmental community's role in crafting positive changes to forestry and mining industry practices over the past two decades and of their links to likeminded American and international organizations which have come back to haunt the Conservatives. Moderate members of the oil and gas, mining, and forestry industries, who have worked hard to develop good working relationships with the environmental and aboriginal communities under the sd framework, view Harper's demonization strategy with alarm. Not only do the lead ministers lack experience in the sector, but they are actively working to undermine trust and social capital that took years to build. Moderate industry leaders and provincial officials know that the wedge politics approach could backfire by stirring public opinion against the oilsands and pipeline projects. Nanos polling reported that public support in Canada for the Keystone pipeline dropped 16% from April to December 2013.[18]

Oliver has gone out of his way to actively demonize the scientific community. Regarding the impact of oilsands expansion on greenhouse gas emissions, he attacked world-renowned American scientist James Hansen.[19] Twelve leading Canadian climate change scientists criticized Oliver's presentation of the climate change and Keystone debate in an open letter to the government and were quickly dismissed by Oliver.[20] Andrew Weaver, a leading Canadian scientist, responded to "the debate" between Hansen and Oliver noting that Oliver's claims were based on a poor interpretation of the science and that "policy based on science and evidence is exactly what is needed, and found lacking ... so I don't mind that the Minister has referenced me in debate ... But it is most unfortunate that Mr. Oliver has obviously not taken the time to read the paper he referenced, nor apparently made any effort to understand climate science generally."[21]

REWRITING THE RULES:
FRIENDS WIN, ENEMIES LOSE

Hiding a multitude of reforms within omnibus budget bills avoided the scrutiny of rigorous, clause-by-clause review by parliamentary committees. Review by MPs and testimony by expert witnesses was clearly viewed as a threat. Bills C-38 and C-45 diminished federal responsibility for the environment by reducing existing environmental regulations and by cutting funding and programs. The following examples reveal the Conservatives' "slash and dash" approach, but offer only a representative sample as changes to the Fisheries Act, the Species at Risk Act, and others are not explored in detail in this chapter.

C-38, the Jobs, Growth, and Long-Term Prosperity Act, was tabled March 28, 2012 and significantly diminished the scope of the Canadian Environmental Assessment Act (CEAA). A key change was the "substitution" rule allowing the transfer of environmental assessments to provincial governments. Offloading responsibilities to provincial governments is problematic because of the inconsistency of regulations from province to province. The definition of environmental effects was narrowed to preclude the effects of a project on climate, for example. New limits of one year for standard environmental assessments and two years for panel reviews were legislated. This change was in response to claims from resource companies that public hearings take too long and slow the pace of development.

Moreover, the NEB is now exempt from the Species at Risk Act. The environment minster now has discretion to decide which assessments are necessary and cabinet the power to over-rule decisions. These changes "may make it easier for Harper and his ministers to meddle in the ultimate approval of the contentious Northern Gateway pipeline."[22] This coincides with limiting public participation before review panels to "people directly affected by the project"; a determination also now made at federal discretion.[23]

The Navigable Water Protection Act (NWPA) was altered radically when C-38 removed pipelines and interprovincial power lines from the definition of "works." This change eases the scrutiny required for pipelines traversing waterways. C-45 went further renaming NWPA the Navigation Protection Act (NPA), elevating navigation and diminishing protection of navigable waters are covered. The previous act applied to 32,000 lakes across the country and most rivers; now only 97 lakes, 62 rivers, and 3 oceans (less than 1% of Canada's waterways) listed in the new Act require review and permits from the Minister of Transport before development. For instance, Northern Gateway is proposed to move along the Kitimat and Upper Fraser Rivers in BC, and both rivers will no longer be considered for review. "Transport Canada officials say big projects on waterways will still be assessed by the National Energy Board ... But the NEB only looks at technical feasibility of building a project, not its environmental effects."[24]

Two of the most dramatic moves were repealing the Kyoto Protocol Implementation Act and killing the NRTEE. This terminated Canada's legal requirement to even prepare a Climate Change Plan. In March of 2013 – a year after the NRTEE funding was eliminated – Environment Minister Peter Kent actually forbid the posting of NRTEE reports online[25] underscoring the government's fear of transparency and public access to publically funded research.

STIR THE CONFLICTS AND MAN THE BARRICADES

In light of this information the question is, how is the wedge politics approach working in this critical area of Canadian public policy? While oilsands projects continue to grow despite some local First Nations opposition in Alberta, it is the politics of the pipeline projects to move bitumen to markets that reveals the dynamics of the wedge politics approach. And while it is not yet possible to answer the question definitively as decisions have not yet been made on any the major pipelines projects to move bitumen to tidewater, it is clear that intentionally stirring conflict has ensured rough sailing for the government despite its ability to ram radical legislative changes through Parliament.

Wedge politics on energy / environment issues in this era is a high-risk approach. There are just too many other actors with 'policy and political capacity' who can influence outcomes. A leaked memo from the Prime Minister's Office used explicit "friends and enemies" language to designate the opposition, bureaucracy, media, scientists and environmentalists as "enemies."[26] Above all, and this reveals the utter naivety of the Harper polarization strategy, it is the government's non-performance on climate change that is undermining its aspirations for oilsands development. Harper and several of his ministers are climate change skeptics or outright deniers and Barack Obama caricatured such deniers as dangerous "flat earth society" types in his Georgetown University speech on June 25, 2013.[27] Obama announced that building the Keystone pipeline "requires a finding that doing so would be in our nation's interest. And our national interest will be served only if this project does not significantly exacerbate the problem of carbon pollution. The net effects of the pipeline's impact on our climate will be absolutely critical to determining whether this project is allowed to go forward."[28]

Keystone XL

The Harper government resents deeply the fact that the American government has such influence over the pace of oilsands development. Harper flippantly called Keystone a "no brainer," but as opposition grew Oliver and Harper became regular Washington lobbyists for TransCanada Corp. In Washington, Oliver stuck to the script demonizing prominent American scientists, environmentalists and journalists. The US backlash resulted in public protests and intensive lobbying against Keystone. This campaign focused precisely on the scientific issues that Harper wanted to avoid; that the 700,000 barrels per day Keystone XL would facilitate an even rapider expansion of high emission bitumen. The US media raised doubts about Keystone's employment benefits for Americans – one of its key selling points – and Obama shared these doubts in public. A New York Times editorial supported blocking Keystone in an effort to send a message regarding the value of the science and importance of climate change.[29]

Obama's Georgetown speech panicked the Conservatives. "Briefing notes prepared for ... Oliver before a trip to Chicago to promote Keystone ... noted that "the pipeline network must be expanded" but only a month later in Washington his notes removed any notice of expansion."[30] This represented a shift in rhetoric, not fact, to downplay oilsands emissions increases in response to Obama. Oliver responded that if the pipeline approval failed, bitumen would be transported south by rail and the associated increase in emissions will still take place. Later Harper, would send a letter directly to Obama (apparently without Oliver's knowledge) asking him what the Conservatives could do to address GHG emissions in the oil and gas sector that would, cynically, provide Obama "political cover" to allow to approve Keystone XL.[31]

The Conservatives once again expended tax dollars to mount a PR campaign in the US just as the Economic Action Plan promotion of RRD at home was being assessed as an annoying and expensive dud.[32] American observers were stunned by the barrage of ads and events and the overt public lobbying for one project, which is out of character for any foreign government and especially Canada. Journalist Paul Koring noted that "an ad campaign touting Canada as a friendly, reliable – even green – supplier of oil launched Monday as the Harper government seeks to prop up its case for the controversial Keystone XL pipeline" and that it was "targeted at lobbyists and lawmakers … the ads … touted Keystone as a big part of the answer to America's energy needs" while attempting to deflect attacks by anti-Keystone XL groups.[33] Oliver's and Harper's many lobbying trips suggest Keystone XL may not be a "no-brainer."

The Northern Gateway Pipeline and a Canadian Energy Strategy

The BC NDP opposition party opposed both Enbridge's Northern Gateway project and Kinder Morgan's twinning of the Trans Mountain pipeline into Vancouver and was defeated by the incumbent Liberals in the 2013 BC provincial election. Premier Christy Clark raised doubts about bitumen pipelines running from Alberta through BC to coastal ports, arguing that Alberta reaps the rewards while BC takes the risks. But Clark championed liquefied natural gas (LNG) pipelines and coastal terminals as a "made in BC" solution to increase autonomy from Alberta resources.[34] Confrontations over Gateway between Clark and Alberta premier Alison Redford at the 2012 premiers meetings undermined provincial consensus on the need for and design of a pan-Canadian energy strategy. Such a strategy would have to apply to all the energy production and transmission systems in Canada and go well beyond simply producing and exporting more bitumen. However, the Harper government showed little interest, and the strategy struggles to emerge.[35]

With little political support in BC, Enbridge soldiered on through the joint review process that had been tilted in its favour. The Conservatives kept advertising to offset the negativity surrounding Gateway. Indeed, "the statement of work provided to the ad company a year ago noted that media coverage had been critical of legislative changes that gave the federal cabinet power to override the NEB recommendations on project approval."[36] A couple of months before the NEB recommendation was due, Harper launched a rather oddly dubbed "charm offensive" aimed at the First Nations Chiefs in BC.[37] The Chiefs viewed the rushed meetings as a pro-forma exercise as Oliver repeated his taking points 'ad nauseum' confirming the suspicion that the exercise was really about showing a track record of 'consultation' in the event that the decision ends up in the courts.[38] Indeed, legal experts are predicting that the project will be tied up in a 'legal quagmire' for years because the federal government has not satisfied a legal requirement for meaningful consultation. The federal government is "trying to integrate native consultations with the environmental review process," and "Grand Chief Stewart Phillip, head of the Union of BC Indian Chiefs, said First Nations are prepared for a fight and if the federal government tries to "ram these proposals through," it will create a "watershed moment in Canadian history ... governments have unfortunately, in a provocative way, pitted the economy against the environment and it will prove to be incredibly divisive to Canadians who will find themselves on one side or the other ... We will carry this fight through the courts and on the land if necessary."[39] As expected, in December 2013 the NEB recommended conditional approval of Northern Gateway while laying out 209 conditions. The next steps lie with Harper.

Energy East

The Harper government was initially skeptical of the idea of a cross-Canada pipeline and the development of more domestic refining capacity for bitumen. But as Keystone, Gateway, and Trans-Mountain (a further proposed project) became increasingly troubled, the government threw its support behind Energy East which requires 1,400 km of new pipe and the conversion of 3,000 km of existing pipeline. In August 2013, TransCanada initiated public information sessions to begin the process of receiving regulatory approval by promoting the pipeline's potential contribution to the Canadian economy, largely from tidewater access to new international markets.[40]

Proponents ratcheted up the patronization rhetoric deploying the image of "nation building" to woo public opinion. TransCanada CEO Russ Girling compared Energy East to the Canadian Pacific Railway, with Oliver referencing the James Bay hydro and St Lawrence Seaway infrastructure initiatives. Oliver wants Canadians to believe that oil pipelines offer a "silver bullet" for Canadian prosperity. The "with us or against us" rhetoric elevates the demonization strategy allowing no room for questions; in fact, Oliver went a step further saying that in his historic examples "the odds were long, the challenges great, and the opposition fierce ... But in each case, Canadians responded with the eloquence of action. Nation building is not confined to our history ... it is an obligation to the future, and every generation must honour that obligation."[41] This is a sly approach with the rather obvious conclusion that if you have any doubts about the pipelines or oilsands expansion, you are not only on the wrong side of history, but also a bad Canadian.

CONCLUSIONS

Intentionally politicizing energy/environment policy is high risk. Harper's obsession with bitumen exports, to the exclusion of almost all other Canadian

energy systems, and the demonization of those who disagree with him, is divisive. The partisan compulsion to kill s d and institutionalize r r d can trigger bizarre behaviour such as Harper's attack on Obama in New York where
Harper seemed to accept that Keystone x l is dead, but refused to "take no
for an answer." He went on to accuse Obama of playing "bad politics" on the
pipeline, implying Harper will get his approval when the Republicans replace
Obama in the Oval Office.[42]

Venturing, in such an openly partisan way, into the domestic politics of your
largest trading partner is yet another example of the high risk roll of the dice.[43]
Harper's rhetoric in that press conference, where he argued that Keystone
underscored the danger of being dependent on a "single market," might best
be understood as Harper preparing the ground domestically for his approval
of the two West coast pipeline projects on "national interest" grounds. This will
put him in direct confrontation, at the very least, with Vancouver regional
mayors, First Nations, and possibly the b c government. Harper now has the
opportunity to approve Northern Gateway, but as Jim Prentice noted above
"The real risk is not regulatory rejection but regulatory approval, undermined
by subsequent legal challenges and the absence of 'social licence' to operate."
It is an understatement to say that such an outcome will "stoke" a high profile,
crisis-riddled future for the bitumen production and transportation sector. It
may play well to the Conservative base, but ratcheting up tensions in a critical
policy field in the interests of enticing 40% of voters is potentially problematic
for the Conservatives. There is no guarantee the wedge will break their way.[44]

NOTES

1 Jason Fekete, "Develop Resources Now or Never, Oliver Says," *Ottawa Citizen*
   (August 27, 2013).
2 Even conservative apologist Peter Foster questioned Harper's methods in "forcing
   through the bulging grab bag of legislation contained in omnibus bill C-38," noting
   that the government is failing at distinguish between streamlining and steamroll-
   ering, because right now it looks like the environment has been "thrown under the
   omnibus." See Peter Foster, "Right Strategy, Blunt Tactics," *Financial Post* (May 9,
   2012).
3 Glen Toner and James Meadowcroft, "The Struggle of the Canadian Federal
   Government to Implement Sustainable Development," in Deborah VanNijnatten
   and Robert Boardman, eds., *Canadian Environmental Policy and Politics* (Toronto:
   Oxford University Press, 2009), 77–90.
4 An example of the polarization approach was Public Security Minister Vic Toews's
   demonization of everyone who disagreed with his bill on internet monitoring as
   supporters of child pornography and pedophiles. David Pugliese, "Toews Fires
   Back: Minister Suggests Those Who Question New Surveillance Law are Supporting
   Pedophiles," *Ottawa Citizen* (February 13, 2012).

5 Several party militants involved in the robocalls and ethical oil campaigns gained wedge politics experience working on Republican campaigns. Linda Diebel, "Robocalls: Tory M P s Used Top US Republican Firms during May election," *Toronto Star* (March 3, 2012).

6 Canadian Association of Petroleum Producers, "A New Benchmark of Responsible Resource Development" (2010).

7 In several speeches early on Harper called "for international consensus on climate change" (see for example, Prime Minister's Office, "Harper Calls for International Consensus on Climate Change" [Berlin, June 4, 2007]); he also made multiple speeches supporting renewable energy and biofuels, arguing that the "global appetite for more environmentally friendly sources of energy is growing by the day" (see for example, Prime Minister's Office, "Prime Minister Announces Substantial Investment to Boost Canada's Production of Biofuels" [Stongfield Saskatchewan, July 5, 2007]); he also said that "Canada's new government takes its responsibility for the environment very seriously" (Prime Minister's Office, "P M Unveils ecoENERGY Renewable Initiative" [Victoria, January 19, 2007]).

8 Joe Oliver, "System-wide Responsible Resource Development," speech to Automatic Coating Limited Facility (Toronto, April 17, 2012).

9 Tom Siddon, David Anderson, John Fraser, and Herb Dhaliwal, "An Open Letter to Stephen Harper on Fisheries," *Globe and Mail* (June 1, 2012).

10 John Ivison, "Tories Stick to Their Secretive Ways in Trying to Hide Major Policy Shift," *National Post* (April 18, 2012).

11 Charlie Smith, "Former Conservative Cabinet Minister Jim Prentice Issues a Veiled Warning to Stephen Harper," *Straight* (July 1, 2012).

12 Terry Glavin, "B C Pipeline Follies," *Ottawa Citizen* (April 3, 2013).

13 Bob Weber, "Oilsands Lawsuits Loom: Alberta Aboriginals Have Long Case List Pending or Planned," *Ottawa Citizen* (January 3, 2014).

14 Natural Resources Canada, "An open letter from the Honourable Joe Oliver, Minister of Natural Resources, on Canada's commitment to diversify our energy markets and the need to further streamline the regulatory process in order to advance Canada's national economic interest," (January 9, 2012).

15 See Shawn McCarthy, "C R A Audits charitable status of Tides Canada amid Tory attack," *Globe and Mail* (May 7, 2012); and Kate Webb, "One Year and $5 million Later, Harper's Charity Crackdown Nets Just One Bad Egg," *Metro News* (March 30, 2013).

16 Canadian Press, "Green Charities Don't Get the Most Greenbacks: Foundations Fear 'Chill' from Harper Government's Focus on Cracking Down on Charities," C B C News (May 10, 2012).

17 Shawn McCarthy, "C S I S, R C M P Monitor Activist Groups before Northern Gateway Hearings," *Globe and Mail* (November 21, 2013).

18 "Nanos Number Pipeline Politics – New Poll Shows Support for Keystone X L Pipeline Has Waned," C B C News (January 15, 2014).

19 "Joe Oliver Slams Scientist's Oilsands Claims," *C B C News* (April 24, 2013).

20 Max Paris, "Government should grow up on climate change, scientists say," *C B C News* (May 8, 2013).

21 Green Party of Canada, "Joe Oliver Attempts to Use Science, Gets Schooled by Greens' Andrew Weaver," *Media Release* (April 29, 2013).

22 Greg Weston, "Harper's Real Agenda Visible in Budget Bill," CBC *News* (May 2, 2012).

23 "Natural resource industries were delighted with the changes and did not lobby for anything further. They were pleased as punch." See Heather Scoffield, "Omnibus Bill Only the Latest Move in Profound Changes for Environment, Natives," *Maclean's* (October 21, 2012).

24 Margo McDiarmid, "Waterways Changes in Budget Bill Seen as Eroding Protections," CBC *News* (October 18, 2012).

25 "Ottawa Nixes former environment Panel's Data Sharing Plan," CBC *News* (March 26, 2013).

26 "Anger erupts over PMOS 'enemies' list: Echoes of Watergate-era Nixon's list," *Ottawa Citizen* (July 17, 2013).

27 Even the Conservative friendly editorial board of the Ottawa Citizen denounced Oliver's tendency to make "favourable references to climate-change deniers." Having someone with this attitude serve as Canada's lobbyist in Washington is a highly suspect management strategy. The editorial goes on to say that the Harper government's "long ambivalence toward climate change" makes it difficult to come to the US and offer last minute participation in joint efforts to cut carbon emissions in the oil and gas sector in order to get the President's approval for the Keystone pipeline. "Climate change Is Deal Breaker," *Ottawa Citizen* (September 9, 2013).

28 Barack Obama, "Remarks by the President on Climate Change," Georgetown University, Washington (June 23, 2013).

29 "The EPA's Keystone Report Card," *New York Times* (April 26, 2013).

30 Ian Austen, "Canadian Documents Suggest Shift on Pipeline," *New York Times* (August 25 2013).

31 Shawn McCarty and Jeff Jones, "Harper Asks Obama for Joint Oil Strategy: Letter to Washington Says Ottawa Would Work with Washington to Provide Political Cover," *Globe and Mail* (September 7, 2013).

32 Dean Beeby, "Economic Action Plan Ads Ignored, Poll Finds: Toll-free Number Listed in Ads Got No Calls Whatsoever," *Ottawa Citizen* (September 17, 2013).

33 Paul Koring, "Harper Government Touts Keystone in US Ad Campaign," *Globe and Mail* (May 13, 2013).

34 Tim Harper, "British Columbia election: Irresistible Alberta oil meets immovable BC," *Toronto Star* (May 13, 2013).

35 Mark Winfield, "'Dirty Oil,' 'Responsible Resource Development,' and the Prospects for a National Conversation about Energy Sustainability in Canada," *Journal of Environmental Law and Practice* 25 (2013): 19–39.

36 Dene Moore, "Ottawa was concerned about negative Gateway publicity," *Globe and Mail* (March 25, 2013).

37 Jason Fekete, "Harper Seeking Pipeline Support: Ministers Dispatched to BC to Meet with First Nations chiefs," *Ottawa Citizen* (September 14, 2013).

38 In response to the Conservative lobby, BC's coastal First Nations initiated an anti-oil tanker media campaign targeting PM Harper. The campaign video juxtaposes the

Exxon Valdez oil spill with the words "British Columbians have spoken. Will Stephen Harper listen?" See Mark Hume, "Kill Northern Gateway Now, First Nations Leaders Say amid Ad Campaign," *Globe and Mail* (September 23, 2013).

39   Kim Pemberton, "Expect Legal Battle if Ottawa Forces Oil Pipeline through, UBC Legal Expert Warns," *Vancouver Sun* (September 25, 2013).

40   Shawn McCarthy, "Where Oil Meets Water: The Final Stop for the Energy East Pipeline," *Globe and Mail* (August 13, 2013).

41   Paul Vieira, "Canadian Government Invokes History to Build Support for Pipeline Projects," *Wall Street Journal* (August 26, 2013).

42   William Marsden, "Canada Won't Back Down on Keystone-PM: 'It won't be final until the pipeline is approved,' Harper Says in New York," *Ottawa Citizen* (September 27, 2013).

43   Monica Gattinger, "Canada-United States Energy Relations: Making a MESS of Energy Policy," *American Review of Canadian Studies* 42, 4 (2012): 460–73.

44   Gary Mason, "Gateway Is a War that Ottawa Can't Win," *Globe and Mail* (December 21, 2013).

PART TWO

Selected Policy and Departmental Issues and Realms

9 One of These Things Is Not Like the Other? Bottom-Up Reform, Open Information, Collaboration, and the Harper Government

AMANDA CLARKE

When characterizing government under the Harper administration, the adjectives "bottom-up," "open," and "collaborative" rarely enter the lexicon. Instead, since becoming Canada's prime minister, many have argued that Stephen Harper has produced a federal government that is more top-down, closed, and uncooperative than ever before. We read of micromanagement, a disregard for the guidance of civil servants, "muzzled" scientists, and partisan interference in the work of the bureaucracy. Add to these reports the cutbacks implemented via the Deficit Reduction Action Plan, and one might reasonably assume that the past seven years have represented a dark time in the lives of federal public servants.

Yet, during this same period, the public service has made impressive advances in the area of internal information sharing, experimenting with web 2.0[1] technologies to challenge the "siloed" information control traditionally associated with government bureaucracies. Feeding off of this development, civil servants passionate about improving public management have formed a vibrant online and offline community, fuelling an unprecedented grassroots public sector reform movement that has emerged outside the formal structures of the government. Of late, this movement's aspirations and concerns have caught the attention of officials within the bureaucracy, inspiring creative discussion on the reforms required to strengthen the civil service through web-enabled information exchange and collaboration. And in the spirit of such information exchange and collaboration, the government is experimenting with web-based tools to ensure this reform movement is driven by the bottom-up participation of civil servants themselves, a twist on tactics adopted for previous reform efforts.

This narrative of bottom-up reform, open information and collaborative public service does not square neatly with the "doom and gloom" descriptions typically associated with life in government since 2006. In this chapter, I explore this alternative narrative to shed light on these less publicized, but nonetheless significant, developments that have arisen in the federal public service under Harper's watch.

The chapter develops in three parts. First, I explore the narrative typically relayed when Harper's civil service is described. According to this perspective, since 2006, government bureaucracy has been marked by an ever-increasing emphasis on top-down control, coupled with a general disregard for the value of the federal public service as a source of evidence and guidance. I next describe the initial grassroots, and now more institutionalized movement by which the federal civil service is experimenting with new forms of information sharing and collaboration in the name of improved public management, offering an alternative perspective on life in government under Harper's watch. Finally, the chapter questions the extent to which this alternative narrative can progress, in particular, in a context of budget cutbacks and under the leadership of a government that gives the civil service little scope to engage with those outside its walls.

HARPER'S CIVIL SERVICE: TOP-DOWN CONTROL, POLITICIZATION, AND RECENT CUTBACKS

When describing life in the federal public service under Harper's reign, the image conjured is rarely a rosy one. Insight generated through Access to Information requests and admissions from former political insiders and bureaucratic officials suggest that under Harper, the civil service's influence, autonomy and resources have degraded significantly.

Harper set the stage for a rocky relationship with the civil service early on; in the 2006 election, Harper claimed that the bureaucracy was largely composed of Liberal sympathizers. Reflecting his mistrust of the public service, after becoming prime minister, Harper developed a "shadow bureaucracy" of partisan political staffers who, combined with the Prime Minister's Office (PMO) have concentrated power in the political executive to an extent not seen before in Canadian federal policy processes. In turn, some argue that Harper is "plunging [the civil service] into irrelevance."[2] As Jeffrey summarizes, "large sections of the bureaucracy remain virtually unoccupied and largely fettered. Most have never experienced an era in which all policy development occurs in a top-down fashion, and few will be prepared to remain for a significant period of time if this situation does not change.[3]

Combined with this "top-down," partisan approach to policy development is an apparent disregard for research and evidence that might contradict the government's policy preferences. The elimination of the long-form census, the pursuit of controversial policies with scant evidence bases – such as the "tough on crime" agenda – and cuts to scientific research[4] likely suggest to civil servants that their primary function of providing non-partisan advice to decision makers is equally discounted by the Harper government.

As influence over policy decisions has waned, so too has the bureaucracy's independence from the partisan objectives of the political leadership. Under Harper, the P M O began using the Privy Council Office (P C O) to exert a greater control over departmental communications and engagement activities. Through detailed "message event proposals" bureaucrats must now ensure that the P M O approves all interactions they have with outsiders to ensure they are "on message."[5] Similarly, scientists in the federal public service claim they are being "muzzled" by tight restrictions on communications. They report being asked to exclude or alter technical information in government documents and claim to be afforded a limited capacity to engage with media and the public.[6] And as the line between the partisan political executive and the civil service has blurred, civil servants have, in certain cases, been called to act in ways that they perceive as jeopardizing their commitment to the public service values and ethics code. For example, a series of exchanges in Industry Canada reveal that the directive to replace the standard reference to the "Government of Canada" in official communications with "the Harper Government" frustrated civil servants committed to the notion of non-partisan public service.[7]

Denied meaningful influence over policy decisions, afforded little capacity to act independently, and increasingly drawn into controversial and potentially partisan communications strategies, civil servants today are hardly working in the golden age of federal public administration. Add to this the recent cutbacks to the civil service, implemented as part of the Deficit Reduction Action Plan, and one might reasonably assume that morale in the federal service is hitting all time lows.

HARPER'S CIVIL SERVICE: BOTTOM-UP REFORM, OPEN INFORMATION, AND COLLABORATION

As the Harper administration instituted stringent top-down policy processes and an increasing emphasis on information control in the federal public service, a body of academic literature emerged that, in essence, called for the exact opposite approach to public management than that taken by Harper since 2006. Variously labeled as digital era governance,[8] Wiki Government,[9] government as platform,[10] and government 2.0,[11] these theories contended that effective public policy making and service delivery can and should benefit from the impressive forms of information sharing and networked collaboration made possible by the World Wide Web. Authors describing these models argued that civil servants should be empowered to share information freely amongst themselves and to engage with external information networks to tap into outsiders' insights.

While Harper's approach to state management has not heeded these calls, civil servants within the federal bureaucracy have. That is, unlike in other jurisdictions, notably, the United Kingdom,[12] and the United States,[13] where election promises, high-level directives and well-funded initiatives reflected these new theories of state management, in Canada, these ideas were introduced to the civil service through "bottom-up" processes. On the one hand, this was achieved through the development of an internal information sharing platform – GCpedia – and on the other, by a grassroots movement of civil servants advocating for the brand of digitally enabled information sharing and collaboration that had been promoted in academic literature in recent years.

The first of these initiatives, GCPedia, was officially launched in 2008. GCpedia is a "wiki," an online platform that allows multiple users to contribute pieces of text or multimedia such that they can collaboratively develop a collection of information linked together via the same hyperlinking technology that underpins the World Wide Web. GCpedia can only be accessed from the Government of Canada's internal servers, but it looks and feels like the wiki with which most individuals will be familiar – Wikipedia – because the two wikis run on the same software.

Playing off the success of a wiki developed by Natural Resources Canada (NRCan), a small group of individuals within the Chief Information Officer Branch of Treasury Board Secretariat developed GCpedia to serve as an online space where civil servants across the government could more easily share information and collaborate in the development of policy, research and organizational documents (meeting minutes, for example). Its creators believed that such a space was needed to better reflect the cross-cutting nature of policy issues and the overlap in certain non-policy sector specific areas of the government's work (for example, human resources and information management). Advocates also argued that GCpedia would better meet the expectations and needs of new civil servants (whom they presumed to be digitally savvy) and to capture the knowledge of seasoned civil servants expected to retire en masse in coming years.[14]

The launch of GCpedia was a significant moment in the history of Canada's federal public administration. Prior to GCpedia, access to information, and the ability to collaborate in its creation, was restricted by department, section and in many cases, by desktop computer. With GCpedia, for the first time, any civil servant with access to the government's intranet could, in theory, access, comment on, and edit the same information simultaneously, and with relative ease. In turn GCpedia challenged the "siloed" information control commonly associated with government organizations.[15]

"In theory" is an important caveat because, as is typically the case when new technologies are introduced to an organization,[16] adoption of GCpedia was not universal upon its launch. While now GCpedia has just under 43,000 registered users, 22,000 articles and over one million edits,[17] its earliest and most prolific contributors certainly represented a minority tranche of the general civil service, whose enthusiasm for GCpedia was unknown to, or questioned by, a majority of civil servants.[18]

Partially in response to such critiques, early advocates of GCpedia formed an ad hoc, grassroots movement inspired by initiatives in other jurisdictions (in particular, those in the UK and the US) and in the literature that had cropped up around the subject of government and web 2.0 technologies in recent years.[19] Members of this movement saw these new technologies, and the models of collaboration surrounding them, as a hopeful avenue for renewing the public service and challenging what they perceived to be the inefficiency and ineffectiveness of traditional bureaucratic culture.

Fitting with their focus on digitally enabled collaboration, the movement relied, and continues to rely, heavily on the web to coordinate its activities and attract members. In 2009, these members began tweeting with the hashtag #w2p, a shorthand for the community of civil servants interested in web 2.0 and its applications to government.[20] This hashtag has become a rallying point around which members of this grassroots movement share information on new technologies and public sector reform, and over the course of one 40-day period of analysis, the #w2p Twitter conversation engaged 492 individuals.[21] Twitter is also used by the #w2p community to organize offline gatherings, scheduled monthly, during which participants share updates on their work, and in many cases, express frustration about the slow speed of change and restrictive bureaucratic culture in which they operate. Individual members of the #w2p community have also developed their own blogs to discuss web-enabled forms of information sharing and collaboration as they relate to the work of government.[22]

Certain members of this community view themselves as covert revolutionaries, working to change the system with what they see as radical but necessary reforms that challenge existing ways of working and power structures within government. One leading group of bloggers in this movement reflects this sentiment by describing their efforts as "scheming virtuously," and invoking images of "rock stars" and "ninjas" to describe those advocating for greater information exchange and collaboration in the civil service. As they explain in their co-authored blog:

> Rockstars are iconic, they're sexy, they sell, and quite honestly their typically rebellious nature is the closest that government workers can get to raging against the machine. Ninjas are stealthy, skillful, and their clandestine nature offers public servants a means of bringing down the system from within. You know what else these images share? An undercurrent of insurgency. We meet in cafés, trade information, and disrupt traditional business models and hierarchies. We embrace asymmetry if it suits our needs, and at times our outputs cannot easily be reintegrated into the collective. We vilify the old guard and celebrate our successes.[23]

This rhetoric is not the brand normally associated with civil servants, who are typically stereotyped as conservative, submissive and risk-averse. But even those who do not employ this more militant language still break the mold of traditional civil servants simply by virtue of participating in the grassroots movement that has cropped up around the issues of information sharing and collaboration in the federal government. Using their real names and pictures, and engaging in highly public online fora, these civil servants blend the personal and professional in ways that challenge the notion of the neutral, faceless bureaucrat, a fiction long perpetuated in the study of public administration and in public sector values and ethics codes.[24] In particular, the #w2p community, with its online Twitter exchanges and publicly accessible blogs represents an interesting development in administrator-citizen relations. Members of the public are now able to follow and participate in conversations about the work of government with civil servants directly, as opposed to relying on official communications channels.[25]

This online community is also noteworthy for its non-conventional, broad-based membership. Its participants are not typically in high-ranking management positions, nor are they necessarily operating in central agencies responsible for questions of public management reform. Instead, the movement attracts membership from a range of functions, ages and levels of authority across the government.[26] And finally, while a number of the concerns driving these individuals are familiar, animating earlier reform efforts such as the Glassco Commission and Public Service 2000, this movement is unique because it arose outside of institutional or sanctioned venues, on the initiative of civil servants from the bottom-up.

As time has passed, this bottom-up pressure for change has received the attention of actors more commonly associated with such public sector reform efforts. In particular, the past two Clerks of the Privy Council have expressed their support for technology-enabled information sharing and collaboration. In 2008[27] and 2009[28] Kevin Lynch praised the use of wikis and other collaborative technologies in NRCan and amongst the Science and Technology Community in the federal public service. In his 2010,[29] 2011,[30] and 2012[31] annual reports to the prime minister, Wayne Wouters also echoed the concerns and aspirations of the grassroots movement focused on information exchange and collaboration. Wouters referenced "the need for culture change in the Public Service" and argued that "We need to nurture a more performance-oriented, collaborative and innovative culture by, for example, taking greater advantage of Web 2.0 tools to deliver on our business."[32]

In this spirit, the Clerk continues to regularly advocate for use of GCpedia, and two other internal social media tools developed subsequently, GCconnex, a Facebook-like directory, and GCforums, an online discussion space. And in 2010 Wouters lent his support to the efforts of the #w2p community specifically by speaking at an event they organized titled "Government of Canada Collaborative Culture Camp." In his address to the #w2p community, the clerk noted: "I hope you and others take my attendance here as a further signal of my commitment to fostering collaboration and innovation in the workplace. To ensure that we continue to offer Canadians excellent service we must make silos, as an organizational structure, a thing of the past."[33]

In 2013, this grassroots movement gained deeper institutional grounding, and a stronger emphasis on *external* online collaboration (with members of the public) through two Clerk-led initiatives: Blueprint 2020 and the Deputy Minister Committee on Social Media and Policy Development.[34] Blueprint 2020 is a cross-government initiative that seeks to "develop a vision of a revitalized and world-class public service equipped to serve Canada and Canadians."[35] The initiative began with the release of a document developed by senior deputy heads that outlines four guiding principles for the reform effort. These four principles are a near verbatim replication of the reforms that GCpedia advocates and the #w2p community had called for since 2008–09. The document, titled *Blueprint 2020 – Getting Started – Getting Your Views* underscores the need to develop: (1) an "open and networked environment"; (2) "whole-of-government" approaches to services; (3) a "modern workplace" that employs new technologies for networking, improved access to data, and better services; and (4) the embrace of "new ways of working" which capitalize on a "diversity of talent" located within and outside the civil service.[36]

Following this document's release, the Blueprint 2020 initiative is now focused on a cross-government engagement effort. While components of this effort follow a more traditional model – with deputies consulting their employees in order that feedback can be channeled back to the clerk's office – some of the non-conventional engagement techniques employed by the earlier grassroots movement have also become central components of Blueprint 2020. For example, the Twitter hashtag #gc2020 has become a rallying point for discussion on Blueprint 2020, with civil servants granted the scope to discuss the initiative on their own terms outside institutionalized, government controlled engagement processes.

This is not to say that this institutional voice is absent, however. Analysis of the #gc2020 conversation reveals that the initiative's official account (@BlueprintGC2020), the commissioner of the Canada Revenue Agency, Andrew Treusch (@andrewtreusch), and Assistant Deputy Minister (Finance) Louise Levonian (@louiselevonian) are amongst the most central actors in the conversation; of the approximately 222 participants tweeting about Blueprint 2020, the largest proportion of tweets are either directed at these institutional voices, or issued from them.[37] Finally, as with #w2p, this online activity has also carried over to offline gatherings. For example, one of the architects of GCpedia organized a meeting under Chatham House Rule in which a group of approximately thirty civil servants joined to discuss their ideas for Blueprint 2020 outside a formal government setting.

Blueprint 2020 is complemented by a second initiative launched by the clerk in 2013, the Deputy Minister Committee on Social Media and Policy

Development. The committee is mandated "to explore the linkages between social media and policy making, including new models for policy development, public engagement and the role of the public servant in the social media sphere."[38] With this committee, the movement is shifting further from its initial emphasis on internal information sharing and collaboration, to include a greater emphasis on information sharing and collaboration with the public. And representing another interesting twist on traditional "top-down" reform efforts, the committee is experimenting with a "reverse mentoring" model, in which seasoned deputies are partnered with junior civil servants that are more attune to social media's applications in the public sector. As with Blueprint 2020, this committee also engages online with civil servants via its own Twitter account (@DM_SMPD) and under the hashtag #dmsmpd (a Twitter conversation that engaged 162 users and produced 357 tweets over a thirty-two-day period).[39] Finally, the committee is partnering with a grassroots initiative titled "Policy Ignite" and using a "Dragon's Den" format to vet proposals from civil servants on the best ways to employ social media for policy development.[40]

The introduction of collaborative tools like GCpedia, the emergence and positive reception of a grassroots public sector reform movement and experimentation with bottom-up engagement processes suggest that the Harper years have proven themselves a relatively innovative and empowering period in the history of federal public administration. Under Harper, civil servants have been afforded considerable scope to discuss their work in public fora and to question "ways of working" in government. Civil servants have also been appreciated for the insight they can contribute to broader discussions on reforms required to create a more innovative, collaborative culture of public service in the years to come.

This image is at odds with those that are typically drawn when describing life as a civil servant under Harper. As outlined initially, academic and media accounts emphasize the culture of control that has taken hold in the federal government under his watch. Cutbacks and a perceived disregard for the advice of bureaucrats suggest that far from feeling empowered, civil servants likely feel that their value has been discounted in recent years. The initiatives detailed here complicate this narrative. In the final section I question the extent to which these two facets of Harper's civil service can be reconciled, before suggesting how the tension between them may undermine efforts underway to expand the information sharing and collaboration agenda, in particular, as it involves engagement between the government and the public.

RECONCILING NARRATIVES: SEPARATE TRACKS ON COURSE FOR COLLISION?

One way of reconciling these two contradictory narratives is to suggest that they are simply a reflection of the enduring autonomy of the public service.

According to this perspective, the federal public service has a "life of its own" that persists across different administrations, and as such it is entirely plausible that a separate agenda focused on internal management and, in some cases, relatively mundane aspects of daily life in the public service (such as how offices are organized, and information is stored and shared) has emerged under Harper. After all, such discussions likely always took place: this is not the first time that civil servants have been frustrated with the ways of their workplace, sharing their perspective on the need for change with colleagues.

Perhaps what is innovative now is the venue in which such conversations take place. No longer restricted to the water cooler and coffee break, the Internet offers civil servants a new space to discuss their work, and the opportunity to form and sustain a community with relative ease owing to the reduced costs of information sharing and coordination that accompany the Web. One might argue, then, that today the public service is better equipped than ever before to foster and protect an autonomous culture that is distinct from the government of the day. Applied here, this argument suggests that despite working under an administration intent on tightly managing and controlling the bureaucracy, civil servants nonetheless enjoy a great degree of latitude to act independently in the digital age.

However, this argument only explains why the extra-institutional initiatives described here, such as the #w2p community, have been able to emerge under Harper's watch. GCpedia, Blueprint 2020, and the Deputy Minister Committee on Social Media and Policy Development, on the other hand, are all official government initiatives for which Harper has given his open consent. How do we explain support for initiatives that promote information sharing and seek to strengthen the civil service from a Prime Minister seemingly intent on reducing information flows and diminishing the role of the civil service?

One might argue that, in the end, initiatives like GCpedia, Blueprint 2020, and the deputy minister committee are perceived to be inconsequential relative to the broader range of activities that are of more immediate concern to a government attempting to maintain a tight grip on the activities of the public service. After all, thus far, these are primarily internal, and as suggested above, relatively mundane initiatives for which the Harper administration is unlikely to receive negative press coverage, or any coverage at all. In fact, one might even argue that if these initiatives were to receive more attention, they would support the government in pursuing its political objectives. These initiatives have grown out of a sense that the public service can be more efficient, effective and lower-cost by reducing overlap and making better use of its resources, an imperative that any government, and surely one with a neoliberal ideology and base of supporters, can happily stand by.

Perhaps, then, these two facets of Harper's civil service have been able to co-exist because they run on separate tracks. #w2p, GCPedia, Blueprint 2020, and the deputy minister committee have largely focused on the internal affairs of the federal bureaucracy. As long as they do not intersect with the public-facing side of government in which the Harper government has more political ground to gain and lose, these initiatives can continue under the autonomous control of civil servants themselves with little reprieve from the political leadership.

That said, we might question the compatibility between these initiatives and Harper's approach to the federal bureaucracy in the years to come. As the movement for greater information sharing and collaboration has become more mainstream and institutionalized, the resources required to sustain it have grown. In particular, the civil service will need funding and new skills to achieve the goals set out in Blueprint 2020 and by the Deputy Minister Committee on Social Media and Policy Development.

Experimentation and change do not come free. In this case, the once internal and mundane intersects with the government's program of public sector cutbacks, an initiative that is much closer to its political agenda. When the goals of this internal movement are in competition with the political strategic goals of the Harper administration it is likely that the latter will win out, leaving little scope to fund the new initiatives that Blueprint 2020 and the deputy minister committee call for.

Similarly, these two tracks may collide as the movement for information sharing and collaboration continues to extend its gaze outwards, emphasizing the use of digital technologies to involve the public in policy making and service delivery. This has been a less prominent component of these initiatives thus far, focused as GCpedia is on internal information sharing, and #w2p has been on engagement amongst civil servants. But as noted above, Blueprint 2020 and the deputy minister committee both call for use of the web to engage with the public. These efforts are more likely to be stifled given that they move beyond the safe-space of internal information sharing and collaboration, and enter into the much more publicized, politically sensitive realm of government-citizen interactions. Harper's control over external communications suggests that when it comes to engaging with the public, he will be unwilling to give civil servants much free reign.

CONCLUSIONS

For many, the chapter on "the Harper years" in the history of Canadian public management would be a very dark read indeed, emphasizing the culture of top-down control that emerged under his reign since first entering office in 2006. Certainly, stories of muzzled scientists, tightly controlled communications, cutbacks and an alleged disregard for evidence-based policy advice suggest that the past seven years have hardly represented a golden age in the federal public service. But at the same time, the Harper years have been host to unprecedented public servant-led reform movements, experimentation with new forms of internal information sharing, and creative, progressive discussions on the reforms required to update the civil service for the digital age.

This chapter has shed light on these developments, complicating the narrative that currently dominates our perceptions of life in the civil service under the Harper government. At the same time, the chapter argued that this alternative trajectory is by no means on a certain path of progress. The #w2p community, GCPedia, Blueprint 2020, and the Deputy Minister Committee on Social Media and Policy Development have thus far restricted their gaze to the internal affairs of the bureaucracy, and as such, their work has not yet posed a significant threat to the more pressing political objectives of the government.

It is likely that as long as these developments continue along this track, Harper will find little reason to expend resources to halt them, preferring instead to tightly manage aspects of the civil service that have a more immediate impact on his capacity to remain in government. But with these initiatives requiring greater resources, and increasingly focusing on engagement with the public, they are beginning to clash with the political imperatives of the government. In other words, while these two narratives may co-exist in relative harmony at present, a collision may be just around the bend.

NOTES

1 Web 2.0 refers to the second generation of web technologies. Web 1.0, the first generation of the web, includes static web pages that allow for a one-way flow of information from the web to the reader. Web 2.0 refers to websites and related tools (ex. smartphones) that enable the user to interact with other users and contribute to online content. Examples of web 2.0 technologies include social media sites like Facebook, Twitter, and YouTube, as well as blogs. See Tim O'Reilly, "What Is Web 2.0?" Available at http://oreilly.com/web2/archive/what-is-web-20.html

2 Brooke Jeffrey, "Strained Relations: The Conflict Between the Harper Conservatives and the Federal Bureaucracy," paper presented to Canadian Political Science Association conference (Waterloo, ON, 2011), 2. Available at http://www.cpsa-acsp.ca/papers-2011/Jeffrey.pdf.

3 Ibid., 13.

4 Mark Taliano, "Why Harper Hates Evidence-Based Data," The Huffington Post September 22, 2013) available at http://www.huffingtonpost.ca/mark-taliano/harper-defund-science_b_3971531.html; and Chris Turner, "Harper's War on Science Continues with a Vengeance," The Toronto Star (October 13, 2013) available at http://www.thestar.com/opinion/commentary/2013/10/13/harpers_war_on_science_continues_with_a_vengeance.html.

5 Mike Blanchfield and Jim Bronskill, "Documents Expose Harper's Obsession with Control," The Toronto Star (June 6, 2010) available at http://www.thestar.com/news/canada/2010/06/06/documents_expose_harpers_obsession_with_control.html.

6   Bruce Cheadle, "Government Scientists Feel Muzzled: 'The Big Chill' Survey," *The Huffington Post* (October 21, 2013) available at http://www.huffingtonpost.ca/2013/10/21/government-scientists-muzzled_n_4137104.html?utm_hp_ref=canada; and Emily Chung, "Muzzling of Federal Scientists Widespread, Survey Suggests," *CBC News* (October 21, 2013) available at http://www.cbc.ca/news/technology/muzzling-of-federal-scientists-widespread-survey-suggests-1.2128859.

7   Canadian Press, "'Harper Government' Not 'Government of Canada': Documents Reveal Wording Directive, Contradict PMO," *The Huffington Post* (November 29, 2011) available at http://www.huffingtonpost.ca/2011/11/29/industry-canada-documents-harper-government-communications_n_1118001.html.

8   Patrick Dunleavy and Helen Margetts, "The Second Wave of Digital Era Governance," paper presented at the American Political Science Association (Washington, DC, 2010), available at http://eprints.lse.ac.uk/27684/1/The_second_wave_of_digital_era_governance_(LSERO).pdf.

9   Beth Simone Noveck, *Wiki Government: How Technology Can Make Government Better, Democracy Stronger, and Citizens More Powerful* (Washington, DC: Brookings Institution Press 2009).

10 Tim O'Reilly, "Government as a Platform." *Innovations* 6, 1 (2011): 13–40.

11 W.D. Eggers, *Government 2.0: Using Technology to Improve Education, Cut Red Tape, Reduce Gridlock, and Enhance Democracy* (Lanham: Rowman & Littlefield, 2007).

12 See the UK's Power of Information Taskforce, http://powerofinformation.wordpress.com/ and the Government Digital Service, http://digital.cabinetoffice.gov.uk/.

13 See the US Open Government Initiative, http://www.whitehouse.gov/open/around.

14 Wayne Wouters, "For Public Servants" (2012), available at http://www.clerk.gc.ca/eng/feature.asp?featureId=23; and Treasury Board Secretariat official, personal communication, March 14, 2013.

15 See C. Bellamy, "From Automation to Knowledge Management: Modernizing British Government with ICTs." *International Review of Administrative Sciences* 68, 2 (2002): 213–30; and K. Layne and J. Lee, "Developing Fully Functional E-government: A Four Stage model." 2001, *Government Information Quarterly* 18, 2 (2001): 122–36.

16 Y. Lee, Kenneth A. Kozar, and Kai R.T. Larsen, "The Technology Acceptance Model: Past, Present, and Future." *Communications of the Association for Information Systems* 12, 50 (2003), available at: http://aisel.aisnet.org/cais/vol12/iss1/50.

17 User statistics recorded as of October 25, 2013. Source: personal communication with Treasury Board Secretariat official.

18 Treasury Board Secretariat official, personal communication, March 14, 2013.

19 In interviews with #w2p members, US President Barack Obama's "Open Government Directive" and the UK government's open data and "Digital by Default" initiatives were frequently cited as models that Canada should be following. Many interviewees also cited academic work on digital government reforms and the social web more generally. In particular, interviewees were captured by the work of Beth Simone Noveck, *Wiki Government: How Technology Can Make Government Better, Democracy Stronger, and Citizens More Powerful* (Washington,

DC: Brookings Institution Press, 2009); and Clay Shirky, *Cognitive Surplus: How Technology Makes Consumers into Collaborators* (New York: Penguin, 2010).

20 A hashtag is a convention of the microblogging service Twitter. Words preceded by a hashtag symbol (#) indicate what a Twitter message (a tweet) refers to. In this case, a tweet including the hashtag #w2p signifies that the tweet discusses something of relevance to those interested in web 2.0 technologies and the public service.

21 Tweets containing #w2p issued between 8–20 April, 8–20 July, and 7–20 October, 2013 were archived using Netlytic (http://netlytic.org/). Note that while 492 individual accounts were detected, these accounts were not all operated by federal civil servants, as anyone with a Twitter account is permitted to use the hashtag #w2p.

22 See "Canadian Public Sector Renewal" (2013), available at http://www.cpsrenewal.ca/; "Government of Canada 2.0" (2011), available at http://blog.gc20.ca/; and "Results for Canadians" (2013), available at http://usability4government.wordpress.com/.

23 Canadian Public Sector Renewal, "On Public Sector Ninjas and Rockstars" (2010) available at http://www.cpsrenewal.ca/2010/07/column-on-public-sector-ninjas-and.html.

24 See M. Lipsky, *Street-level Bureaucracy: Dilemmas of the Individual in Public Services* (New York: Russell Sage Foundation, 2010); and M. Bovens and S. Zouridis, "From Street-Level to System-Level Bureaucracies: How Information and Communication Technology is Transforming Administrative Discretion and Constitutional Control." *Public Administration Review* 62, 2 (2002): 174–84.

25 For example, this author has on occasion posed questions relating to government policy to the #w2p community via Twitter, and received responses despite not being employed by the Government of Canada. Similarly, non-civil servants are invited to attend #w2p gatherings, as long as they are not selling a product or promoting a consulting service.

26 Aboriginal Affairs and Northern Development Canada official, personal communication, March 27, 2013.

27 Kevin Lynch, *Fifteenth Annual Report to the Prime Minister on the Public Service of Canada* (2008), available at http://www.clerk.gc.ca/local_grfx/docs/reports/15rpt-eng.pdf.

28 Kevin Lynch, *Sixteenth Annual Report to the Prime Minister on the Public Service of Canada* (2009), available at http://www.clerk.gc.ca/local_grfx/docs/reports/16rpt-eng.pdf.

29 Wayne Wouters, *Seventeenth Annual Report to the Prime Minister on the Public Service of Canada* (2010), available at http://www.clerk.gc.ca/local_grfx/docs/reports/17rpt-eng.pdf.

30 Wayne Wouters, *Eighteenth Annual Report to the Prime Minister on the Public Service of Canada* (2011), available at http://www.clerk.gc.ca/local_grfx/docs/18rpt-eng.pdf

31 Wayne Wouters, *Nineteenth Annual Report to the Prime Minister on the Public Service of Canada* (2012), available at http://www.clerk.gc.ca/eng/feature.asp?pageId=300

32 Wayne Wouters, *Eighteenth Annual Report to the Prime Minister on the Public Service of Canada* (2011), p. 13, available at http://www.clerk.gc.ca/local_grfx/docs/18rpt-eng.pdf.

33 Clerk of the Privy Council, "Remarks for Wayne G. Wouters for Collaborative Culture Camp" (2010), available at http://www.clerk.gc.ca/eng/feature.asp?pageId=263.

34 Note that in December 2013 this committee changed its name to the Deputy Minister Committee on Policy Innovation.

35 Clerk of the Privy Council, *Blueprint 2020* (2013), available at http://www.clerk.gc.ca/eng/feature.asp?pageId=350.

36 Clerk of the Privy Council, *Blueprint 2020 – Getting Started – Getting Your Views, Building Tomorrow's Public Service Together* (2013), available at http://www.clerk.gc.ca/eng/feature.asp?pageId=349.

37 Tweets containing #gc2020 were archived between 16–20 October 2013 using Netlytic. Between this time, 476 tweets were issued, an average of 34 tweets per day. Centrality was measured using "total degree," the combination of all incoming and outgoing tweets issued to and from a user in the network of individuals tweeting with the hashtag #gc2020.

38 Privy Council Office, *Deputy Minister Committee Mandates and Membership* (2013), available at http://www.pco.gc.ca/index.asp?lang=eng&page=secretariats&sub=spsp-psps&doc=comm/mandat-eng.htm.

39 Tweets issued to or from the Deputy Minister Committee's Twitter account (@DM_SMPD) between 9–16 April, 8–19 July, and 8–19 October 2013 were archived using Netlytic.

40 See Policy Ignite, http://policyignite.eventsbot.com/.

10   How Foundations Spend: Is the Current 3.5% Asset Disbursement the Right Public Policy?

IRYNA KRYVORUCHKO AND KEN RASMUSSEN

INTRODUCTION

One of the fastest growing, but least examined elements of Canada's ever expanding charitable sector is philanthropic foundations. At present, there are close to 12,000 foundations in Canada, accounting for 10% of charitable activity. At a time when government funding is under tremendous strain, foundations can be a positive source of revenue for charitable organizations. This is because foundations are legislated to disburse funds regularly to support charitable activities, a prevailing portion of which is spent on grants to other charities.

Yet the role of foundations is not well known beyond those who interact with them. More importantly, their tax treatment by Canada Revenue Agency (CRA) poses a set of concerns related to the suitability of existing tax rules and their policy intention. The question about the appropriate treatment of foundations' disbursements on charitable activities has drawn considerable attention in recent budgets. This chapter explores whether the existing disbursement policy is suitable for Canadian foundations in the current economic and political environment.

Governments have used a variety of tools to encourage the financial support of activities that are considered socially desirable, mainly by providing charities with favorable tax treatment. Charities of all types receive tax-exempt status enabling them to raise revenue for the services they provide without incurring an income tax. Differences in the tax treatment arise depending on whether CRA classifies charities as *grant makers* or *service providers*. If more than 50 percent of an organization's activity is devoted to grant-making then CRA designates it as a foundation and it is subject to further restrictions. In particular, when foundations are classified as private as opposed to public they face tighter rules because they are controlled by a few non-arm's length individuals (e.g., family). The assumption underpinning the distinction between public and private foundations is that if a foundation is closely controlled there is more room for abuse of the organization. In order to limit the use of private foundations for tax-sheltering purposes and curtail an excessive accumulation of income within these organizations, the government designed differential disbursement rules for public and private foundations subjecting the latter type to more restrictions.

Foundation disbursements are based on legislated percentages of assets (defined as the endowment and property) and revenues (defined as annual donations from individuals and other charities) that foundations must spend in order to maintain their tax-exempt status. Private foundations have been treated differently in terms of the portions of assets and revenues they must dedicate to supporting charitable activities. This different treatment between public and private foundations was in place from 1976 to 2010. When the disbursement requirement was initially introduced in 1976 private foundations were legislated to pay out 5% of the fair market value of their assets towards charitable purposes. Public foundations, on the other hand, were not subject to any asset disbursement rules. In 1984 disbursement reform extended the asset disbursement requirements to public foundations as well, but differences in the treatment of disbursements between the two foundation types continued to exist on the revenue side. In particular, private foundations were required to spend a higher percentage of their revenues on charitable activities compared to public foundations.

In the 2010 budget the federal government announced it would completely eliminate the revenue disbursement requirement for all foundations, which had been in place for nearly thirty years. Disbursements of public and private foundations are now identical. As the 2010 budget ends the differential treatment between the two foundations types, the remaining issue is whether the asset disbursement rate of 3.5% is suitable given the current economic conditions and political environment in Canada. An attempt to address the suitability of the asset disbursement rate occurred in 2004, when the federal government reduced the rate from 4.5% to 3.5% to "ensure that [foundations'] capital endowments can provide a stable and suitable flow of funds for the delivery of charitable programs and services."[1]

After the 2008–09 recession, discussions about the rate suitability emerged again within the foundation sector. Many foundations were struggling to raise enough money to provide funding for other charities and were having difficulties in coping with the demands of existing disbursement requirements.[2] The resulting crash of the stock market has posed issues of mere existence especially for foundations with smaller asset bases, which is about a third of all foundations in Canada. Therefore, the disbursement regulation needs to allow for the varying conditions of the capital markets.

Our chapter is concerned with the appropriate nature of the disbursement requirement or what is known as the *disbursement quota* in legal terms. The issue of a suitable disbursement quota is a classic public policy question and we focus our discussion on two broad issues. The first issue relates to the debate about the overall need for any disbursement quota. Given its highly arbitrary nature, it is argued to be non-equitable and unenforceable in its current form, imposing a costly administrative burden on many foundations.[3] The second issue pertains to restructuring the current disbursement regulation with a goal of achieving a more robust foundation sector.

The potential reform would focus on the following three aspects. First, a regular review of the disbursement rate is needed in order to keep it up-to-date with the stock market conditions. Second, establishing disbursement rates that would capture differences in the size of foundation assets rather than making the rates specific to CRA designations. Finally, the government should consider rules that provide a balance between meeting short-term vs. long-term investment goals. This would involve helping foundations in diversifying their investment portfolios by combining their investments in the traditional markets with strategic investing. As the composition of the foundation sector is evolving, a feasible disbursement regulation is a necessary step towards a stronger foundation sector and needs to be taken seriously in the public policy forum.

WHY FOUNDATIONS?

As an alternative to setting up a charitable organization, individuals can use their wealth to support charitable causes through the establishment of foundations. The advantage of a foundation is that donors get the same favorable tax treatment, but it provides them with greater control over the distribution of their funds than if these were simply donated to a charitable organization. In addition, foundations can be redirected to other purposes depending on the wishes of the founder, and they can exist in perpetuity if their trustees make wise investments of its assets.

The arguments that allow the creation of foundations are often the same as for the entire charitable sector. That is, foundations encourage pluralism by playing an important role in the provision of public goods and services by supplying them to minority interests that have not yet achieved the attention of government or broader public support. The other rationale is the discovery argument in which they serve as mechanisms of experimentation in social policy or in pushing the frontiers of scientific research beyond short-term horizons of governments and businesses. That is, they provide functions that neither governments nor private markets can or want to deliver.

Foundations are found in most free market economies in which individuals not only accumulate their wealth, but can share it for the purposes of public benefit. This aspect is not without controversy and many are critical of foundations as they see them as elements of a plutocracy imposing its particular policy preferences, with taxpayer support, on society as a whole. Yet overall, a robust foundation sector is generally regarded as a positive attribute of a healthy democratic society. While Canadian and European foundation sectors are not as big as the one in the United States, it remains something that all countries appear interested in cultivating and encouraging.[4]

There are many studies that have analyzed the impact of foundation spending rules on the operation of foundations in the US.[5] All American foundations must meet or exceed an annual rate of 5% of the average market value of its assets to avoid paying any excise taxes. While this amount includes grants to charities, it also covers some administrative costs associated with grant-making. This figure has been in place since 1976, after a downward revision from 6% which was initially established in 1969. Contrary to the United States, European foundations are not required by the government to disburse any portions of their assets or revenues.[6] Any grant-making occurs on a purely voluntary basis.

The research in the area of foundation disbursements has been less robust in Canada. However, Canada is similar to the United States in subjecting all foundations to the same payout rules regardless of the foundation type. While anecdotal evidence suggests that the Canadian asset disbursement rate of 3.5% is set to be in line with the conditions of the capital market, its inflexibility has become an important issue especially after 2008–09 economic downturn. The analysis in this chapter contributes to a debate on the changing treatment of foundations' disbursements with the aim of making foundations a more robust tool for supporting activities of the broader charitable sector.

FEDERAL REGULATION OF FOUNDATION SPENDING PRACTICES: PAST AND PRESENT

The development of the first disbursement regulation began in the 1950s, but it was only in 1976, when the federal government introduced an official disbursement quota to help limit spiralling fundraising costs and the accumulation of monies within foundations. The imposition of a disbursement quota required foundations to devote a certain portion of their resources towards a charitable purpose by either transferring gifts to other charities or by carrying out their own charitable activities. Failure to meet the government's minimum spending requirement could result in the termination of foundation's registered charity status.

The 1976 disbursement reform in Canada adopted the model of American disbursement rules that had been formally legislated in 1969. The first asset disbursement requirement was only for private foundations, which had to pay out 5% of their assets averaged over the previous two years. No such rules were adopted for public foundations because they were not operating under the same level of scrutiny. On the revenue side, both foundation types were required to disburse similar portions of their revenues received in the previous fiscal year (see Table 10.1).[7]

The 5% asset disbursement rule adopted exclusively for private foundations produced substantial opposition from the foundation sector which argued that this rate would not allow for its sustainable growth. After some reflection, the government responded with a revised proposal to impose a 4.5% asset disbursement quota on both public and private foundations as part of the 1984 disbursement reform. On the revenue side, both public and private foundations were required to disburse 80% of tax-receipted donations from the previous year. Yet some unequal treatment of private foundations was found in requiring them to disburse 100% of grants from other charities in the following year, while public foundations were required to disburse only 80%. As Abigail Payne argues, the government's rationale for the special treatment of private foundations was not clear.[8] Yet William Innes and Patrick Boyel counter by emphasizing that this distinction was necessary to curb abuse by closely controlled private foundations.[9]

For the next twenty years from 1984 to 2004, foundations did not see any significant updating to the regulatory regime yet they have considerably strengthened their presence since the early 1990s. As Figure 10.1 shows, the total number of public and private foundations almost doubled between 1992 and 2008. Prior to 2004, however, this growth occurred at a decreasing rate. Was this an intentional gap on the policy making front? During 1984–2003, there were a number of upheavals in the Canadian economy including double digit inflation with matching interest rates, the signing of the North American Free Trade Agreement, a spending crisis in Ottawa and considerable political turmoil within Canada's two dominant political parties. These issues took precedence leaving little room for policy initiatives related to charities and social economy in general.

The Liberal minority government of Paul Martin was however more interested in social reform than his Liberal predecessor or his Conservative successor. In his first Speech from the Throne, Martin emphasized that the voluntary sector is an essential contributor to the "quality, fairness and vitality of [Canadian] communities" and that the government is committed to strengthening "the capacity and voice of the philanthropic and charitable organizations."[10] The voluntary sector was in great need of improvements in its regulatory environment including the simplification of rules around disbursements, which had remained unchanged since 1984.[11] Foundations were also expressing concern about generating enough income to meet the 1984 disbursement quota in respect of investment capital because of low interest

Table 10.1

Disbursement rules for public and private foundations, 1976–2010

	1976 Disbursement Rules	*1984 Disbursement Rules*	*2004 Disbursement Rules*	*2010 Disbursement Rules*
Private Foundations	*Assets:* Disburse the greater of: (a) 5% of fair market value of capital assets from previous fiscal year or (b) 90% of income earned from capital assets in previous fiscal year.	*Assets:* Disburse 4.5% of average value of assets over previous two years.	*Assets:* Disburse 3.5% of average value of assets over previous two, provided this value is above $25,000. Otherwise, no disbursement required.	*Assets:* No change.
	Revenues: Disburse 90% of difference in foundation's income in previous fiscal year and foundation's earned income from its capital assets in previous fiscal year.	*Revenues:* Disburse (1) 80% of tax-receipted and 100% of gifts from other charities received in previous fiscal year and (2) 80% of 10-year gifts and bequests spent from current fiscal year.	*Revenues:* Disburse (1) 80% of tax-receipted donations and 100% of gifts from other charities received in previous fiscal year and (2) 100% of 10-year gifts and bequests spent from current fiscal year.	*Revenues:* All rules are eliminated.
Public Foundations	*Assets:* None.	*Assets:* Same rules as private foundations.	*Assets:* Same rules as private foundations.	*Assets:* No change.
	Revenues: Disburse the greater of: (a) 80% of tax-receipted donations from previous fiscal period or (b) 90% of foundation's income in previous fiscal year.	*Revenues:* Same rules as private foundations.	*Revenues:* Same rules as private foundations except disburse 80% gifts from other charities received in previous fiscal year and	*Revenues:* All rules are eliminated.

Notes: According to the Income Tax Act of 1976, "foundation's income" is defined as income from the following sources: government, other registered charities, individuals, corporations, investment or business income. A 10-year gift is a donation made to a foundation that is subject to the donor's direction that the gift be held within a foundation for ten years. A bequest is a donated property that a foundation receives from the will of the deceased person.

Figure 10.1
Growth in public and private foundations, 1992–2008

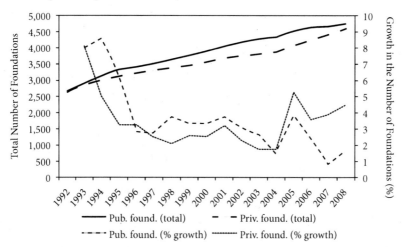

Source: Canada Revenue Agency (cra) data accessed at Public Economics Data Laboratory, McMaster University

rates and weaker stock market following the dot.com crash. While between 1981 and 1984 the Bank of Canada interest rate averaged 15%, between 2001 and 2004 the average interest rate was just above 3%.[12] With such low interest rates, it was not surprising that foundations were at risk of not meeting the 1984 asset disbursement rate of 4.5%. By identifying the voluntary sector as the "a focal piece of Canada's social tool kit," the federal government could no longer delay the response to the sector's issues including its outdated disbursement quotas.[13]

In its 2004 Budget, the government revised the asset disbursement rate down from 4.5% to 3.5% for public and private foundations. The government also instituted the exemption from the asset disbursement rate for both foundation types with assets of $25,000 or less averaged over the previous two years. These small foundations, however, were still responsible for meeting the revenue disbursement requirement.

Despite these positive changes brought on by the 2004 disbursement reform, key stakeholders such as Imagine Canada, the National Charities, and the not-for-profit law section of the Canadian Bar Association continued to urge the government to consider a complete elimination of the disbursement quota as is the case in most of Europe.[14] In particular, they wrote letters to the Finance Minister James Flaherty, Assistant Deputy Minister Louise Levonian, and assistant commissioner at the Canada Revenue Agency Brian McCauley in July 2009 where they raised concerns about the existing treatment of disbursements and difficulties it posed for the development of the charitable sector.[15] Furthermore, Imagine Canada followed up in October 2009 with its presentation to the Standing Committee on Finance to seriously consider revising the existing disbursement regime on the grounds of it being distortive, non-equitable and unenforceable in its current form. The report released in December 2009 by the Standing Committee on Finance incorporated earlier recommendations as part of 2010 pre-budget consultations. With extensive lobbying by the charitable sector the Harper government announced the new reform to the disbursement requirements on March 4, 2010. The main change was a complete elimination of the revenue disbursement quota for all foundations. This also meant that foundations with assets below $25,000 became fully exempt from any disbursement requirements. The new reform appears to have fulfilled stakeholder demands to remove a large portion of the disbursement burden for smaller organizations. Additionally, the 2010 reform has marked the end of the regulatory gap around the treatment of disbursements for public and private foundations that existed since 1976. At present all foundations with assets above $25,000 face only a 3.5% asset disbursement rate, which is substantially less than the 5% payout rule in the United States.

POLICY IMPLICATIONS AND FUTURE REFORMS

With successful pressure from the charitable sector to completely eliminate any existing revenue spending rules, what would be the consequences for the Canadian government and the charitable sector of additionally removing the asset disbursement requirement?[16] Certainly, Canada would not be the first jurisdiction to exempt foundations from any disbursement rules since most of the European governments have never required their foundations to disburse any assets or revenues. While the exemption from the quota would provide an immediate relief for many foundations, there is greater uncertainty as to the benefits for the charitable sector as a whole. Would we strengthen the foundation sector at the expense of the broader charitable sector?

With ongoing budgetary cuts governments are struggling to finance the provision of goods and services, while charitable foundations appear to be taking a more active role as providers of many local goods. The existence of disbursement requirements offers a form of assurance that necessary goods and services will continue to be provided when governments (or markets) fail.[17] Charities also need to know that they can rely on foundation grants because they help to promote charitable operations, provide stability during the times of economic downturn, and even serve as a signal of charity quality to individual givers which can help in attracting more private donations to charitable organizations.[18] Spending on gifts to charities by public foundations increased from just under $1 billion in 1992 to over $2.3 billion in 2008. Total grants made to other charities by private foundations have increased by over 175%

during the same sixteen-year period. Yet there is a real concern that foundations may cut back on grants as they try to preserve assets.

Disbursement rules are not necessarily a bad regulatory tool and the ongoing debate is more about how consistent the quota rates are with changing economic conditions and how well they are administered and met.[19] Table 10.2 illustrates that over the past twenty years foundations have been on track in meeting their disbursement requirements. While recent reforms have contributed to simplifying the regulation around disbursements, only the 2004 reform has adjusted the asset disbursement rates to account for changing economic conditions. Before eliminating the asset spending rule altogether, it may be worthwhile for the government to introduce a regular review of disbursement rates (e.g., every three or four years) to keep them in line with varying stock market conditions and inflation rates. The review will address the arbitrary nature of the asset disbursement rate making it less distortive and potentially more equitable. The federal government is already familiar with the concept of program review, according to which all government programs are evaluated on a four-year cycle.[20] Extending this concept to foundation disbursements should be a simple task.

With growing similarities in the operation of the two foundation types, interesting differences arise when foundations are classified based on the size of their assets. Table 10.3 illustrates considerable differences across the average amount of grants disbursed to other charities by public and private foundations of various asset sizes between 1992 and 2008. Since 2010, all foundations with the asset threshold of $25,000 (denoted as small) are subject to a 0% disbursement rate. Yet it appears that the size of their grants is rather similar to the size of grants paid out to other charities by medium-sized foundations (with assets more than $25,000 and never more than $1 million in any given year). From the fairness perspective, this suggests that medium-sized foundations may also need to be exempt from disbursement rules. If the government is taking steps towards implementing a *size-based* disbursement regulation for foundations, it needs to provide clear guidelines as to how this regulation is crafted for foundations of different sizes.

When it comes to large foundations (with assets of $1 million in at least one year), the question about governmental support of their operations including a suitable disbursement rate is even more concerning. The largest Canadian foundation is the Andre and Lucie Chagnon Foundation with total assets worth $2 billion, while the Gates Foundation (United States) has a $37.1 billion endowment or the Wellcome Trust (United Kingdom) has assets worth $22.9 billion. Yet it is these large foundations that have the capacity to provide meaningful financial support. One way for the government to encourage giving by large foundations is to create favourable conditions for mission investing also known as program related investments (PRIs). Foundations that directly invest their assets into community or social enterprises consistent

Table 10.2.
Ratio of actual to estimated disbursements by public and private foundations

	Public Foundations	Private Foundations
	Actual total disbursements / estimated disbursements	
1994-1998	1.6	1.3
1999-2003	1.3	1.0
2004-2008	1.2	1.0

Notes: The ratios are calculated in two steps. First, estimated disbursements are obtained by determining the disbursement amount for a foundation if it exactly followed its spending requirement. Then the estimated amount is compared to the amount the foundation has actually disbursed in a given year. The calculations allow for changes to the asset disbursement rate in 2004.

with their missions are considered to be making mission investments. For example, the Internal Revenue Service (IRS) in the US allows American foundations to count PRIs as part of their required 5% annual payout.[21] Current CRA policies say little about such investments.[22] The Canadian Task Force on Social Finance recommends that foundations invest 10 percent of their capital towards such initiatives.[23] While mission investing is becoming popular amongst many American foundations, the Canadian government will need to take a stronger role in educating foundations about mission investing until they are aware of the risks and benefits associated with it.

CONCLUSIONS

At the heart of the debate about disbursement rules is the question about suitability of the existing disbursement quota. Its policy intention should be to achieve the right balance between encouraging foundations to give and ensuring that they have the needed flexibility to find an investment strategy for the perpetuation of their endowments. In reality, the treatment of disbursements has been criticized for being inequitable and highly distortive. Moreover, the 2008–09 recession contributed to the rate suitability debate since for many foundations the asset disbursement rate of 3.5% introduced in 2004 became overly demanding on their resources. It appears that Canadian government needs to find the right balance between maximizing current foundation spending and strategically planning for foundations' long-term spending in the light of recent asset growth.

In this chapter we argue that the elimination of the disbursement quota may not be a viable option at this point considering the many benefits that foundation disbursements provide to both the government and the charitable

Table 10.3
Average spending on grants to other charities by size and foundation type

Average Total Grants to Other Charities ($2001 millions)	Public Foundations			Private Foundations		
	Small (N=1,533)	Medium (N=2,826)	Large (N=1,520)	Small (N=1,664)	Medium (N=2,561)	Large (N=1,543)
1992-1998	10.0	57.8	857.0	28.5	51.1	390.0
1999-2003	8.6	121.1	1430.0	23.4	65.1	725.7
2004-2008	9.0	116.7	1940.8	19.2	89.3	815.7
Disbursement rate since 2010	0%	3.5%	3.5%	0%	3.5%	3.5%

Notes: Small foundations are with assets always less than $25,000; medium foundations are those with assets more than $25,000 and never more than $1 million in any given year; large foundations are with assets of $1 million in at least one year. Foundations with assets great than $100 million (N=56) are excluded from this sample.

sector. At a time when government is facing budgetary cuts and is no longer able to finance the provision of many goods and services, foundations can offer their resources to some extent as a substitute to government spending. Funds from foundations disbursed as grants to other charities can play an important role in supporting charity operations and additionally can serve as a signal of quality to individuals about these charities leading to a higher pool of private donations.[24]

The main issue around foundation disbursements is rather how to create better policies for the treatment of foundation spending. We offer three recommendations to assist the government in aligning social goals with market conditions. First, the government may need to look into establishing a regular review cycle of the existing disbursement rate, which will in the least avoid disbursement policies becoming outdated. Our second recommendation pertains to the government building disbursement rules around the size of foundations rather than their CRA designations as has been done in the past. With large foundations having the potential to create social change, their successful operation will depend on government's encouragement and policy support. Finally, the Canadian government needs to educate foundations about mission investing and consider the option of including mission-related investments in the calculation of the asset disbursement rate as is the case in the United States.

The implementation of these policy recommendations will certainly require a great deal of additional analysis. Determining an appropriate review cycle should be subject to a cost-benefit analysis and administrative costs should be taken into consideration. A better understanding of the current landscape of foundations and how these entities operate will assist in developing a sized-based regulatory system for foundations.[25] It will also help answer questions concerning if and how foundations are refocusing their priorities as governments step back from being the sole provider of many public goods and services. As foundations grow in number and size government decision-makers will need to pay attention to the treatment of disbursements and determine if an immediate benefit is more important than the long-term viability of charitable foundations.

NOTES

1 Canada, Budget 2004, "New Agenda for Achievement," 177.
2 Steve Lawrence, "Foundations Address the Impact of the Economic Crisis." Research Advisory, Foundation Center, 2009.
3 Imagine Canada, presentation to the House of Commons Standing Committee on Finance, available at http://www.imaginecanada.ca/files/www/en/publicaffairs/presentation_to_finance_com_10082009.pdf.
4 Historically, foundations in the United States played a bigger role when the federal state may have provided limited support to a particular area. Kenneth Prewitt, "American Foundations: What Justifies Their Unique Privileges and Powers." In *Legitimacy of Philanthropic Foundations: United States and European Perspectives*, edited by Kenneth Prewitt, Mattei Dogan, Steven Heydemann, and Stefan Toepler (New York: Russell Sage Foundation, 2006): 27–46.
5 See R. Sansing and R. Yetman, "Prudent Stewards or Pyramid Builders? Distribution Policies of Private Foundations" (2002), available at http://mba.tuck.dartmouth.edu/pages/faculty/Richard.sansing/payout.doc; and A. Deep and P. Frumkin, "The Foundation Payout Puzzle." *Taking Philanthropy Seriously*, edited by W.V.B. Damon and S. Verducci (Bloomington: Indiana University Press, 2006): 44–59.
6 Exceptions are foundations in Finland, Germany, Spain, Sweden, and United Kingdom which are required to disburse some portion of foundations' revenue. Foundations Comparative Highlights of Foundation Laws (2002), available at http://www.efc.be/programmes_services/resources/Documents/ComparativeHighlightsOfFoundationsLaws_2011.pdf.
7 Table 10.1 is adapted from Iryna Kryvoruchko, "Foundations in Canada: Policies, Operations, and Financial Structure." PhD Dissertation (McMaster University, June 2013), chapter 2.
8 Abigail Payne, *Firm Foundations: Putting Private and Public Foundations on Level Ground* (C.D. Howe Institute, 2005) http://www.cdhowe.org/pdf/backgrounder_88.pdf.
9 William Innes and Patrick Boyle, "Shaky Foundations? A Defence of Special Rules for Private Foundations" (C.D. Howe Institute, 2005).
10 Canada, *Speech from the Throne* 2004. http://www.pco-bcp.gc.ca/index.asp?lang=eng&page=information&sub=publications&doc=aarchives/sft-ddt/2004_1-eng.htm.

11 Donald Burgeois, "Eliminating the Disbursement Quota: Gold or Fool's Gold." *The Philanthropist* 23, 2 (2010): 184–9.

12 Bank of Canada interest rates: http://www.bankofcanada.ca/rates/interest-rates/key-interest-rates/?page_moved=1.

13 James Rice and Michael Prince, "Martin's Moment: The Social Policy Agenda of a New Prime Minister." In *How Ottawa Spends, 2004–2005: Mandate Change in the Paul Martin Era*, edited by Bruce Doern (Montreal and Kingston: McGill-Queen's University Press), 114.

14 Canada, *Budget 2010* "Leading the Way on Jobs and Growth," 128. More about the role of Imagine Canada in the Canadian charitable sector can be found here http://www.imaginecanada.ca/node/9.

15 Imagine Canada wrote the letter to Finance Minister James Flaherty on July 23 2009: http://www.imaginecanada.ca/files/www/en/publicaffairs/disbursement_quota_letter_23072009.pdf. The president of the Canadian Bar Association wrote a letter to Assistant Deputy Minister of Finance Louise Levonian and assistant commissioner at the Canada Revenue Agency Brian McCauley on July 20, 2009, available at http://www.cba.org/cba/submissions/pdf/09-40-eng.pdf.

16 Canada, Budget 2010.

17 Helmet Anheier and Siobhan Daly, "Role of Foundations in Europe: A Comparison." In *Legitimacy of Philanthropic Foundations: United States and European Perspectives*, edited by Kenneth Prewitt, Mattei Dogan, Steven Heydemann, and Stefan Toepler (New York: Russell Sage Foundation 2006): 27–46.

18 James Andreoni, "Leadership Giving in Charitable Fundraising." *Journal of Public Economic Theory* 8, 1 (2006): 1–22; and Susan Rose-Ackerman, "United Charities: An Economic Analysis." In *Community Organizations: Studies in Resource Mobilization and Exchange*, edited by Carl Milofsky, (Oxford University Press, 1988).

19 Payne, *Firm Foundations.*

20 For a description of the Strategic Review Process see http://www.tbs-sct.gc.ca/sr-es/faq-eng.asp.

21 Mark Kramer and Sarah Cooch, "The Power of Strategic Mission Investing." *Stanford Social Innovation Review* (2007): 43–51

22 Laird Hunter, Susan Manwaring, and Margaret Mason, "Mission Investing for Foundations: The Legal Considerations." A report of Community Foundations of Canada and Philanthropic Foundations Canada (2012).

23 Task Force on Social Finance, *Report: Mobilizing Private Capital for Public Good* (2010).

24 Andreoni, "Leadership Giving."

25 Abigail Payne, "Changing Landscapes of Charities in Canada: Where Should We Go?" (University of Calgary, 2012), available at http://www.policyschool.ucalgary.ca/?q=content/changing-landscapes-charities-canada-where-should-we-go; and Kryvoruchko, "Foundations in Canada: Policies, Operations and Financial Structure."

11 Managing Canada's Water: The Harper Era

DAVIDE P. CARGNELLO, MARK BRUNET,
MATTHEW RETALLACK, AND ROBERT SLATER

INTRODUCTION

In Canada, as elsewhere, getting water management right is a condition of continued economic, environmental, and cultural prosperity, as well as of moral and political legitimacy. Getting it wrong will entail high costs and onerous social burdens. Water is a unique resource, too valuable for its management to be left to chance.

Water management has yet to be claimed, politically. It does not fall neatly into any one ideological camp. It is central to the wellbeing of all Canadians, but also complex, requiring original policy crafting, flexible and cooperative governance, investment, leadership, and foresight. Despite promising initial gestures, water appears to have been largely forgotten under the current government. This is especially troubling given the current federal focus on natural resource development.

We argue that the importance of water and of the risks associated with its misuse speak to the need for a comprehensive Canadian water strategy tailored to the unique characteristics of this resource – characteristics that determine the most effective, efficient, and equitable means of managing it. We begin by discussing some of the ways in which water is valuable and unique: why should we care about water management? Second, we frame our discussion by introducing two influential ethical and political traditions: how should we think about water management? Third, we canvas recent Harper era Canadian efforts: where do we stand? We conclude by arguing for an approach that 'moves water into the mainstream' and recognizes the key role the federal government must play in helping to meet Canada's water management needs.

A VALUABLE AND UNIQUE RESOURCE

Essential to life and the health of our ecosystems, water is valuable, versatile, and unique. We drink it, grow and process our food with it, use it to dispose of our waste and to keep our bodies healthy. Water contributes an estimated $7.8 to $22.9 billion annually to the Canadian economy.[1] It is crucial to energy production,[2] recreation, and the manufacture and transportation of goods, and it plays a fittingly central, symbolic role in nearly all cultures and religions.[3] The ecosystem services provided by our watersheds support our activities in essential, irreplaceable ways.

As the 2013 Calgary and Toronto floods attest, water is also a damaging force. It can wreck neighbourhoods, level buildings, disrupt transportation and shipping lines, and claim lives. Flooding, chemical spills, and bacterial contamination can render it unsafe for human consumption, for growing crops, or raising livestock; rivers and streams can become too polluted for fishing or swimming. Worldwide, rising sea levels and water-related climatic events endanger densely populated areas, and intense exploitation of aquifers threatens important farmlands.

Perhaps especially in Canada, we often take for granted that, when turning the tap on for a drink or to brush our teeth, clean, fresh water will flow.[4] We also take for granted that floods and other water-related disturbances are aberrations, interruptions in an otherwise stable hydrologic cycle. We can likely no longer afford this confidence. Much of the rest of the world certainly cannot. While approximately 70% of the earth's surface is covered in water, fresh water accounts for only about 3% of it.[5] Further, water-related risks have become so unpredictable that recorded data often no longer provide adequate bases for decision-making, challenging our ability to respond in fundamental ways.[6] As populations continue to grow, fresh water is increasingly scarce. Competition for rights of access has become fierce. The world over, access to water is often a battle for survival – and the battles are not always figurative. The current turmoil in Syria, for example, can be traced to unrest over lack of access to water, among other causes.[7]

But should this worry us in Canada? The truth is that we don't know how worried we should be about our water or how careful we should be with it. We do know that, while Canadians enjoy approximately 7% of the world's renewable fresh water supplies (that is, supplies which, if properly managed, can be replenished through the natural cycle of evaporation and precipitation), most of our water drains into the Arctic, away from our most densely populated and intensively farmed areas, where we need it most. We also know that from 1972 to 1990, with a population growth of about 34%, rates of fresh water withdrawal in Canada grew by 90%.[8] Can we continue depleting our water wealth at this pace? As the old adage says, "We never know the worth of water, till the well is dry." We must address these issues before the well runs dry.

Water is a unique resource. Its management poses singular conceptual challenges. We have become relatively adept at managing our behaviour in many domains – at regulating economic and commercial activity, administering criminal justice, protecting property rights, delivering social and medical services, and maintaining professional and educational standards, for example. But many of our administrative practices are ill suited to managing water. Commercial and financial institutions can be made to respect jurisdictions; educational, medical, and legal institutions, to meet established standards of access and quality. Moreover, the majority of our goods occupy discrete physical locations, tend not to move unless moved, and can be distinguished the one from the other with relative ease. This greatly facilitates the adjudication of claims concerning ownership, transfer and use rights, and related obligations. People, too, fall under legal and institutional jurisdictions: as citizens, employees, subscribers, etc. But water is different.

Unlike people, institutions, and businesses, water does not follow the rules of the human world. It respects neither borders nor jurisdictions, does not respond to incentives, and can be neither punished nor persuaded to comply with regulations. Unlike lumber, buildings, or books, water does not stay put. When we place it somewhere, it ends up somewhere else. We pour it on the ground and it vanishes. We spill something in part of it and all of it becomes contaminated. It is dynamic and malleable; it flows, solidifies, evaporates – its condition varies in space and time. It is often abundant when we do not want it around and unavailable when we need it most. For all these reasons, water exhibits regional challenges on a national scale with upstream and downstream users in dispersed geographic areas affecting each other's wellbeing in often unanticipated ways. The upshot is that we must rethink our approach to water management.

WATER ETHICS

So, how should we think about water? Water has not, until recently, received the sustained attention it deserves in the ethical canon. Nonetheless, two overarching – and often opposing – traditions emerge within mainstream moral and political theory. For our purposes, what is noteworthy about these traditions is not their disagreements, but the underlying consensus that can be teased from them.

The utilitarian tradition provides much of the theoretical foundation of modern day microeconomic theory and policy analysis. Championed most famously in the eighteenth and nineteenth centuries by Jeremy Bentham and John Stuart Mill, utilitarianism focuses on the moral imperative to generate the "greatest happiness of the greatest number."[9] According to utilitarians, a resource like water should be thought of as an important welfare enhancing good, and its distribution, use, and protection should be guided by the ideal of welfare maximization. In many instances, utilitarians will recommend the adoption of market-based systems of exchange: welfare is maximized when impediments to the free exchange of goods are minimized.

But this recommendation does not hold for all goods in all markets and all circumstances. In some cases, particularly those involving common property resources, free exchange may lead to market failure. Externality-driven collapses, or "tragedies of the commons," as they have come to be known, occur when each market agent's acting rationally to maximize her welfare (say, by drawing on a freely available resource) yields a globally suboptimal outcome (destruction of the resource). Overfishing provides the classic example. Regulations designed to protect fishery stocks can ensure continued fishing under responsible conditions. Where there exist dangers of overexploitation and where the collapse of a given resource would prove highly detrimental to human welfare (as in the case of water), utilitarians must recommend the adoption of measures designed to ensure responsible use of that resource.

A second approach, whose roots lie in the natural law and contractualist traditions, receives its most influential exposition in the works of John Locke and Immanuel Kant. This rights-centred approach focuses on the duties, claims, and rights of individuals, providing the conceptual and philosophical bases for (a) the modern conception of human rights (access to water, for example), and (b) a system of private property rights. The Lockean conception of property rights has proven especially influential. It takes as fundamental the principle that 'mixing one's labour' with an unclaimed resource gives rise to ownership claims. Interestingly, Locke stresses that such ownership claims should be circumscribed by the proviso that each must leave "enough, and as good" of that resource for others[10] – a counterweight, which can help prevent the kind of overuse that leads to the market-failures and commons tragedies described by microeconomic theory. In a time of increasing uncertainty concerning the health of natural resources, this Lockean proviso becomes central to resource management ethics, especially when our obligations to future generations are taken into account.

Strikingly then, despite their traditional antagonism, each of these approaches can recognize the need for societies to manage their natural heritage. Whether for reasons relating to human rights or welfare maximization, both utilitarians and rights-based theorists must support the ideal of resource stewardship: responsible management of humanity's greatest assets.[11] We must see ourselves as trustees of our water.[12]

Given its uniqueness, its importance, and the risks associated with its misuse, Canadian governments of all types have a central role to play in managing our water. They alone possess the democratic legitimacy and the technical, financial, and coordinating capacity to meet the water-related challenges that lie ahead. They alone are in a position to assess the state of Canada's water (to determine how much of it there is, where, and of what quality), to assess the

cumulative impacts of how we use it, and to mobilize the governance structures best suited to its management, so as to integrate the ecological, social,
and economic services that water provides.

CANADA'S CURRENT WATER MANAGEMENT EFFORTS

Where do we currently stand? In this section we canvas key federal documents
and offer a snapshot of recent federal water-related expenditure initiatives. We
discuss legislative changes introduced under Bill C-38 (the 2012 omnibus bill)
and relevant provincial and territorial efforts. We find that while the current
government initially appreciated the need for a national water strategy, eight
years on, none has materialized. Resource extraction has been privileged at
the expense of water management, and the government's approach to water
has been piecemeal and disjointed rather than systematic.

Key Documents

Shortly after the 2006 election, Rona Ambrose, the Harper government's first
environment minister, noted that "Canada is very far behind ... in any sort
of a national water strategy." She added, "it is very important to address this
early on."[13] The government's approach was initially encouraging. Its 2006
electoral platform promised a "Made in Canada" water strategy focused on
aquifer mapping to identify groundwater resources, protection of the Great
Lakes, a ban on inter-basin water transfers, penalties for bilge oil dumping,
investments in watershed management, and water quantity and quality assurance. The National Water Strategy announced in the following year's budget
did not explicitly mention the latter four issues, but included $30 million to
support the cleanup of the Great Lakes, Lake Winnipeg, and Lake Simcoe,
$44 million for fisheries and water levels research, and $19 million for oceans
research and protection.

The 2007 budget announced the first tougher municipal waste regulations
under the Fisheries Act, and funding for First Nations water infrastructure.
While offering substantially less than the sums required to meet national
water infrastructure needs (estimates put the replacement value of water
infrastructure in "fair" to "very poor" condition at $80.7 billion),[14] the an-
nouncement was a step in the right direction, particularly since Ambrose also
noted in parliament that the federal government was "beginning discussions
with the provinces on a national water strategy to share information about
water quality and water quantity, to ensure Canadians have access to safe and
clean drinking water, and to identify the quantity and resource related issues
that are emerging throughout Canada today."[15]

Progress has since stalled. Analysis of speeches from the throne, budget
speeches, and election platforms suggests that the Harper government's

Table 11.1
Key documents: water-related initiatives and commitments

Initiatives and Commitments	Election Platform			Federal Budget								Throne Speech						
	2006	2008	2011	2006	2007	2008	2009	2010	2011	2012	2013	2006	2007	2008	2009	2010	2011	2013
Leadership and strategy	✓			✓								✓						
High profile projects	✓	✓	✓	✓		✓	✓	✓		✓			✓					
Monitoring and assessment	✓			✓		✓	✓											
First Nations water				✓	✓	✓	✓	✓	✓	✓	✓		✓				✓	✓
Municipal infrastructure				✓	✓	✓	✓	✓	✓	✓	✓		✓					
Legislative changes						✓		✓	✓	✓								

interest in water was at its greatest in 2007 (see Table 11.1). Since then, it has waned in the face of overwhelming focus on natural resources such as energy, mining, and forestry. The 2008 election platform made fewer water-related commitments than its predecessor and, while the 2008 throne speech contained a pledge to "ensure protection of our vital resources … [and] ban all bulk water transfers or exports from Canadian freshwater basins," the following year's speech did not mention water at all. The 2009 budget highlighted funding for First Nations water infrastructure and municipal water infrastructure (through the Economic Action Plan), identified a $28.4 million dollar initiative to improve reporting on environmental indicators (including water), and announced changes to the Navigable Waters Protection Act.

2010 and 2011 saw renewed pledges concerning First Nations and municipal water infrastructure, as well as funding for Great Lakes water quality research, further improved reporting on environmental indicators, and the extension of the Arctic Waters Pollution Prevention Act. In 2012 the Experimental Lakes Area research station and the National Roundtable on the Environment and the Economy were defunded or abolished. Bill C-38 introduced profound and controversial changes to legislation relating to environmental protection. The Transboundary Waters Protection Act (Bill C-383), which effectively blocks future bulk water exports, received unanimous support in the House (2013). The 2013 budget increased infrastructure funding to municipalities (including water infrastructure), outlined smaller research initiatives, discussed ballast water regulations to protect against invasive species, and proposed stricter regulations for pulp and paper mills. The 2013 throne speech promised that the "polluter pays" principle would be given statutory basis but without much explanation. In 2013 Canada withdrew from the UN Convention to Combat Desertification, making Canada the only country outside the agreement. All the while, there has been little to no public disclosure of water related cuts and reallocations.

Since 2007, ministerial statements relating to water have generally focused on discrete initiatives. Ambrose's successors in the environment portfolio have demonstrated little appetite for leadership on a Canadian water strategy.

Snapshot: Federal Expenditure Initiatives

Our analysis suggests that initial attempts to engage the water agenda have been sidelined. Water has returned to its afterthought position. Despite the early promise of a national strategy, federal water-related initiatives have fallen consistently into three traditional spending categories: municipal infrastructure (including water infrastructure), First Nations water infrastructure, and some priority watersheds.

- Municipalities receive the lion's share of expenditures (for the construction of drinking water treatment plants, water distribution systems, sewerage systems, and storm water management facilities, among other projects). Under both iterations of the Building Canada Plan (2007, 2013) infrastructure funding to provinces, territories, and municipalities increased significantly (to $53 billion over ten years, in 2013). As noted above, however, water infrastructure needs alone surpass $80 billion. While expenditures by all governments are substantial, needs continue to grow. The first Canada-wide regulations proclaimed under the Fisheries Act in 2012 will further increase demands on municipalities.
- The federal government has a fiduciary responsibility toward Canada's First Nations. This responsibility includes safe drinking water, sewage treatment, and flood damage protection. The current government's commitments to First Nations water infrastructure have been relatively consistent, with expenditures announced in each budget from 2006 to 2013. The performance record in this category is wanting, as judged by the number of First Nations communities subject to boil water advisories. From 2007 to 2013, this number has generally hovered between 115 and 125, with a low of 97 (July 2008) and peak of 127 (just over 20% of communities) in October 2011. Between 2006 and 2014, approximately $3 billion will have been spent on First Nations water infrastructure and related projects,[16] with no discernible trend in the number of communities under advisories – suggesting operational challenges. Aboriginal Affairs and Northern Development Canada recognizes the need for "better management practices, improved operator training, increased system capacity, and the construction of new infrastructure," at an estimated cost of $1.2 billion.[17]

- The government has committed to expenditures in certain watersheds that are showing clear evidence of stress caused by pollution or land use changes. These include Lake Winnipeg, the Great Lakes, Lake Simcoe, and the Athabasca River. Resources have been directed to monitoring, research, remedial projects, and public engagement. Funding for high profile projects and monitoring was announced in 2007, 2009, 2010, 2011, and 2013. In a number of cases, however, announcements reemphasise previously existing initiatives.

Outside these categories, few water-related projects have been initiated since 2006 and there is little evidence of federal involvement in the emergence of a Canadian strategy. It should also be noted that, except in the case of First Nations water infrastructure, clear information on water-related expenditures is not available through publicly accessible sources.

Legislative Changes

The 2012 omnibus bill (Bill C-38: Jobs, Growth, and Long Term Prosperity Act) includes substantive changes to five relevant pieces of legislation. Four categories of changes emerge: (1) streamlining approval processes for projects with potential environmental impacts, (2) narrowing the federal mandate, (3) strengthening environmental enforcement and compliance mechanisms, and (4) limiting opportunities for public consultation on projects with potential environmental impacts. (See Table 11.2.)

Notable changes:

- The Navigable Waters Act now applies only to listed bodies – currently: 3 oceans, 97 lakes, and portions of 62 rivers (a drastic reduction from 32,000 lakes and roughly 2.25 million rivers). Under the National Energy Board Act, the National Energy Board may authorize interference with navigable waters.
- Under the Canadian Environmental Assessment Act some provincial assessments can be substituted for federal assessments. The Fisheries Act may be suspended where equivalent provincial legislation already exists.
- Enforcement powers have been strengthened, for example, through the adoption of Administrative Monetary Penalty regimes under the Navigable Waters Act and the National Energy Board Act.
- Assessments under the Canadian Environmental Assessment Act apply to a more limited set of projects and must be completed within tighter deadlines.

The declared intent of these changes was to accelerate the pace of "responsible resource management." It is not clear whether the intention was also to reduce federal capacity to meet constitutional obligations for water-related issues as these have developed since confederation, or whether this was collateral damage resulting from the drive to intensify resource extraction.

Table 11.2
Bill C-38 key water-related changes

	Streamlined approval process	Narrowed federal mandate	Strengthened enforcement/ compliance	Reduced public consultation
Fisheries Act	✓	✓	✓	
Species at Risk Act	✓			
Navigable Waters Act	✓	✓	✓	✓
National Energy Board Act	✓		✓	✓
Environmental Assessment Act	✓	✓	✓	✓

The consequences of these changes will become evident over time and will undoubtedly engage the courts.

Provincial and Territorial Initiatives

While federal involvement remains uneven and contentious, action by provincial and territorial governments has been somewhat more consistent.

- The premier of British Columbia placed water policy on the agenda of the Council of the Federation (2010), leading to the development of a provincial Water Charter (2011) that promotes individual and collective accountability for Canada's water resources. Performance reports will merit careful consideration to determine whether early promise is converted into action.
- British Columbia is at the consultation phase in its attempt to modernize its Water Sustainability Act and adopt an areas-based management approach that takes local conditions into consideration.
- Saskatchewan is adopting new water legislation (slated for 2014), has a twenty-five-year water security plan, and a new Water Security Agency. The plan addresses increased demand for water and creates a new water allocation system.
- In Manitoba, Lake Winnipeg was named Threatened Lake of the Year in 2013. The Save Lake Winnipeg Act (2011) allows Cabinet to designate Crown lands as provincially significant wetlands, expands control of livestock manure, mandates water and wastewater management planning, and imposes a two-year moratorium on peat harvesting.
- Alberta has not updated its Water Act since 2000, but has renewed its Water for Life Strategy (2003, 2008).
- Ontario's Great Lakes Protection Act (2013) is currently in second reading. The act establishes a Guardians' Council to identify priorities, promote local activities, and formulate recommendations. The Clean Water Act (2006)

is far-reaching and has sought to encourage public participation in source water protection planning.

- Quebec's Water Act (2009) formally recognizes water as part of the province's "collective patrimony" and acknowledges the stewardship responsibilities of government.
- In 2013, Nova Scotia released its Water for Life strategy, which commits the province to an integrated water management approach and is one of the first to report performance against the Water Charter.
- Quebec and Nova Scotia have placed moratoria on hydraulic fracturing ("fracking") in order to study the controversial practice.
- The Northwest Territories has developed a comprehensive strategy structured around the goal of maintaining the ecological integrity of the Mackenzie River Watershed, has set a new standard for First Nations engagement, and is negotiating inter-jurisdictional agreements with upstream governments. Results will be precedent setting.

At the provincial and territorial level, catalyzing events have raised the profile of water-related challenges. These include: the Walkerton and North Battleford contaminated water incidents, and flooding in the Saguenay-Lac-Saint-Jean region, in the Calgary area (at a record-breaking cost $5.6 billion), and in Toronto, where a two-hour storm caused $850 million of insured damage. The result has been increased sensitivity to the need for an integrated approach to water, and recognition that provinces and territories can do more together than alone.

MOVING WATER INTO THE MAINSTREAM

What can we conclude concerning water management in Canada? In short, despite encouraging early signals, federal interest in water has fizzled under the current government.

The crucial mistake of traditional approaches has been to think of water management as an issue that can exist within clearly demarcated jurisdictional boundaries. "When we try to pick out anything by itself," John Muir wrote in 1911, "we find it hitched to everything else in the Universe."[18] In 2011, Margaret Catley-Carlson added that: "A century later, a gathering of the World Economic Forum discovered the same phenomenon. Four hundred top decision makers listed the myriad looming threats to global stability, including famine, terrorism, inequality, disease, poverty and climate change. Yet when we tried to address each diverse force, we found them all attached to one universal security risk: fresh water."[19] Water management is not like other issues.

Still, across the country, progress has been made over the decades – slowly and imperfectly, but steadily. This is one reason why Bill C-38 is worrisome.

Its changes have been significant and unilateral. Scientists have also expressed concerns that their research is being sidelined.[20] In the rush to expedite natural resource extraction, we risk losing sight of some of the most basic conditions of our continued prosperity. Water management is fundamental to that prosperity, and its importance will continue to grow, given increasing resource scarcity and climatic volatility. Canada needs a strategy that acknowledges the national significance of water management, and that ensures we avoid the commons tragedies and market failures that routinely threaten common property resource use. We need a strategy that moves water into the mainstream.

This demands a change in perspective. First, we must be willing to manage water as a resource in its own right. This means learning to play the long game. It takes close to 400 years for the average drop of water to reach the mouth of the St Lawrence from the headwaters of Lake Superior.[21] Managing watershed health is a long-term project. Second, we must recognize that, in nature, everything is "hitched to everything else," as Muir put it. An increase of 1°C in atmospheric temperature, for example, boosts the amount of water vapour in the air by 7%, which provides more atmospheric moisture for rain and snow, but also dries out land surfaces and worsens droughts.[22] Water management must be comprehensive and adaptive. Third, water policy must emerge from within a web of thickly interconnected jurisdictional constraints. Responsibility over water resources must be assigned on a watershed-by-watershed basis. Managing shared responsibility is a necessity.

CONCLUSIONS: A STRENGTHENED FEDERAL ROLE

Since its promising early announcements recognizing the need for a national water strategy, the Harper government has retreated, preferring isolated initiatives to systematic planning. Isolated investments, while valuable, do not constitute a strategy and cannot compensate for lack of coordination and integration. Funding must be allocated systematically in order to maximize impact and lower per-project transaction costs. Nor can a piecemeal approach respond to the deep worries that remain concerning the long-term sustainability of our water capital and our ability to ensure that we safeguard 'enough, and as good' of it for all Canadians, present and future.

We have argued that the unique characteristics of water, its value, and the risks associated with its misuse speak to the need for a Canadian strategy that moves water into the mainstream. Such a strategy must recognize: (a) the importance of long-term, adaptive, watershed-based management, (b) the need for shared responsibility and integration of authorities, and (c) the existence of significant research needs relating to data collection and coordination, analysis, and monitoring. These requirements help isolate the principal elements of a strengthened federal role in water management.

First, there is considerable need for federal investment in scientific research relating to water – whether undertaken directly by the federal government, or indirectly, through universities and international initiatives. To craft effective policies we need an accurate, comprehensive picture of the state of our water wealth. Significant economies of scale and barriers to entry relating to the development of facilities and expertise for data collection and monitoring render federal investment both vital and efficient.

Second, the federal government must provide national coordination on water management. The constitution does not discuss water. While responsibility over natural resources rests principally with the provinces, federal action is required through, for example: (a) provision of the legislative tools necessary to meet inter-jurisdictional and shared-management constraints, (b) coordination of data collection requirements (including standardization, prioritization, and communication), and (c) coordination of decisions regarding sitings, assessments, and terms and conditions of approvals. This suite of coordinating instruments and legislative tools must be mobilized in consort with provincial and other players.

Third, we need federal leadership. Water must be placed on the political agenda as an issue of national interest. Provincial and territorial governments have taken important first steps by according water policy a more prominent position on their agendas. While the federal government has allocated funds toward specific projects and in traditional spending categories, it remains largely absent from its key and unique role of ensuring a coherent, systematic framework for the management of Canada's water. The challenges posed by the impact of climate change on water resources, for example, require urgent attention; this, alone, justifies federal leadership.

NOTES

1 See Stephen Renzetti, Diane P. Dupont, and Chris Wood, "Running through Our Fingers: How Canada Fails to Capture the Value of Its Top Asset" (Blue Economy Initiative, November 2011).
2 See Roger Gibbins and Larissa Somerfeld, "National Strategies for Energy and Water: The Illusion of Convergence" (Canada West Foundation, 2012).
3 See Peter G. Brown and Jeremy J. Schmidt, eds., *Water Ethics: Foundational Readings for Students and Professionals* (Washington, DC: Island Press, 2010).
4 Peter H. Pearse, "Developments in Canada's Water Policy." In *The Management of Canada's Water Resources* (The Institute of Public Administration of Canada, 1986), 1.
5 United States Geological Survey, http://ga.water.usgs.gov. Accessed October 25, 2013.

6   See P.C.D. Milly, Julio Betancourt, Malin Falkenmark, Robert M. Hirsch, Zbigniew
    W. Kundzewicz, Dennis P. Lettenmaier, and Ronald J. Stouffer, "Stationarity Is Dead:
    Whither Water Management?" *Science* 319 (February 2008): 573–4.

7   William Polk and James Fallows, "Your Labor Day Syria Reader, Part 2: William
    Polk," *The Atlantic* (September 2, 2013). Accessed October 25, 2013 via http://www.
    theatlantic.com.

8   Environment Canada, *Water Quantity*. Accessed October 25, 2013 via http://www.
    ec.gc.ca/eau-water.

9   Jeremy Bentham, *A Fragment on Government* (1776), intr. by Ross Harrison
    (Cambridge: Cambridge University Press, 1988).

10 John Locke, *Second Treatise of Government* (1690), ed. by C.B. Macpherson
    (Cambridge, MA: Hackett, 1980), 19.

11 See Peter G. Brown, *Restoring the Public Trust* (Boston, MA: Beacon Press, 1994).

12 See also Ralph Pentland and Chris Wood, *Down the Drain: How We Are Failing to
    Protect Our Water Resources* (Vancouver, BC: Greystone, 2013), 221–3.

13 Renata D'Aliesio, "Canada 'Very Far Behind' on National Water Strategy." *Calgary
    Herald* (February 27, 2006).

14 Federation of Canadian Municipalities, Canadian Construction Association,
    Canadian Public Works Association, and Canadian Society for Civil Engineering,
    *Canadian Infrastructure Report Card, Volume 1: 2012 – Municipal Roads and Water
    Systems* (2012), 64.

15 Parliament of Canada, 39th Parliament, 1st Session, edited Hansard, Number 021,
    May 11, 2006.

16 Aboriginal Affairs and Northern Development Canada (AANDC), "Water." Accessed
    October 25, 2013 via http://www.aadnc-aandc.gc.ca.

17 AANDC, *Fact Sheet – The Results of the National Assessment of First Nations Water and
    Wastewater Systems*. Accessed October 25, 2013 via http://www.aadnc-aandc.gc.ca.

18 John Muir, *My First Summer in the Sierra* (1911) (New York, NY: Houghton Mifflin
    Harcourt, 2011), 104.

19 Margaret Catley-Carlson in The World Economic Forum Water Initiative, *Water
    Security: The Water-Food-Energy-Climate Nexus* (Washington, DC: Island Press,
    2011), xxi.

20 See Chris Turner, *The War on Science: Muzzled Scientists and Wilful Blindness in
    Stephen Harper's Canada* (Vancouver, BC: Greystone, 2013).

21 *Mysteries of the Great Lakes* (Science North, 2008). Available at http://sciencenorth.
    ca/mysteriesofthegreatlakes/

22 National Academy of Science, *Warming World: Impacts by Degree* (National
    Academies Press, 2011).

12 The National Shipbuilding Model for Government Procurement: Separating the Wheat from the Chaff

JENNIFER SPENCE

INTRODUCTION

There are two images that are commonly evoked in the public imagination when referencing government procurement in Canada. The first epitomizes all things disliked about bureaucracy – rule-bound, overly complicated, inefficient and confusing – a backwater of public administration. This persona is contrasted by an alternate image often conjured up when discussing the less savory side of politics – partisanship, favoritism, backroom deals, and corruption. Of course, these two images in no way contradict each other; rather, the public administration literature will often offer them up as two sides of the same coin. How could you possibly unravel the red tape and streamline the procurement process when, to this day, people associate the 2006 defeat of the Liberal Party with the Sponsorship Scandal and the decline of the Progressive Conservative Party with the 1986 political mishandling of CF-18 contracts?[1] Then along comes the procurement of large ships under the National Shipbuilding Procurement Strategy (NSPS) – the largest value procurement project in Canadian history. This chapter, like most of the discourse on the NSPS, is primarily focused on the large vessel procurements. However, the NSPS is a larger strategy that includes other commitments.

Less than eighteen months after the project began, two shipyards were selected to be part of strategic sourcing arrangements[2] and NSPS received with overwhelming praise from industry and politicians of every stripe, as well as the media and procurement specialists nationally and internationally. Newspaper headlines included "Shipbuilding: At last, a cure for procurement"[3] and "All governments should do it this way."[4]

Of course, in the months that have followed, the NSPS has received less flattering media coverage and some critics have suggested that it was always too good to be true. Furthermore, although the Fall Report of the Auditor General of Canada[5] acknowledged the success and effectiveness of the new NSPS model, it echoed concerns that have been raised over the last year in other fora about the timing and process for setting project budgets. So how do we separate the wheat from the chaff in the public discourse on the NSPS? Is this a procurement that has the potential to fundamentally redefine public procurement or a major procurement that was prematurely lauded for its success?

This chapter critically examines the NSPS. The first section provides an overview of the procurement environment in which the NSPS was created. This serves as the foundation for an examination of the core features of the NSPS in order to analyze the NSPS procurement approach, as well as its supporting governance arrangements. How was this procurement different? My central argument is that the NSPS does offer lessons learned that are valuable and potentially transformational for government procurement. However, the failings of previous procurements did not serve as the means to design a new model for complex procurement; rather, what is unique about the NSPS approach is its emphasis on finding solutions by establishing a collaborative relationship between the key players both within and outside government. Furthermore, I argue that the new NSPS model does not directly resolve the challenges and risks generated by the budgeting approach used for the NSPS; however, it may facilitate a working environment that allows for the meaningful consideration of alternative approaches. Finally, I argue that the transferability of the full NSPS model is currently limited to a select group of high-profile, complex projects. This suggests that there is a value in placing further attention on how collaborative governance approaches and principles can inform procurements of different scales and levels of complexity.

FITTING THE NSPS INTO THE FEDERAL
PROCUREMENT LANDSCAPE

Governments are an important player in national economies and are recognized as one of the largest markets in the world. In 2013, the Organisation for Economic Co-operation and Development (OECD) indicated that government procurement totalled €1.3 trillion in OECD countries and averaged approximately 15% of GDP.[6] This means that many industries supply governments with goods and services either directly or indirectly,[7] while in certain industries, including aircraft, shipbuilding, construction, and communication equipment, governments are, and will continue to be, a major direct consumer of goods and services.[8]

The Government of Canada alone procures on average $14 billion annually[9] to support the delivery of federal programs and services to Canadians, recognizing that other levels of government also play an important role in delivering public goods and services. Approximately one-third of the amount spent by the government is committed to large, complex projects, while the remainder is spent on smaller, lower risk, and less complex procurements.[10]

When originally announced on June 3, 2010, the NSPS was valued at $33 billion and was tasked with meeting multiple objectives,[11] including:

- Procuring the next generation of small and large ships for the Canadian Navy and the Canadian Coast Guard, as well as the repair, refit and maintenance of the existing Canadian fleet;
- Supporting Canadian shipyards and the marine industry; and
- Creating jobs in high-tech industries across Canada.

What this illustrates is that the NSPS, like many complex projects, is expected to meet multiple objectives, which at times may be difficult to reconcile. This includes the most obvious and predictable goal of any public or private buyer, which is to procure the best value goods and services on budget and on time that meet the needs of the Government of Canada and Canadians. However, as a government in a modern democracy, the public administration of procurement has the added responsibility of delivering the NSPS within a broader procurement system and processes that ensure respect for core principles, such as integrity, transparency, and fairness.[12] Finally, as mentioned earlier, the government's purchasing power is an important economic and social lever; therefore, it should not be surprising that the NSPS, like many other large procurement projects, is also tasked with fulfilling broader public policy objectives – in this case, introduce an industrial strategy that seeks to bolster economic growth; support Canadian industries to improve domestic and international productivity and competitiveness; and maximize long-term, high-skill Canadian jobs.[13] In the case of the NSPS, this ultimately translated into a policy decision by the government to rebuild Canada's capacity to manufacture modern, high-tech ships and eliminate the "boom and bust" cycle that Canada's shipbuilding industry has historically experienced.[14]

Therefore, although any procurement can attract public attention, it is not surprising that high-cost, high-risk and complex procurement projects, such as the NSPS, are the ones that are most commonly subjected to scrutiny, while often being the most difficult to explain in simple terms. Of course, given the nature of these projects, they are also the procurements where the government has experienced the most complications when adopting "traditional" procurement approaches and tools that have frequently been ineffective at meeting the needs of the Government and suppliers. The NSPS also draws notice because it is a defence-related procurement and, therefore, in the public imagination, runs the risk of joining a long line of military projects in Canada and other Western countries that have frequently suffered from extensive delays and extreme cost overruns. Canadians cannot avoid ongoing public debates about the politically charged F-35 Joint Strike Fighter Program, the Maritime Helicopter Project, or the Joint Support Ship Project. As larger projects they are politically visible, nationally and regionally.

THE ORIGINS OF THE NSPS

In fact, it was the failings of these high-profile procurements, the Joint Support Ship Project in particular, and the general expectation that the NSPS was "doomed to fail," "[destined] to be mired in regional, partisan politics and slow bureaucratic processes"[15] that made the large vessel procurements a political "hot potato" that politicians were willing to separate themselves from the procurement process. Furthermore, many officials were aware of serious weaknesses with the existing approach to managing complex procurements that was frequently ineffective at meeting the needs of government, supporting Canadian industry and realizing the expectations of Canadians. Ultimately, this situation provided officials with the space to try something new. In other words, through the public failing of these complex projects came an opportunity to advance a new procurement approach for the NSPS, as well as highlighting the "starting conditions" that served to shape the NSPS governance model.[16]

However, what specifically was wrong with business as usual? What were these starting conditions that facilitated the development of a new model? To begin, it is helpful to consider what has *not* changed. First, all procurement projects include a full life cycle of activities – from planning an acquisition, to identifying and choosing the right suppliers, to negotiating appropriate contracts, and administering and closing contracts.[17] Irrespective of the complexity of a procurement project, the government has articulated four phases that all procurements go through: precontractual; contracting; contract management; and postcontract.[18]

Secondly, federal procurements are subject to a complex legislative and regulatory framework that all projects are required to respect and work within. Historically, this framework has been translated into a heavy reliance on competition, rigid rules and norms, and performance monitoring, all of which have grown over decades within public administration. This rigidity has served to devalue, and in many cases, explicitly prohibit, the core principles of buyer–supplier relations that are common in the private sector, including durability, consistency, trust, and commitment. This procurement approach has ultimately served to degrade government's relations with its suppliers.[19]

It is this lack of trust that exists between industry and government that has been a common criticism – the government's traditional model of fair, open and transparent procurement dictates that bidders and potential bidders should be kept at arm's length. The government defines its requirements, and industry's role is to respond by submitting proposals. This approach does not require an integrated relationship between the two. In fact, in many cases, it expressly prohibits buyer-supplier interaction. Jonathan Whitworth, the CEO of Seaspan Marine Corporation, indicated that "there was about a hundred years of procurement history that gave us that feeling that in the past, procurement projects were difficult. They were clouded in secrecy. They were black boxes ... So unfortunately, past practices gave us an ill feeling; us, being in the industry, of the next round."[20]

A further challenge to the procurement process that may be less obvious to outside observers is how these projects were also hindered by the silos that exist within Canadian federal public administration – vertical hierarchical organizations created to support a Westminster model, which emphasizes ministerial accountability for specific mandates.[21] For example, in a major military procurement, the Department of National Defence is focused on getting the most advanced equipment that meets its current and future needs, while Industry Canada is focused on the economic benefits for Canada, and Public Works and Government Services Canada is focused on maintaining the integrity of the procurement process.[22] Using the traditional approach to procurement, there are no systematic incentives to reconcile the different mandates and objectives of the departments involved. In fact, the prevailing systems and structures are more likely to facilitate power, resource and knowledge asymmetries and a similar lack of trust. The recognition by key officials of the limitations of the traditional model of procurement allowed those involved in the NSPS to consider how this procurement could be managed differently to create conditions for success.

THE UNIQUE CHARACTERISTICS OF THE NSPS

The NSPS does not circumvent or challenge the existing procurement framework. However, in recognizing the challenges that previous large complex procurements have faced, the NSPS sought to question the rigid and segregating rules and norms that had grown up over decades as an *interpretation* of these legal requirements. In other words, I argue that what makes the NSPS unique is not so much a new model for complex procurement; rather, it was the willingness of officials to question the *interpretation* of certain fundamental principles, such as "fair, open and transparent," which enabled the adoption of a collaborative governance process and principles that fundamentally changed the nature of the relationship between players and provided new conditions to develop trust, a sense of shared accountability, and a focus on achieving collectively recognized outcomes.

In fact, I suggest that Ansell and Gash's model of collaborative governance (see Figure 12.1) provides a clear illustration of the key characteristics of the NSPS that make it unique as a procurement project, as well as capturing the

Figure 12.1
Model of collaborative governance

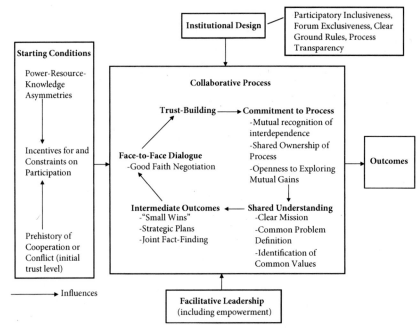

Source: Ansell and Gash, "Collaborative Governance in Theory and Practice," 550.

core components that are contributing to the project's success. As discussed in the previous section, the NSPS exhibited the "starting conditions" outlined in the model both in terms of the internal relations between government departments and between government and industry that provided the incentives for adopting a new governance approach and this new approach was not a new model for how complex procurement should be organized, planned, and managed; rather, it was a commitment from the beginning of the project to a *facilitative leadership* approach that was committed to a *collaborative process* for advancing the project and the adoption of key *institutional design* principles.

In fact, the collaborative engagement of industry, regional stakeholders and other levels of government started *before* the NSPS was created when the government hosted a series of outreach sessions in the summer of 2009 and solicited input on what a long-term shipbuilding strategy should look like. It was through these discussions that critical design elements of the strategy were developed, such as the division of work packages. According to Steve Durrell, then President of Irving Shipbuilding Inc., "what we got back for an outline showed that they had actually listened to industry as to what would be a good way forward."[23]

However, perhaps the greatest shift was that through these discussions it was determined that the objectives of best value for Canadians and support for the long-term viability and competitiveness of the Canadian shipbuilding industry could not be realized by procuring the large vessels on a contract-by-contact basis. Instead, through these discussions, it was concluded that the successful realization of the N S P S required strategic sourcing arrangements for the larger vessels that would provide the marine industry with the certainty required to invest in establishing the necessary technological and human capacity. It was through a collaborative discourse with industry that government officials were able to appreciate the limitations of the traditional contract-by-contract competitive procurement model and recognize the advantages of establishing a long-term relationship for the successful realization of the project's objectives.

In fact, consistent with this early policy discourse, Timothy Choi presents a compelling argument that, in the case of shipbuilding, there is little evidence to suggest that the theory that increased competition will result in reduced costs will hold true.[24] He argues that this logic does not take into consideration the increased costs of constructing the same classes of vessels in different shipyards, and ignores the efficiencies that can be realized from the learning that can be applied with the building of multiple vessels – essentially presenting an economies-of-scale argument. Furthermore, he points out that it does not factor in the reality that increased competition may result in risky investments and "corner cutting" by the marine industry that may compromise the successful completion of projects and may ultimately result in the economic ruin of parts of the industry.

In addition, there is research that suggests that buyer-supplier relationships can be critical to the successful completion of complex projects and that a relationship of commitment and trust developed over an extended period of time can facilitate opportunities for learning and innovation.[25] Furthermore, a strategic supply arrangement with a single supplier can have numerous advantages for facilitating learning and performance improvement,[26] as well as developing the capacity to maintain and repair Canada's fleet. This is not to suggest that it does not also pose risks, such as those pointed out by the auditor general, that Canada will not acquire the ships in an affordable manner,[27] but many of these risks are being mitigated by jointly setting project timelines, ongoing communication, and open-book accounting practices that have been agreed to in the Government's agreements-in-principle with the two shipyards.

These preliminary discussions to develop the N S P S served as the foundation for a new buyer-supplier relationship that was further strengthened following the official announcement of the N S P S and the subsequent launch of the large vessel procurement project. While the project was still in the early stages of planning, potential bidders and other industry representatives were invited on multiple occasions to participate in determining how the objectives of the project could best be met, including the process for qualifying potential bidders, the evaluation criteria and weighting used to assess proposals, and the time frames and milestones that would be set for advancing the project.

In addition to a new collaborative relationship with industry, there were also efforts to address the internal silos that exist between government departments. The NSPS Secretariat was created, bringing together officials from all the relevant departments to implement the strategy and to be the link with their home organizations. This Secretariat is overseen by a committee of assistant deputy ministers from each of the key departments that oversees the development and implementation of the governance process; ensuring that the NSPS is managed in a manner consistent with the Government's principles of fairness, openness and transparency.[28] It is a committee of deputy ministers from these same departments that have final decision-making authority on the implementation of the NSPS, while ministers played no role in the selection of shipyards. In fact, they were advised of the results after the successful shipyards.

The final aspect of the NSPS large vessel procurement that has garnered attention is the extensive use of third-party expertise. For certain aspects, such as the benchmarking of shipyard capabilities undertaken by First Marine International, the argument can be made that this highly technical expertise can most efficiently and effectively be acquired from an outside source. However, in many cases, I would argue that outside expertise, such as fairness monitoring and financial analysis, were brought in because of the Government's unique requirements to ensure a fair, open, and transparent process combined with a recognition of a previous environment of low trust between the various players. This means that these external actors were brought in to lend credibility to the process and demonstrate commitment to a new collaborative governance approach. Therefore, it is misleading to suggest this feature of the NSPS as a unique component of the new governance model. Instead, it should be acknowledged as a means to advance the project, given the constraints generated from the "starting conditions" of the NSPS.

ISSUES NOT ADDRESSED BY THE NSPS MODEL

Military procurement in Canada has never been easy for the military or for the government. The military is managing aging equipment, while any decision taken by the government to replace this equipment has such a large price tag that it is guaranteed to become visibly political.[29] When the Conservatives came to power in 2006, they made a commitment to invest in the Canadian military. Through the Canada First Defence Strategy, the Government committed $490 billion to defence, which included a shopping list of major military equipment that would be replaced, including:

- 15 ships to replace existing destroyers and frigates;
- 10 to 12 maritime patrol aircraft;

- 17 fixed-wing search and rescue aircraft;
- 65 next-generation fighter aircraft; and
- a fleet of land combat vehicles and systems.[30]

In other words, the Government's strategy included a policy decision to invest in *modernizing* Canada's aging military equipment, presumably with the knowledge that this would garner political attention (both good and bad) and involve purchasing equipment that is increasingly costly, as well as highly technical and complex, especially given the need to maintain interoperability with Canada's allies.[31]

It was also a policy decision that should have been made with the knowledge that the process of procuring these types of equipment is known to take decades and that the rate of change in these increasingly technical procurements would make it almost impossible to properly cost at such an early stage.[32] There should be no surprise that a firm budget set in 2006 to procure military equipment, based on only a notional idea of what is needed and even less of an idea of what will be available by the time that contracts are put in place to build this equipment, would ultimately result in the need to reduce the number of vessels and/or their capabilities. Add to this the NSPS policy decision to rebuild the Canadian marine industry and create jobs in Canada, and it is safe to assume that all the NSPS projects will suffer from inadequate funding and to recognize that fixed budgets are impractical.

Combine this with the subsequent global financial crisis, and the cautions and criticism of the Auditor General[33] and others about the potential risk that the military will not get the vessels or capabilities that it needs should come as no surprise. With recent economic changes, the government has decided to shift its attention to lowering the deficit, and that means cuts are being made in many of the government's program areas – this is not an environment where we should expect to see additional investments in high-cost procurements for the Canadian Forces and the Canadian Coast Guard.[34]

Does the NSPS collaborative governance model address these budget issues? Not directly, but it does provide the relevant players with the means to consider this issue in an open and transparent manner where diverse interests, needs and objectives can be assessed and informed decisions can be made. However, it is important to remember that, at the end of the day, this is a policy decision that will be made by the government, which will shape the options available to the public service for how the project is managed and what equipment can ultimately be procured.

CONCLUSIONS

This chapter demonstrates that the NSPS truly has set a new course for government procurement that is worth attention, recognition, and further monitoring. The NSPS collaborative governance approach offers stakeholders the opportunity to build new relationships and establish unique procurement solutions that best meet their needs. I also illustrate that the NSPS has created the initial conditions for real change to the government's procurement system. However, the NSPS is managed within a complex framework that is unique to public procurement and is tasked with meeting multiple policy objectives that may be difficult to reconcile. Furthermore, this governance approach cannot directly resolve the funding shortfalls that the NSPS currently face – nor has it ever claimed to do so. Assigning sufficient resources to fulfill the objectives of the NSPS is ultimately a policy decision made by the government, not an issue to be resolved by the procurement process.

With the public success of the NSPS, the government is highly motivated to consider how the lessons learned from this experience could inform other complex procurements. In the summer of 2011, only two months before the successful shipyards were selected for the large vessel procurement packages, the same collaborative governance model was being applied to the re-launch of the Fixed-Wing Search and Rescue Aircraft Replacement Project (FWSAR). After getting off to a rough start in 2009, a renewed process for the FWSAR project was initiated with an intensive series of consultations with industry and the creation of a secretariat with representatives from all key departments. Now, similar collaborative governance features can be found in a growing number of high-value and complex procurement projects, including the Government Relocation Services Project, the construction of a new bridge to replace the Champlain Bridge in Montreal, and the re-procurement of the Canada Student Loans Program.

However, in considering the broader application of the NSPS model, it is important to point out that the NSPS large vessel procurement process is still ongoing and will not be completed for twenty to thirty years when the vessels are delivered to Canada and all contracts complete the post-contract phase of the procurement. This serves to emphasize that the greatest contribution of the NSPS is to demonstrate the impact of a new collaborative approach to procurement – it is premature to assess its impact on the overall procurement process or framework.

It is also important to highlight that the NSPS large vessel procurement projects were, and continue to be, heavily dependent on the intense investment of senior leaders in multiple departments who are committed to the project's success – at critical points in the process, the input and decisions of assistant deputy ministers and deputy ministers are required to ensure that the projects advance. This may suggest that the exact replication of the leadership-intensive NSPS model will ultimately be limited to a select group of high profile, complex projects where there is sufficient will to invest the necessary time and resources. However, as noted earlier, on average two-thirds of the annual money spent by the government is used to acquire goods and services that are less complex and cost less than $40 million; therefore, one of the critical questions that remains is how can the NSPS collaborative governance approach inform the many procurements that do not attract the limelight? Ultimately, a rule-bound interpretation of "fair, open and transparent" procurement grew up over decades and is well entrenched in the culture and norms of the public administration.

This would suggest that in order for the N S P S approach to achieve a broader applicability, there needs to be careful consideration of how collaborative governance approaches and principles can inform procurements of different sizes and levels of complexity. With this in mind, it is critical that government officials dedicate time, effort and the same facilitative leadership to a comprehensive transformation of the government's procurement system. It is unlikely that the "traditional" approach can be undone on a project-by-project basis.

Finally, what this analysis suggests is that the "lessons learned" from the N S P S approach may not be limited to the transformation of government procurement. The experience gained by adopting a collaborative governance approach has the potential to inform a variety of government policies and programs that could benefit from the development of more fruitful relationships between the diverse interests and needs they are designed to respond to.

NOTES

1 Barbara Allen, "How Ottawa Buys: Procurement Policy and Politics Beyond Gomery," in *How Ottawa Spends, 2006–2007*, ed. G. Bruce Doern (Montreal and Kingston: McGill-Queen's University Press, 2006), 95–115.

2 There has been confusion generated because the October 19, 2011 announcement revealed the results of a competition to select shipyards to be part of strategic sourcing arrangements and not the award of contracts. Although this was an important step in this complex procurement, it was still part of the pre-contractual phase of the project and only provides the platform to move to the contracting phase of the procurement.

3 J. Simpson, "Shipbuilding: At Last, a Cure for Procurement," *The Globe and Mail* (November 26, 2011).

4 Editorial, "All Governments Should Do It This Way," *The Guardian* (November 26, 2011).

5 "National Shipbuilding Procurement Strategy," in *2013 Fall Report of the Auditor General of Canada* (Ottawa: Office of the Auditor General of Canada, 2013).

6 Timothy G. Hawkins, Michael J. Gravier, and Edward H. Powley, "Public Versus Private Sector Procurement Ethics and Strategy: What Each Sector Can Learn from the Other," *Journal of Business Ethics* 103, no. 4 (May 10, 2011): 567–86, doi:10.1007/s10551-011-0881-2.

7 Hawkins et al., "Public Versus Private Sector Procurement Ethics and Strategy."

8 Christopher J. Nekarda and Valerie A. Ramey, "Industry Evidence on the Effects of Government Spending," *American Economic Journal: Macroeconomics* 3, no. 1 (2011): 36–59.

9   Public Works and Government Services Canada, *Public Works and Government Services Canada 2013–14 Report on Plans and Priorities* (Ottawa, 2013), 3.

10 Government of Canada, "PWGSC-Acquisitions Branch Activity – Procurement Value" (Ottawa: PWGSC Spend Cube, 2013).

11 Government of Canada, "Government of Canada Announces National Shipbuilding Procurement Strategy" (Ottawa: Government of Canada, 2010).

12 Timothy G. Hawkins, Michael E. Knipper, and Timothy S. Reed, "Outcome-Focused Market Intelligence: Extracting Better Value and Effectiveness From Strategic Sourcing," in *Tenth Annual Acquisition Research Symposium* (Monterey: Naval Postgraduate School, 2013).

13 Allan Craigie, "The Ways of Federalism in Western Countries and the Horizons of Territorial Autonomy in Spain," in *The Ways of Federalism in Western Countries and the Horizons of Territorial Autonomy in Spain, Vol. 1,* ed. Alberto López Basaguren and Leire Escajedo San Epifanio, vol. 1 (Berlin, Heidelberg: Springer Berlin Heidelberg, 2013), 155–164, doi:10.1007/978-3-642-27720-7; Eric James, "The National Shipbuilding Procurement Strategy: An Update" (Ottawa, 2013), http://books.scholarsportal.info/viewdoc.html?id=577515.

14 Allan Craigie, "Regionalism, Nationalism, and Defence Procurement in Canada," paper presented to CPSA 2013 Annual Conference (Victoria, 2013), available at http://www.cpsa-acsp.ca/papers-2013/Craigie.pdf.

15 Government of Canada, "National Shipbuilding Procurement Strategy Video" (2012), http://www.tpsgc-pwgsc.gc.ca/app-acq/sam-mps/snacn-nsps-video-eng.html.

16 C. Ansell and A. Gash, "Collaborative Governance in Theory and Practice," *Journal of Public Administration Research and Theory* 18, no. 4 (October 17, 2007): 543–71, doi:10.1093/jopart/mum032.

17 Miia Martinsuo and Tuomas Ahola, "Supplier Integration in Complex Delivery Projects: Comparison Between Different Buyer–supplier Relationships," *International Journal of Project Management* 28, no. 2 (February 2010): 107–16, doi:10.1016/j.ijproman.2009.09.004.

18 Government of Canada, "Phases of the Procurement Process" (2013), https://buyandsell.gc.ca/for-government/buying-for-the-government-of-canada/the-procurement-rules-and-process/phases-of-the-procurement-process.

19 Hawkins et al., "Public Versus Private Sector Procurement Ethics"

20 Government of Canada, "National Shipbuilding Procurement Strategy Video."

21 Ruth Hubbard and Gilles Paquet, *The Black Hole of the Public Administration* (Ottawa: University of Ottawa Press, 2010).

22 Craigie, "Regionalism, Nationalism, and Defence Procurement in Canada."

23 Government of Canada, "National Shipbuilding Procurement Strategy Video."

24 "The Costs of 21st Century Shipbuilding: Lessons for Canada from the Littoral Combat Ship Program," *Canadian Naval Review* 8, no. 4 (2013).

25 Martinsuo and Ahola, "Supplier Integration in Complex Delivery Projects," 109.

26 Surya Chadra Raju, Lino Guimarães Marujo, and Raad Yahya Qassim, "An Optimal Investment Model for Single Supplier-Single Customer Partnership Performance

Improvement in Shipbuilding Supply Chains," *International Journal of Business and Management* 8, no. 11 (May 16, 2013): 85–93, doi:10.5539/ijbm.v8n11p85.

27 "National Shipbuilding Procurement Strategy."

28 Government of Canada, "Backgrounder: The National Shipbuilding Procurement Strategy Guiding Principles," 2013, http://www.tpsgc-pwgsc.gc.ca/app-acq/sam-mps/ddi-bkgr-8-eng.html.

29 Craigie, "Regionalism, Nationalism, and Defence Procurement in Canada."

30 Government of Canada, *Canada First Defence Strategy* (Ottawa, 2008), 4.

31 Craigie, "Regionalism, Nationalism, and Defence Procurement in Canada."

32 Aaron Plamondon, *The Politics of Procurement* (Vancouver: UBC Press, 2010).

33 "National Shipbuilding Procurement Strategy."

34 Craigie, "The Ways of Federalism in Western Countries and the Horizons of Territorial Autonomy in Spain"; James, "The National Shipbuilding Procurement Strategy: An Update."

13 How Accurate Is the Harper Government's Misinformation? Scientific Evidence and Scientists in Federal Policy Making

KATHRYN O'HARA AND PAUL DUFOUR

To achieve world excellence in science and technology, Canadians must promote and defend two complementary and indivisible freedoms; the freedom of scientists to investigate and the freedom of entrepreneurs to innovate and market their products to the world.

Industry Canada[1]

INTRODUCTION

A remarkable and unprecedented transformation has taken place in federal government science under the Harper administration. Federal science has not only been subject to the command-control fetish within the current government, but both the media and the scientific community at large have joined forces – albeit in an uncoordinated manner – to help shape a more aggressive campaign in defending the legitimate role of science and the use of advice for decision-making in government. The resulting tension between the appropriate communication of government science and its public profile conflicts with those of Harper's bureaucratic norms and edicts. At its core is the freedom of scientists to investigate, publish and communicate findings pitted against an ideological obsession designed to control any and all policy messages. The full cost of this engagement has yet to be borne out, but it is clear that Canada's image as a democratic federation that uses evidence and promotes a knowledge-based economy has suffered considerably.

Granted, government scientists are civil servants and have multidimensional functions in performing their work within a parliamentary democracy, especially as they provide support in policy and regulatory development. They also have input into related science activities (RSA) regarding product and process assessment in both pre-market and post-market realms of review and analysis. Any science advice provided is also constrained by laws regarding commercial privilege and by laws of cabinet secrecy.[2] And advice is just that: counsel to be taken or ignored. That said, much of what constitutes government scientific advice and research in the past has been quite transparent with previous administrations engaged in stimulating more effective science advice and communication within the public domain. Much ink has been spilled to describe the role of federal scientists in decision making, especially with the earlier work of the now defunct Council of Science and Technology Advisors (CSTA).[3]

In light of the Harper government's incursion into science policy the issues of both the muzzling of government scientists and how the government chose to face intense scrutiny by both the media and the scientific community highlights a changed and charged political landscape. This chapter investigates the emergence of an activist research community.[4]

THE BACK STORY

The 1997–2000 period offers a window on how the previous Liberal administration tried to address the use of scientific evidence in controversial issues – and arguably more successfully (e.g., safe medicines, blood supply, fish stocks). In 1997, a public debate emerged over how science advice was being used in decision-making. Criticisms were levelled at two government departments in particular, Fisheries and Oceans Canada and Health Canada. Was the government ignoring or distorting scientific advice? The public outcry prompted then Secretary of State for Science, Research and Development, Ron Duhamel, to ask the federal government's Council of Science and Technology Advisers (CSTA) to assess the issue and suggest a course of action. Specifically, he asked:

- is there a systematic problem or is this a problem relating to certain departments?
- is the advice received in a manner that can be understood by policy makers?
- is the advice being factored into policy in a timely and appropriate manner?
- is the use of advice being documented so that usage is transparent to subsequent analysis by competent authorities?

The result was a report, *Scientific Advice for Government Excellence* (SAGE), which made several recommendations for improvements. While these guidelines were designed as principles, they were adopted as government policy in a short document labelled "A Framework for Science and Technology Advice: Principles and Guidelines for the Effective Use of Science and Technology Advice in Government Decision Making":

- Government needs to anticipate, as early as possible, those issues for which science advice will be required.

- Advice should be drawn from a variety of scientific sources and from experts in relevant disciplines.
- Government should employ measures to ensure the quality, integrity and objectivity of the science and science advice it uses, and ensure that science advice is considered in decision-making.
- Government should develop a risk management framework that includes guidance on how and when precautionary approaches should be applied.
- Government is expected to employ decision-making processes that are open, as well as transparent, to stakeholders and the public.
- Subsequent review of science-based decisions is required to determine whether recent advances in scientific knowledge have an impact on the science advice used to reach the decision.[5]

The CSTA went on to publish several key reports, including a 2003 report *Science Communications and Opportunities for Public Engagement*. This report made four key recommendations, also adopted by the government of the day:

1 Embrace the concept of participatory science communications;
2 Adopt communications as an integral part of the management and conduct of S&T and S&T informed policy;
3 Develop comprehensive S&T communications strategies;
4 Invest in S&T communications planning, training and delivery.

These guidelines were adapted from existing global standards to better communicate science to the public. Unfortunately, little progress was made when the Conservative government abolished the CSTA, the national science advisor, and the Canadian Biotechnology Advisory Committee.[6] These three councils were replaced by a Science, Technology, and Innovation Council (STIC) made up of eminent Canadians whose advice, in breaking with past tradition of open and transparent advisory bodies, was to remain confidential.[7] This decision, along with other matters – to deliberately keep science policy advice secret – was a contributing factor that led to the increasing mistrust of the Harper government by the research community and media alike.

THE HARPER ERA: THE MUZZLING OF SCIENCE AND SCIENTISTS

In the 2007–14 period, numerous examples of Harper administration engagement in controlling evidence and muzzling scientists emerged. Of course, the issue was broader than that of science; the Harper obsession for message control[8] extended to all aspects of the machinery of government, including some notable cases affecting Library and Archives Canada and Statistics Canada, both of which are likely to have profound implications on how Canada is to maintain repositories of knowledge and long-term data analysis for public policy.[9]

What made the muzzling issue especially egregious was the assault on fundamental tenets of a knowledge community, one that views democracy and freedom of expression as its touchstone. Initially, the science community and its endogenous leadership remained quiet for fear of retribution and did little in the way of advocacy.

But this silence could not continue, especially with international pressures from science groups and media who questioned the legitimacy of the Harper apparatchik in clamping down on science communication and belittling or ignoring evidence-based expertise. Advocacy awareness among civic society and scientific and research associations began to surface. Government science, regarded as a largely slumbering elite known for its whine and wimp approach to lobbying, showed signs of an awakening and a willingness to engage in civic society. The issue became more than a question about funding. It was to be a matter of principle around which the norms of scientific autonomy and research integrity were challenged by bureaucracy and political power.

THE DEATH OF EVIDENCE MARCH: ADVOCACY IN ACTION AND SCIENCE FINDS A POLITICAL VOICE

On July 10, 2012, an unusual sight could be witnessed as over 2,000 scientists and their allies swept down Wellington Street in Ottawa on their way to Parliament Hill. They chanted "no science, no evidence, no truth, no democracy." The occasion was the Death of Evidence march. At issue was the federal government's erosion through cuts or outright elimination of its own evidence collecting capacity, especially science. The list was long.[10] The march garnered considerable media coverage. *Nature* argued that "governments come and go, but scientific expertise and experience cannot be chopped and changed as the mood suits and still be expected to function. Nor can applied research thrive when basic research is struggling."[11] The argument had been placed front and centre in February of that year, when a special symposium organized by Canada's two, non-partisan, science writers' associations took place at the American Association for the Advancement of Science meeting in Vancouver. The panel explored the issue of "un-muzzling government scientists and how to re-open the discourse." Numerous organizations and commentators came out in support of government researchers' right to speak publicly and freely about the results of their work to the taxpaying public through the media.

Meanwhile, federal bureaucrats were announcing cuts to public science. The poster child was the Experimental Lakes Area research project – a long-standing experiment created in the late 1960s by the renowned scientist David Schindler. The ELA's $2M annual budget was cut from the host federal department, Fisheries and Oceans Canada, as part of overall reductions in spending during the 2012–13 program review exercise. But while this skirmish resulted in an agreement to transfer most of the ELA research to a Manitoba-based institute with support from the Ontario and Manitoba Governments, the outcome was far from ideal. More advocacy was to follow.

The federal opposition parties, especially the New Democratic Party, mounted a strong effort addressing muzzling issues. The NDP used their official opposition day in the House on March 19 to protest both the cuts and the silencing of government scientists. In further action, borrowing from the Obama administration's support for government research integrity, the NDP introduced a motion in the House on September 18, 2013 arguing in part that federal departments and agencies should "actively support and encourage federal scientists to speak freely to the media and the public about scientific and technical matters based on their official research, including scientific and technical ideas, approaches, findings, and conclusions."[12]

MOUNTING EVIDENCE

As a result of the Death of Evidence march, a new advocacy group, Evidence for Democracy, was formed. Its objectives were to promote the generation and open dissemination of science and evidence-based knowledge as well as to develop resources to help the public evaluate the use of evidence in government decision-making. The first order of business was to host a series of rallies in September 2013 across 17 cities in Canada to build on the momentum of the July demonstration.

The Canadian Association of University Teachers (CAUT) in the autumn began a series of consultations across Canada asking interested researchers about their views on relevant issues, including muzzling scientists and changes to research funding. Its website chronicles stories from scientists on the impacts of basic research and ways to become more engaged in communicating science to the public and decision-makers.[13] Another group based at the University of Toronto launched a campaign Scientists for the Right to Know. Supporters argued that the Canadian federal government has been "waging a systematic assault on science as the basis of relevant information for policy making, and for knowing ourselves as a country and a nation."[14]

And in October 2013, the Professional Institute for the Public Service (PIPSC) released a survey – the first of its kind in Canada with over 4,000 respondents from a pool of 15,398 – examined a series of challenges facing government scientists. Conducted by Environics, the survey asked PIPSC members for their assessment of the overall climate for science, political interference, muzzling and impacts on policy affecting several science departments and agencies such as Fisheries and Oceans Canada, Environment Canada and the National Research Council. The results were disquieting:

I am allowed to speak freely and without constraints to the media about work I do at my Department/Agency. 90% No (10% Yes)

If I knew of a departmental decision or action that, based on my scientific knowledge, could bring harm to the public interest, including to health, safety, or the environment, I could share these concerns with the public or media without fear of censure or retaliation from my Department/Agency.
87% Disagree (4% Strongly agree, 10% Somewhat agree, 28% Somewhat disagree, 59% Strongly disagree)

Our ability to develop policy, law, and programs that are based on scientific evidence and facts has been compromised by political interference.
71% Agree (24% Strongly Agree, 47% Somewhat Agree, 14% Somewhat disagree, 14% Strongly disagree)

Over the last 5 years, do you feel that the sharing of government science findings with the Canadian public has become too restricted or too unrestricted?
Too Restricted – 74%
Too Unrestricted – 4%
No Change – 22%[15]

Also in 2013, the Environmental Law Clinic and Democracy Watch sent a request to the Office of the Information Commissioner (OIC) asking that she investigate the federal government's policies and actions to obstruct the right of the public and the media to speak to government scientists. In May, the OIC agreed to examine the issue. And in October, an unusual political response to the Harper approach to science came from the PQ government in Quebec. Apart from announcing a National Research and Innovation Policy, the Quebec document criticized the Harper administration's relationship with science and its own scientists, arguing that it goes against the very core of a knowledge-based society.[16]

THE MUZZLED AND THE MEDIA

While a group of eighty-five prominent Canadian scientists were the first to issue a statement concerning the government's "mishandling and mistreatment of science and due processes" under the banner of Canadian Scientists against the Politicization of Science in October of 2008,[17] Canadian journalists quickly picked up the scent. Specialist science reporters, spearheaded by Margaret Munro of Postmedia News, were particularly instrumental in sounding the alarm over the way federal scientists were stopped from communicating freely with the media. Munro reported how the new communication policy for Environment Canada from 2008 meant scientists could not talk to media until they were issued talking points scripted through the minister's office, a process that typically took days. "It effectively prevented timely access and ensured missed deadlines," said Munro.[18] The word "muzzling" became a popular heuristic in headlines describing the way the Harper government was treating its scientists who laboured for the Canadian taxpaying public.

This label had never factored in Canadian federal politics even though previous governments had issues with some of their government scientists' advice, notably with the cod fisheries[19] moratorium and the Kyoto Accord[20] talks under the Liberals' watch.[18] Consider, however, that from 2007 onwards just under 2,000 news items appeared in the Canadian and foreign press headlines that linked the muzzling of scientists to specific federal government ministries and the Harper government. This trend consistently increases as shown in Figure 13.1 below.[21]

Even accounting for repeat references, the number of links is not inconsequential. The media successfully framed the treatment of science and scientists as "muzzling." Especially at risk were departments where scientists' regulatory research, a mainstay of governmental science, could potentially impede natural resource development. The press picked up on the changes Harper was fomenting and reported accordingly: in March 2010, the public learned that, at Natural Resources Canada, ministerial approval is needed for scientists to speak to media and in 2013, new Department of Fisheries and Oceans (DFO) rules mandated ministerial approval to publish research. The clampdown began with Environment Canada's media policy document of February 2008, leaked to Postmedia News, which contained a series of FAQ's along with the directive for the department to speak with "one voice." For example, one question; Who is approving responses to the media? The answer: Media responses are evaluated by the appropriate experts and their managers to ensure accurate and consistent responses. Ministerial Communications Services approves responses on a case-by-case basis and consults with their core clients as necessary. Through yet another access to information request about specifics of the Environment Canada policy, Postmedia News learned more about "approved media lines," which uncovered the practice of sending requests for interviews to the Privy Council Office if they concerned

- Any calls from Press Gallery affiliated reporters, major news outlets, domestic and international
- Any issue related to the Minister's priorities, legislation, and/or policy decisions
- Policy related questions, especially related to climate change, wildlife, water quality, and supply
- International issues, including COP Conference of the Parties
- Funding issues, such as programs, grants, and contributions
- Questions related to current or proposed legislation

Figure 13.1

Muzzle graph. The number of instances of news coverage that included the words muzzle, Canada, government and scientist (captured by Lexis-Nexis), quarterly, January 2007–October 2013.

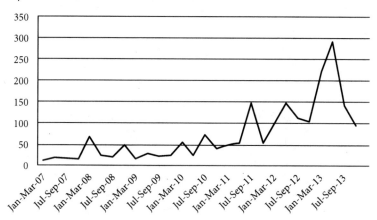

- Questions on the process or proposed process to protect species such as the polar bear and caribou.[22]

For some foreign media, the perception that Canada was in seeming lock step with the former Bush Jr. policy on controlling federal research was, in itself, newsworthy.[23] Further cuts to science would not have made much of an international story if not for the undertones of muzzling and suppression of evidence-generating that came with the closing of well known research tools like the long form census, facilities like PEARL[24] and ELA[25] (notable among many others), the elimination of the office the National Science Advisor,[26] and the shuttering of the National Roundtable on the Environment and the Economy.[27] These were topped off by the inability of reporters to talk to researchers in a timely fashion. As a result, the BBC,[28] The Guardian,[29] and The Economist[30] ran stories, as did the journals Nature[31] and Science, through Science Insider[32] expressing dismay over the clamp down on science.[33] In the autumn of 2013 the New York Times ran an editorial branding the Harper policies as "an attempt to guarantee public ignorance."[34]

Canada had previously enjoyed an international reputation for open, accessible and collaborative research. Under Harper, the Conservatives are five-time winners of the Fossil Award, given by environmental groups for obstructing climate change talks and pulling out of the Kyoto Accord. "We are becoming somewhat of a pariah on the international stage," stated the director of the Pacific Institute for Climate Studies, Tom Pedersen, in 2010. "This wasn't the case five or six years ago."[35]

NO ROOM FOR DISCUSSION:
A HARPER MOUTHPIECE

In 2013, then natural resources minister Joe Oliver's branding of groups as "rad-icals" who sought to have input into the Northern Gateway pipeline hearings was telling. The media picked up on his strident, reckless tone which clearly signalled a huge disrespect for Canadians' legitimate concerns about the safety of pipelines and transporting bitumen. Again, in 2013, the former investment banker famously attacked NASA's climate change scientist James Hansen as an "alarmist" and called the scientist's warning on the toll of unregulated tar/oil sands development "nonsense." He is also quoted using by-the-book cli-mate denial language when telling *Maclean's* magazine "that scientists have re-cently told us that our fears are exaggerated." He repeated this sentiment in an interview with the editorial board of the French-language paper *La Presse*.[36] The *Globe and Mail* also reported that pieces of the second omnibus budget bill C-45, which gutted fisheries regulation, overrode protection for water-ways and hijacked environmental assessment, did contain sections that were taken verbatim from a wish list of the pipeline industry lobby.[37]

Critics do say Harper is not targeting science per se, that he is simply de-termined to achieve his economic agenda at all costs. However, the evidence mounts that his combined efforts constitute an attack on science, especially environmental science, through muzzling, communication control, cuts to research and research facilities including the dismantling of research libraries and a decided change in how and why government science is conducted in the first place. This frame around Harper's government has led science writers like Chris Turner, in his 2013 book, to call Harper's tactics tantamount to "a war on science."[38]

The Harper approach can be captured in a simple phrase: how accurate is the misinformation? In a democratic society, the interaction between sound evidence and effective public policy needs to be based on trust, integrity and mutual respect. Anne Glover, the chief scientific advisor for the European Union, has said that when rigorously reviewed and publicly funded sci-ence is not used to shape policy, if it is ignored or thrown away, then the tax-paying public has a right to know why.[39] Unfortunately, as a result of the debasing of scientific evidence-often through purely ideological and political overtures-Canada's image as a well-respected democracy that values evidence has suffered.

The Harper government has never formally responded to muzzling charges; instead, it has side-stepped the issue completely and argued that it has spent more money on R&D than any previous government. Of course, this is a bit of a canard, since it is the emphasis that is being placed on research investment that has changed; the government is investing more in science tied to business to "grow the economy," or as Harper has stated, "science powers commerce."[40]

Government science has consequently taken a significant hit. When adjusted to 2007 dollars, funding for public research has actually decreased by 7% over that period. In fact, data from Statistics Canada show a continuing drop in research and development investment: Canada's gross expenditures on R&D as a percentage of GDP fell to 1.74 in 2012, down sharply from 1.92 in 2010 and a high of 2.09 in 2001. For the fiscal year 2013–14, intended spending for S&T activities was $10.5 billion, a decline of 3.3% from 2012–13.[41] Further, the anticipated total of 35,192 full-time equivalent (FTE) positions engaged in S&T is a decline of 2.9% from 2012–13.[42]

CONCLUSIONS

Canada has witnessed a tipping point in the relationship between science, media, and the Harper administration. The attacks on government science have led to a mobilization of the research community signalling an increased militancy and participation in political action. The media, both in Canada and abroad, continue to cover more misinformation. Lack of transparency and overall disrespect for targeted scientists, and for the use of science in decision-making is being scrutinized. Campaigns, rallies and petitions are continuing to expose the Harper government's treatment of a critical public policy issue.[43] More commentary is expected with the release of Harper's promised second science and innovation strategy.

A continued campaign is needed to ensure that change will happen, and that accountability, if not actionable in Parliament, is present at the polls. On a constructive note, the Union of Concerned Scientists has developed a system for grading the transparency of US government science. This initiative gives each agency two letter grades: one for media policy and the other for social media policy. The scoring rubric is based on six measures of open communication, which ascertain if the policy is accessible, current, clear, and consistent; protects scientific free speech; safeguards against abuse; is consistent with legal requirements; promotes openness and timeliness; and includes handling of misconduct and disputes.[44] As it now stands, none of the Harper government's communications / media-relations policies would make the grade. But ongoing scrutiny with a press-friendly report card could help public understanding and form a basis for comparison of use to citizens, scientists and media. Still, important questions need to be addressed. Jeffrey Hutchings, then a scientist with DFO, in a seminal paper published in 1997 called for a separate arms-length body to conduct federal science away from the bureaucrats and, one can surmise, the Privy Council Office.[45] To be sure, Canada has experimented with many models to free up public science advice and decision making but to little avail under the current regime. An invigorated campaign by the research community, propelled by diligent journalism, to open up government science does present an opportunity to take up Hutchings' challenge.

The awakening of new science-based advocacy groups can only be a healthy incursion into Canadian society. If there is a lesson to be learned, and it may be a simple one, it is this: government scientists have a responsibility to speak out about topics when they hold expert knowledge, particularly if this understanding can better inform policy. Civic society shares a responsibility, in turn, to protect scientists when they do. The government, for its part, needs to take seriously its duty to protect and defend the freedom of scientists to investigate and, in the spirit of scientific integrity, efficiently communicate research – a commitment made by Mr Harper in his first public statement about science. Along with his assurance of an open, transparent, and accountable government this pledge, too, is missing in action.

NOTES

1 *Mobilizing Science and Technology for Canadians: Canada's New Government* (2007), federal strategy announced by Prime Minister Harper in Waterloo, Ontario.
2 See G. Bruce Doern, *Science and Scientists in Federal Policy and Decision-Making*. Discussion paper, project for the Policy Research Secretariat, Government of Canada (1999).
3 For a review of advisory councils and Canada's experience, see Jeff Kinder, "Science Advisory Mechanisms in Canada: An Institutional Analysis," in *Policy: From Ideas to Implementation* edited by Glen Toner, Leslie Pal, and Michael Prince (Montreal and Kingston: McGill-Queen's University Press, 2010), 119–41.
4 It is worth noting here that the word "muzzling" has never appeared regarding previous administrations. Indeed, the Harper government seems to be the first to earn this moniker in relation to government scientists.
5 Council of Science and Technology Advisers, SAGE report for Industry Canada, "A Framework for Science and Technology Advice: Principles and Guidelines for the Effective Use of Science and Technology Advice in Government Decision-making" (2000), 3–14. The document can be found at http://publications.gc.ca/collections/Collection/C2-500-2000E.pdf.
6 As a matter of record, one Conservative, Edmonton MP James Rajotte, who was chairing the House of Commons Committee on Industry, Science, and Technology, argued in November 2006 for an upgrading of the national science advisor by having the position report directly to Parliament.
7 See Paul Dufour, "The Trouble with Voiceless Science Advice," *Research Money* (9 November 2012).
8 See for example, Allan Gregg's speech at Carleton University, "1984 in 2012," which underscored other areas where Harper's government was controlling the media message (September 5, 2012), http:// allangregg.com/ 1984-in-2012-%E2%80%93- the-assault-on-reason/.
9 See the special issue of *Academic Matters*, on "The War on Knowledge," May 2013.

10 See the map that details various cuts and shutdowns in government science at https://
maps.google.com/maps/ms?ie=UTF8&oe=UTF8&msa=0&msid=2156312915128011
93422.0004c54303a5c215725ab

11 "Death of Evidence," *Nature* 487 (July 19, 2012): 271–2.

12 The short version is available here: http://kennedystewart.ndp.ca/ndp-tables-plan-
to-end-conservative-muzzling-of-federal-scientists. The full Hansard from that day,
March 20, 2013, is available here, under "Business of Supply; Opposition Motion –
Science": http://www.parl.gc.ca/HousePublications/Publication.aspx?Mode=1&DocI
d=6049662&Language=E#Int-7937281.

13 CAUT also has a position paper on science policy available at getscienceright.ca.

14 http://scientistsfortherighttoknow.wildapricot.org/

15 For more results see Professional Institute of the Public Service of Canada, *The Big
Chill: Silencing Public Interest, A Survey, October 21, 2013.*

16 "Politique nationale de la recherche et de l'innovation" (Quebec, 2013).

17 http://www.cbc.ca/news/technology/canadian-researchers-call-for-end-to-
politicization-of-science-1.756697.

18 Margaret Munro said this at a symposium, Unmuzzling Government Scientists: How
to Reopen the Discourse, held at the American Association for the Advancement of
Science annual meeting (February 17, 2012, Vancouver, BC).

19 Industry successfully argued that fish stocks were probably fine because they were
able to catch more each season. This was despite worrying signs from in-shore fisher-
men and DFO scientists. The crash in 1993 came the year after the highest catch ever.
See http://news.bbc.co.uk/2/hi/science/nature/2580733.stm; and http://www.thestar.
com/opinion/commentary/2013/09/20/remove_the_muzzle_from_government_
scientists.html.

20 When the Kyoto Accord was being negotiated in 1997, it was significantly weakened
despite cries from scientists and environmentalists. Canada signed on after being allowed to count "carbon sinks" such as forests and farmland to make Canada's reduction targets much less aggressive.

21 The exact Lexis-Nexis search used was <muzzl! AND Canad! AND government
AND scien!> in order to capture all variants of the search terms (i.e. muzzle,
muzzled, muzzling, science, scientist, scientists, etc.) but also to ensure that the
journalists using the rhetoric of muzzling were doing it specifically in the context
of Canadian government science. The searches were repeated to find the number of
articles published during three month intervals beginning in 2007.

22 See http://www.scribd.com/doc/114076515/EC-Media-Policy-Released-to-Margaret
Munro-under-Access-to-Information-Act-2012. Munro is Postmedia News' senior
science reporter.

23 See, for example, Verlyn Klinkenborg, "Silencing Scientists." *New York Times*
(September 21, 2013), http://www.nytimes.com/2013/09/22/opinion/sunday/silen-
cing-scientists.html?_r=0.

24 The closure of PEARL was widely seen to have the aim of choking arctic research.
See, for example, Meagan Fitzpatrick, "'Science and Sovereignty' Key to New Arctic

Research Centre," C B C News (August 23, 2012), http://www.cbc.ca/news/politics/ science-and-sovereignty-key-to-new-arctic-research-centre-1.1231516.

25 The E L A shutdown was even more widely covered than the closure of PEARL, which is understandable given its track record of groundbreaking research and relatively inexpensive operating costs. Much of the coverage stuck to the narrative that this was part of a broader assault on environmental science. See, for example, Stephen Bede Scharper, "Closure of Experimental Lakes Area Part of Assault on Science," *Toronto Star* (March 25, 2013). http://www.thestar.com/opinion/commentary/2013/03/25/ closure_of_experimental_lakes_area_part_of_assault_on_science_scharper.html.

26 See, for example, Hannah Hoag, "Canada Abolishes Its National Science Advisor," *Nature News* (January 30, 2008), doi:10.1038/451505a.

27 See, Jeffrey Simpson, "Ottawa Kills the Emissions Messenger," *The Globe and Mail* (June 20, 2012), http://www.theglobeandmail.com/commentary/ ottawa-kills-the-emissions-messenger/article4350552/.

28 See Pallab Ghosh, "Risks of Placing Scientists 'On Message,'" B B C News (February 17, 2012), http://www.bbc.co.uk/news/science-environment-16881087; and Pallab Ghosh, "Canadian Government Is 'Muzzling Its Scientists,'" B B C News (February 17, 2012), http://www.bbc.co.uk/news/science-environment-16861468.

29 See Suzanne Goldenberg, "Canada's P M Stephen Harper Faces Revolt by Scientists," *The Guardian* (July 9, 2012), http://www.theguardian.com/environment/2012/jul/09/ canada-stephen-harper-revolt-scientists.

30 See "Scientific Freedom in Canada," *The Economist* (March 7, 2013), http://www. economist.com/blogs/americasview/2013/03/scientific-freedom-canada

31 See Kathryn O'Hara, "Canada Must Free Scientists to Talk to Journalists," *Nature* (September 29, 2010), doi:10.1038/467501a.

32 See in particular, Jane J. Lee, "Canada's Restrictions on Scientists' Speech Raises Concerns," *Science Insider* (February 24th, 2012), http://news.sciencemag. org/2012/02/canadas-restrictions-scientists-speech-raise-concerns; and also Sara Reardon, "Canadian Fish Scientist 'Muzzled' by Government," *Science Insider* (July 28, 2011), http://news.sciencemag.org/2011/07/ canadian-fish-scientist-muzzled-government.

33 See John Dupuis's meticulous, though still far from complete, list on *ScienceBlogs*: "The Canadian War on Science: A Long, Unexaggerated, Devastating Chronological Indictment" (May 20th, 2013).

34 See endnote 22. Verlyn Klinkenborg, "Silencing Scientists." *New York Times* (September 21, 2013), http://www.nytimes.com/2013/09/22/opinion/sunday/ silencing-scientists.html?_r=0

35 Quoted by Janet Davison, "Are Canada's Federal Scientists Being 'Muzzled'?" C B C *News* (March 27, 2012), http://www.cbc.ca/news/canada/are-canada-s-federal-scientists-being-muzzled-1.1278183. Note also when Minister Joe Oliver calls opponents of Northern Gateway, "radicals" in "An open letter from the Honourable Joe Oliver, Minister of Natural Resources, on Canada's commitment to diversify our energy markets and the need to further streamline the regulatory process in order to

advance Canada's national economic interest," Natural Resources Canada (January 9, 2012), http://www.nrcan.gc.ca/media-room/news-release/2012/1/3520. And also Oliver's attack on James Hansen, *cbc News* (April 24, 2013), http://www.cbc.ca/news/politics/joe-oliver-slams-scientist-s-oilsands-claims-as-nonsense-1.1304476. Finally, "our fears are exaggerated" is quoted from http://www.theglobeandmail.com/news/politics/pipeline-industry-pushed-environmental-changes-made-in-omnibus-bill-documents-show/article8894850/.

36 *Maclean's* (April 12, 2013) and a similar quote from Minister Joe Oliver's interview can be found in "Le ministre Oliver: Des sables bitumineux sans limite, une menace climatique 'exagérée,'" *La Presse* (April 12, 2013).

37 See Heather Scoffield, "Pipeline Industry Pushed Environmental Changes Made to Omnibus Bill, Documents Show," *The Globe and Mail* (February 20, 2013), http://www.theglobeandmail.com/news/politics/pipeline-industry-pushed-environmental-changes-made-in-omnibus-bill-documents-show/article8894850/.

38 Chris Turner, *The War on Science: Muzzled Scientists and Wilful Blindness in Stephen Harper's Canada* (Vancouver: Greystone Books, 2013). This is the first Canadian book specifically dealing with science under Harper.

39 Quoted in Kathryn O'Hara, "Evidence of Democracy?" http://pencanada.ca/blog/evidence-of-democracy/.

40 Remarks by the Prime Minister announcing Banting Postdoctoral Fellowships, support for Next Einstein Initiative , Waterloo , July 6 2010

41 Statistics Canada, "Federal Expenditures on Science and Technology and Its Components in Current Dollars and 2007 Constant Dollars" (2013), Table 358-0142.

42 Statistics Canada, "Federal Personnel – Engaged in Science and Technology Activities, by Category and Activity" (2013) Table 8. http://www.statcan.gc.ca/pub/88-204-x/2013001/t008-eng.htm.

43 See Paul Dufour, "Let Canadian Science off the Leash," *iPolitics* (14 October 2013).

44 Union of Concerned Scientists, *Grading Government Transparency: Freedom to Speak (and Tweet) at Federal Agencies* (Union of Concerned Scientists, 2013).

45 Jeffrey Hutchings. "Is Scientific Inquiry Incompatible with Government Information Control?" *Canadian Journal of Fisheries and Aquatic Science* 54 (1997), 1,198–210.

14 CIDA, the Mining Sector, and the Orthodoxy of Economic Conservatism in Harper Decision Making

RUBY DAGHER

INTRODUCTION

When the Conservative Party came to power in 2006, many non-conservative thinkers and analysts pondered about the level of transformation that this event would have on the Canadian public sphere and the lives of Canadians. As it turns out, Prime Minister Harper has made many changes to the Canadian public arena. One of the most notable examples is the transformation that has befallen on the Canadian International Development Agency (CIDA), or more recently the "Development" part of the Department of Foreign Affairs, Trade, and Development.

While many argue that these changes to CIDA and the Canadian aid envelope are in line with Harper's increased efficiency and accountability agenda, I argue that these changes are a result of decision-making that is based on Canadian self-interest and the orthodoxy of economic conservatism. The analysis in this chapter demonstrates the strong linkages between Canadian economic interests and the delivery of aid and the lack of rigorous evidence in support of Harper's development agenda.

The chapter begins by examining Prime Minister Harper's vision for development aid and the two underlying important aspects of the theory behind economic conservatism: free markets and free trade. Given the importance of the mining industry to Harper's natural resource-focused government, the analysis then shifts to the role of mining in development. Finally, the analysis turns to the role of free trade and mining in Harper's agenda and the resulting impacts on CIDA's approaches to development.

AID VERSUS FREE TRADE: THE DEBATE

The "aid versus trade" debate has been ongoing since the early 1960s and has redefined the meaning of trade. As is demonstrated below, arguments for and against free trade have overtaken discussions related to trade and refocused the debate on "free trade versus aid." A quick scan of the academic and other literature reveals an enormous amount dedicated to each side of the debate. The following is a quick overview of some of the major arguments.

Benefits of Free Trade

Free trade is an important aspect of the neoliberal ideology which tends to favor privatization, liberalization, and independent central banks that focus on inflation. This push for a market-oriented vision, or market-supremacy, took hold following the rebuilding of Europe following World War II. Subsequently, a school of economists developed lessons learned and transformed them into a package of ten policy prescriptions known more broadly as the "Washington Consensus."[1] These policy prescriptions required the reduction of the state from the economy, the placement of the private sector at the heart of development, and the removal of all barriers to market access (trade liberalization). The World Bank promoted these policies through its Structural Adjustment Programs (SAPs) and made its assistance conditional upon their implementation. Then British prime minister Thatcher and US president Reagan, whom Harper holds in high regard, were powerful supporters of the neoliberal ideology and the Washington Consensus.[2]

Following the disastrous failures of the SAPs, neoliberals maintained their belief in the supremacy of the market and turned their attention to the business-enabling environment (organizational capacity and market-friendly regulations) – the area now deemed vital for the success of the market. These adjustments and the continued ultimate goal of market efficiency or supremacy has led most donors and scholars to prioritize free trade over aid[3] and use aid as a means to support organizational capacity building, improvements in business regulations, and movement towards full trade liberalization.[4]

The proponents of free trade refer to the positive link between free trade and increased demand for labour in unskilled-labour-intensive goods and light manufacturing. Consequently, according to the theory, the more people work, the greater the consumption, the higher the growth, the higher the income levels, the lower the income inequality,[5] and the greater the decrease in poverty.[6] The benefits of free trade, according to neoliberals, can also be reflected through the exploitation of scale economies, better quality and lower prices and increased competition, market size, economic opportunities, rates of return, as well as local and foreign direct investment. Some economists have linked the presence of free trade with democracy promotion and decreases in trade-related corruption, monopolies, and market inefficiencies. Hong Kong, Singapore, South Korea, and Taiwan (the East Asian Tigers) are often presented as case-studies in support of market liberalization[7] and limited governments[8].

Another important assumption underlying the preference for free trade is the belief in the market's moral supremacy. While most supporters of free trade admit to the possible corruptness or immorality of some players in the market, there is a tendency to believe that governments and politicians (unlike technocrats) are more corrupt.[9] Moreover, there is a belief that the size of the market is capable of tempering the impact of corrupt or immoral market players, especially when supported by the appropriate business-enabling environment.[10] This trait, some believe, "has made the market the greatest bottom-up system in history for meeting people's needs."[11] This bodes well with many who claim the need to eliminate all non-market friendly interference, including aid.

Putting the Benefits of Free Trade into Perspective

The idea of market supremacy has been questioned by many, including two of the most famous economists the world has known. Adam Smith, the economist who coined the term 'the invisible hand' and the one who is often quoted in support of market liberalization, cautioned against a belief in the supremacy of the market and noted the possibility of corruption in the market by those looking to protect their wealth and position in society. John Maynard Keynes, the father of Keynesian economics and arguably the most influential economist of the twentieth century, famously cautioned, "to suppose that there exists some smoothly functioning automatic mechanism of adjustment that preserves equilibrium if only we trust to methods of laissez-faire is a doctrinaire delusion which disregards the lessons of historical experience without having behind it the support of sound theory."[12] Even proponents of free trade have questioned the research of earlier economists that highlighted a significant positive correlation between increased trade and economic growth.[13] They have noted the weaknesses in the empirical research and have reached more mixed results when adjusting for the inaccuracies.

Furthermore, current research has validated the negative impact of trade liberalization on the performance of low-income countries, countries that are usually found behind the technology frontier.[14] This research has argued that trade liberalization leads these countries to specialize in low-skill and low-technology goods with little hope for significant technological advancements. This is significant since the neoliberal theory clearly states the important link between patents, technological advancement, and growth.

The likely confinement to trading in low-skilled and labour-intensive products may also increase income inequality within low-income countries since what is considered low-skilled in Western economic terms is often considered relatively-skilled in poor countries.[15] Furthermore, those that produce quality goods are often paid the most followed by skilled workers producing substandard goods. The poor with limited or no skills are excluded from the market and consume so little that they do not matter economically.[16] The situation becomes even more complex when dealing with exported goods that have lower world prices and profit margins and/or when production requires the use of cheaper non-national labour.[17]

There is also a misalignment between the blame laid on politicians or unscrupulous developing country leaders and the trade actions of developed countries. As Wraight argues, developed countries push for the opening of developing countries markets while maintaining their trade barriers, exposing developing countries "to economic 'shock therapy' that wouldn't be tolerated in Europe or America,"[18] treating them unequally at the World Trade Organization (WTO), and taking all the gains of free trade by buying cheap raw products (with little economic value-added) and selling the final products (wherein long-term gains lie) for much higher.

While some believe that certain changes to the system might respond to these criticisms (e.g. making the WTO more representative of all members, supporting skills development, enhancing the business-enabling environment), Rodrik has demonstrated a clear mismatch between the theoretical benefits of free trade and the realistic possibilities for developing countries.[19] There seems to be a long list of impossible conditions that developing countries need to meet as a prerequisite to benefiting from trade liberalization: elimination or negation of all microeconomic imperfections, maintenance of a small economy, maintenance of full economic employment, and the use of strong tools to correct the economy.

Other academics have demonstrated the weak theoretical underpinnings of such "benefits." For his part, Chang (2008) highlights the questionable neoliberal conventional wisdom regarding the rise of the East Asian Tigers. He demonstrates that the success of the East Asian Tigers is very much linked to the active involvement of the state in nurturing new industries that were selected by the government, often in consultation with the private sector, in a bid to make them strong enough to compete internationally. This protection involved using tariffs and subsidies, temporarily nationalizing struggling companies, controlling foreign investment and practising reverse engineering and pirating. This analysis ironically demonstrates that export success is linked to an active intervening government with temporary protectionist policies, similar to the experiences of 'all of today's developed countries, including Britain and the US, the supposed homes of the free market and free trade.'[20] This is an important lesson for developing countries, especially those with mostly infant industries and low-skilled labour and products.[21]

Thus, one can conclude that the mainstream history of capitalism is inaccurate[22] and the theory behind the recommendations, including free trade, is shaky at best and a "grab-bag of ideas based on the fundamentalist notion that markets are self-correcting, allocate resources efficiently, and serve the public interest well."[23] This orthodoxy has led to disastrous effects on struggling developing countries,[24] has made the benefits of trade unattainable to most, increased income inequality,[25] and, while giving us more choices as consumers, it has placed a severe strain on our basic freedoms.[26] Clearly, while trade has been proven to be beneficial, its benefits have not come from free markets, limited governments and liberalization. Consequently, we need to go beyond the market-focused ideology of neoliberal economists and assess development through "an integrated, holistic approach to capture ... economic, political, sociological, and even ... psychological dimensions."[27]

THE ROLE OF THE MINING SECTOR IN DEVELOPMENT

In general, it is difficult to find unquestionable supporters for the role of the mining sector in development. Certain economists, even free-market economists, have identified highly profitable mining and other natural resources as long-term traps.[28] References are often made to the "Dutch Disease" and its effects or the consequences of an increase in the country's currency due to increases in revenues from natural resources, the subsequent increase in the price of exports, a resulting decrease in the competitiveness of exports, a consequential unwillingness and inability to diversify into manufacturing and services exports, and an ensuing decline in manufacturing. This phenomenon is even more important in countries that rely on exporting agricultural products with minimal potential for mark-up. Many economists believe that these factors have had a major harmful impact on the long-term development of many banana republics (single-commodity countries).

Political scientists have also drawn attention to the political economy issues that impact resource-rich countries. They often note that governments stand to increase the size of their coffers from the mining of natural resources if commodity prices remain stable or increase. However, this gain does not necessarily translate into increased growth for the country as a whole. The ability of the system to control autocratic or corrupt rulers[29] and the presence of democratic restraints are often cited as necessary checks to ensure that benefits reach citizens. This thinking has led donor countries, civil society groups, resource endowed countries, and resource companies to develop the Extractive Industry Transparency Initiative (EITI). It maintains standards that countries need to abide by to disclose taxes and other payments made by producing oil, gas and mining companies. It is presumed that by allowing citizens to "see for themselves how much their government is receiving from a country's natural resources" the result is improved "openness and accountable management of revenues from natural resources."[30]

Social and environmental scientists have highlighted the negative impacts that mineral endowments have had on a country's social fabric and environmental conditions.[31] Some of these impacts include the dispossession of local inhabitants from their land; health problems related to insects that thrive in still water, unhealthy migrant workers, and chemicals found in the air, ground, agricultural products, and drinking water; diversion of water resources; accidents in vegetation-filled pits; erosion; destruction of plants and vegetation that are used for self sustenance, income production or medical purposes; and the dislocation of communities. Much of these environmental consequences have had a negative impact on tensions between the various ethnic groups in the mined area.

Several authors have also addressed the impact of the resource rush on the relationship between corporations, developed countries (the corporate home-base) and the developing country. Their analysis looks beyond the deficiencies of the developing country governance system and assesses the political power and influence that the extractive industry has over its home government and the developing country decision makers. Reed (2002) argues that the oligopolistic structure of the industry, its large coffers, and the dependence of developing countries on resource extraction for survival afford corporate leaders influence over political players. The result is regulatory and income bargaining on the part of resource-rich developing countries leading to lax regulations and low shares of the benefits.

Some might rightly argue that the increase in the number of mining players has provided these countries with an ability to benefit from competition. Nevertheless, it is important to note that the industry is still oligopolistic and while the bargaining position of the developing countries has somewhat improved, there is little evidence to suggest that the benefits of such an improvement have translated into significant gains for the resource rich countries.[32] Moreover, when these interactions are guided by organizations like EITI that claim moral supremacy and make statements regarding government corruption (and none or little regarding corporate abuse), it becomes clear that the power struggle has shifted to the halls of multilateral institutions and that incoherence in the free-market theoretical framework remains unchallenged.

Finally, there is also substantial literature on the imbalance of power between extractive firms and the locally empowered communities that live on resource-rich land.[33] Communities that have been empowered through local decision making and ownership are being disempowered by the unequal distribution of power and knowledge between them and rich companies[34] and by the dispossession of their small local or artisanal miners.[35] This often leads to less conservation, more environmental damage, and further economic hardship resulting from very low percentages of profit; amounts that are cannot compensate for the damages.

Some might view the corporate social responsibility (CSR) activities of resource extracting companies as tools to deal with some of the issues that arise from this type of industry. While they can undoubtedly negate some of this negative impact, Campbell[36] convincingly argues that these tools tend to work at micro-level outcomes rather than solving the underlying causes of mining problems and the mining-led unequal approaches to in-country development. In addition, CSR proponents tend to ignore the negative impact that these activities have on issues of accountability and governmental legitimacy.[37]

FREE TRADE, MINING, AND THE HARPER
GOVERNMENT

In a June 2003 Civitas meeting in Toronto, Stephan Harper (then leader of the Alliance Party of Canada) proclaimed the need to promote social and economic conservatism. The primary value of economic conservatism, according to Harper, "is individual freedom, and to that end it stresses private enterprise, free trade, religious toleration, limited government and the rule of law."[38] In his speech, Harper drew on the work of Adam Smith and P.J. O'Rourke related to the "moral and civilizing importance of markets' by reminding us that [p]rivate enterprise and trade ... can turn individual selfishness into useful social outcomes."[39]

In a 2011 speech, Harper claimed the following: "Canadian businesses and their workers succeed and prosper when they have stable and secure access to markets and customers around the world ... Deepening our trading relationships is key to the Next Phase of Canada's Economic Action Plan in order to complete our recovery, create jobs and strengthen families' financial security."[40] Harper's enthusiasm for free trade is also expressed on the Conservative Party's official website where it is claimed that "[i]n contrast, during its 13 years in power, the previous Liberal Government signed only three new trade agreements. Fortunately, under Stephen Harper's Conservative Government, we are making up for lost time, opening new markets for Canadian businesses and creating good new jobs for Canadian workers."[41]

Since taking office, Harper's government has concluded and updated free trade agreements (FTAs) with eleven countries and two multilateral organizations (including the European Union). It is currently negotiating FTAs with 10 countries and one multilateral organization and exploring with another two countries and one multilateral organization. It has also concluded Foreign Investment Promotion and Protection Agreements (FIPAs) with twenty-one countries, and is negotiating with another eleven. Interestingly, slightly over one third of these countries rank in the top 40 receiving Canadian official development assistance and more than 45 percent of them are deemed, by the Government of Canada, to have significant importance for Canadian mining companies. These agreements support the following statement made by the Minister of International Trade at the World Trade Organization in May 2013: "As a government that has put Canada at the forefront of trade liberalization, we believe that trade and investment represent the twin engines of growth for the global economy ... My message to my counterparts this week has been clear: there is no better creator of jobs, growth and long-term prosperity than freer and more open trade ... our goal as legislators must be to turn border bottlenecks into global gateways."[42]

Moreover, the trend of placing mining at the forefront of the agenda was clearly stated by Harper in his speech at the 2012 Summit of the Americas. During that speech, Harper touted the benefits of the mining sector for Canada and highlighted his vision by stating: "Looking to the future, we see increased Canadian mining investment throughout the Americas – something that will be good for our mutual prosperity and is therefore a priority of our government. We are prepared to share our expertise in this area."[43]

THE RECENT SHIFT IN CIDA'S POLICIES
AND APPROACH

One can interpret the following segment of Harper's 2007 Speech From the Throne as a possible initiator of a change in CIDA's policies and approaches: "The best hope for fostering development and our common security in the hemisphere and beyond is through bolstering international trade ... Our Government will keep advancing Canada's trade interests in the Americas and around the world to open up new markets for Canada's innovators."[44]

Subsequently in 2008, CIDA was asked to refocus its funding. The decision was to be based on the local situation in the countries, the level of need (as per the Human Development Index (HDI)), CIDA's expertise and Canada's foreign policy desires. The process led to the demotion of several countries, including eight African countries (six with low and two with medium HDI numbers), and the ascension of three countries, all of which are in Latin America.

However, a few interesting trends appear when one looks deeper into the numbers. As Table 14.1 indicates, funding to all eight African countries has actually increased by $143.06 million or $89.02 million when humanitarian assistance is excluded. Overall, Canada has increased Official Development Funding (ODA) by $37.06 million to six of the ten most important African mining countries for Canada.[45] When adjusted to exclude humanitarian assistance, the numbers indicate an increase of $45.19 million to seven out of the 10 countries. Seven of these countries are ranked in the top 40 countries receiving aid from CIDA,[46] five are ranked in the top twenty-five ahead of Peru, Colombia, Bolivia, and Ukraine, and four of which are countries of focus.

Table 14.1
CIDA's demoted african countries

Country	CIDA-ODA Funding 2007/08	Rank in CIDA-ODA Funding 2007/08	CIDA-ODA Funding 2011/12	Rank in CIDA-ODA Funding 2011/12	Change in Funding	Change in Funding Adjusted to Humanitarian Assistance	Declared Mining Interests	Declared Trade Position
Benin	$6.72M	47	$12.96M	43	$6.24M (93%)	$6.27M (94%)		Low with much potential (share a FIPA)
Burkina Faso	$20.19M	22	$37.07M	20	$16.88M (84%)	$14.91M (74%)	Canadian presence in mining precious stones	Increased substantially
Cameroon	$7.5 M	44	$9.43M	46	$1.93M (26%)	$1.16M (40%)	Canadian companies with moderate assets	Established modest trade
Kenya	$24.89M	20	$80.82M	9	$55.93M (225%)	$16.8M (91%)	Significant increase in Canadian mining investment since 2010	Well established trading relationship
Malawi	$16.29M	28	$46.45M	15	$30.16M (185%)	$29.77 (184%)		Modest but increasing
Niger	$25.6 M	30	$27.84M	28	$12.68M (83%)	$3.27M (36%)	Canadian companies involved in uranium, gold and oil	Modest
Rwanda	$14.65M	32	$33.88M	21	$19.23M (131%)	$18.76M (128%)		Largest trading partner in Central Africa
Zambia	$20.17M	24	$20.18M	33	$0.01M (<1%)	$1.08M (6%)	Most important mining partner in Africa	Dynamic and growing

Finally, CIDA's funding for the countries landing in the top ninety-four HDI rankings (of which three are countries of focus and one is a member of the Caribbean program) has increased by $41.66 million from $101.10 million (adjusted for the earthquake relief in China) in 2007/08 to $142.67 million in 2011/12.[47]

This amount represents only about seven percent of CIDA's ODA budget that reaches countries. Yet, it is significant enough to allow one to question the validity of this expenditure and the lost opportunity of helping a poorer and more vulnerable country. As the Organisation for Economic Co-operation and Development noted in its peer review of Canada's development assistance: "there should be no confusion between development objectives and the promotion of commercial interests."[48]

CONCLUSION

The chapter has examined Prime Minister Harper's vision for development aid and the two underlying important aspects of the theory behind economic conservatism: free markets and free trade. It has shown the importance of the mining industry to Harper's natural resources-focused government, the role of free trade and mining in Harper's agenda, and the resulting impact on CIDA's approaches to development.

Drawing definitive correlations between the numbers on Canadian mining activities, trade and official development assistance is difficult to demonstrate with complete certainty. Still, the statements made by Harper and his representatives regarding mining and trade, the establishment of the Canadian International Institute for Extractive Industries and Development, and Canada's contribution to the EITI and the African Mineral Development Centre all indicate a heavy emphasis on free trade and mining. This emphasis is clearly based on the neoliberal ideology, including a clear disdain for government interference, a great enthusiasm for the power or morality of the market, and the belief in the enabling business environment. This is especially potent given that several researchers have found "that greater trade stimulates capital accumulation in high-income countries but affects capital accumulation negatively in low-income ones."[49]

From the analysis presented in this chapter, the Harper government's decision-making process seems to give only lip service to accountability and efficiency. The evidence has demonstrated a strong reliance on the neoliberal orthodoxy, one that eliminates more equitable policy options and is devoid of policies that are needed for a more holistic development model. Finally, the strong link with Canadian interests is unsettling. Statements made by Ministers Baird (Foreign Affairs) and Fantino (former Minister of International Cooperation) linking CIDA's interests to that of the promotion of Canadian businesses abroad and to bringing jobs, growth and prosperity to Canadians clearly reflect non-development-based objectives. It is thus clear that the Harper Government's decision-making process at best reflects a normative ideological assumption and, at worst, it represents a pillaging of the markets and resources of poorer countries for the benefit of a powerful group of Canadians.

NOTES

1   Ashraf Ghani and Clare Lockhart, *Fixing Failed States: A Framework for Rebuilding a Fractured World* (New York: Oxford University Press, 2008).

2   See Michael Sandel, *What Money Can't Buy: The Moral Limits of Markets* (New York: Farrar, Straus and Giroux, 2013); and Eric Helleiner, *States and the Emergence of Global Finance: From Bretton Woods to the 1990s* (New York: Cornell University Press, 1996).

3   William Easterly, *White Man's Burden: Why the West's Efforts to Aid the Rest Have Done So Much Ill and So Little Good* (London: The Penguin Press, 2006).

4   Support for full trade liberalization involves assistance with trade policies and regulations, trade development, trade-related infrastructure, productive capacity, trade-related adjustment, and other trade-related needs. See World Trade Organization, "Operationalising Aid for Trade" (Geneva, 26 September 2006).

5   Jagdish Bhagwati, *In Defense of Globalization* (New York: Oxford University Press, 2007).

6   David Dollar, "Outward-oriented developing economies really do grow more rapidly: Evidence from 95 LDCs, 1976–85," *Economic Development and Cultural Change* (1992): 523–44.

7   Ha-Joon Chang, *Bad Samaritans: Rich Nations, Poor Policies, and the Threat to the Developing World* (New York: Random House, 2007).

8   Easterly, *White Man's Burden*, 2006; Bhagwati, *In Defense of Globalization*, 2007.

9   Deepak Lal, *The Poverty of "Development Economics"* (London: The Institute of Economic Affairs, 1983); Deepak Lal and Sarath Rajapatirana, "Foreign Trade Regimes and Economic Growth in Developing Countries," *World Bank Research Observer*, World Bank Group, 2, 2 (July 1987): 189–217.

10 The business-enabling environment includes basic infrastructure, strong macroeconomic policies, skilled human resources and managerial capacity. See Massimiliano Calì and Dirk Willem Te Velde, "Does Aid for Trade Really Improve Trade Performance?" *World Development* 39, 5 (2001), 725–40; Dong-Hyeon Kim, Shu-Chin Lin, and Yu-Bo Suen, "Nonlinearity between Trade Openness and Economic Development," *Review of Development Economics* 15, 2 (2011): 279–92.

11 Easterly, *White Man's Burden*, 76.

12 John Maynard Keynes, *The Collected Writings of John Maynard Keynes*, Vol. 25, eds. Johnson and Moggridge (London: Cambridge University Press, 1980), 21–2.

13 Robert Wade, *Governing the Market: Economic Theory and the Role of Government in East Asian Industrialization* (New Jersey: Princeton University Press, 1990).

14   Kim et al., "Nonlinearity."
15   Isabelle Bensidoun, Sébastien Jean, and Aude Sztulman, "International Trade and Income Distribution: Reconsidering the Evidence," *Review of World Economics* 147 (2011): 593–619; and Eunyoung Ha, "Globalization, Government Ideology, and Income Inequality in Developing Countries," *The Journal of Politics* 74, 2 (April 2012).
16   Susan George, "Globalisation and War," *Transnational Institute* (March 10, 2008).
17   Elizabeth Blunt, "Is Aid for Trade an Effective Tool for Reducing Poverty?" IRINI (15 March 2013).
18   Christopher D. Wraight, *The Ethics of Trade and Aid: Development, Charity or Waste?* (New York: Continuum International Publishing Group, 2011), 133.
19   Dani Rodrik, *The New Global Economy and Developing Countries: Making Openness Work* (Washington, DC: Overseas Development Council, 1999).
20   Chang, *Bad Samaritans*, 15.
21   Wraight, *The Ethics of Trade and Aid*.
22   Chang, *Bad Samaritans*.
23   Joseph Stiglitz, "We May Be Nearing the Truth on Neo-liberal Failure." *The Daily Star* (July 14, 2008).
24   Manfred Bienefeld, "Globalization and Development: The Promise of Success without Substance." Paper presented at the Fifth Annual Conference on Globalization and Development, Cuba, February 1982.
25   While economic growth has increased, the benefits, when adjusted to China and India (both implementing many non-free trade policies), have shown rising inequalities between developed and developing countries and within the majority of all countries (see the Conference Board of Canada, http://www.conferenceboard.ca/hcp/hot-topics/worldinequality.aspx).
26   Amartya Sen, *Development as Freedom* (Oxford: Oxford University Press, 1999).
27   Ramgopal Agrawala and P.N. Schwartz, "Sub-Sahara Africa: A Long-Term Perspective Study." Paper for World Bank's Learning Process on Participatory Development (May 1994), 93.
28   Paul Collier, *The Bottom Billion: Why the Poorest Countries are Failing and What Can Be Done about It* (New York: Oxford University Press, 2007).
29   Robert I. Rotberg, *When States Fail: Causes and Consequences* (New Jersey: Princeton University Press, 2004).
30   Extractive Industry Transparency Initiative (EITI) Website: http://eiti.org/. It is ironic that there is no indication of the impact this will have in increasing the amounts paid to developing country governments.
31   Daryl Reed, "Resource Extraction Industries in Developing Countries," *Journal of Business Ethics* 39 (2002): 199–226; Kaakpema Yelpaala and Saleem H. Ali, "Multiple Scales of Diamond Mining in Akwatia, Ghana: Addressing Environmental and Human Development Impact," *Resources Policy* 30 (2005): 145–55.
32   Chinese mining companies have also committed serious abuses of people's rights (see Human Rights Watch, http://www.hrw.org/news/2011/11/03/zambia-workers-detail-abuse-chinese-owned-mines).

33 Daryl Reed, "Resource Extraction Industries in Developing Countries"; and Stephanie Engel and Charles Palmer, "Complexities of Decentralization in a Globalizing World," *Environmental and Resource Economics* 50 (2011): 157–74.

34 Engle and Palmer, *Complexities of Decentralization in a Globalizing World*, 2011.

35 S.W.J. Luning, "Liberalisation of the Gold Mining Sector in Burkina Faso," *Review of African Political Economy* 117 (2008): 25–39.

36 Bonnie Campbell, "Corporate Social Responsibility and development in Africa: Redefining the roles and responsibilities of public and private actors in the mining sector," *Resource Policy* 37 (2012): 138–43.

37 Campbell, "Corporate Social Responsibility and development in Africa."

38 Stephen Harper, "Rediscovering the Right Agenda," Citizens Centre Report, Edmonton: Vol. 30, 10 (June 2003), 73.

39 Ibid.

40 Conservative Hamilton East–Stoney Creek website.

41 http://www.conservative.ca/?page_id=1452.

42 http://www.international.gc.ca/media_commerce/comm/news-communiques/2013/05/30a.aspx.

43 Mark Kennedy, "Stephen Harper Touts Canada's Mining Industry as Americas Summit Gets off to Rocky Start," *The National Post* (April 14, 2012).

44 Speech From the Throne, http://www.parl.gc.ca/Parlinfo/Documents/ThroneSpeech/39-2-e.html. Canada is not the only donor following a free trade agenda. The World Bank, United States, European Union, Britain, and Germany have identified the WTO's aid for trade agenda as their goal. The United States and Britain have also pushed to have American or British private companies involved in opening up the developing country markets. Norway and Japan have a more balanced approach.

45 The top ten countries listed in decreasing importance are: Zambia, Mauritania, South Africa, Madagascar, Democratic Republic of Congo, Ghana, Tanzania, Mali, Senegal, and Eritrea (Source: Natural Resources Canada).

46 These account for about 90 percent of Canadian funding reaching countries either through bilateral or non-bilateral means.

47 All figures were taken from CIDA's website. It is important to note that this spending is not all on trade-related or mining activities. However, it does represent a convenient manner in which to leverage Canadian interests by taking over some of the government's responsibility, helping it meet its responsibility or providing support to citizens.

48 Organisation for Economic Co-operation and Development, *Canada – Peer Review 2012* (Organisation for Economic Co-operation and Development, 2012), 11.

49 Kim et al., "Nonlinearity," 288.

Contributors

MARK BRUNET is a graduate of Carleton University's School of Public Policy and Administration. He is currently working as an evaluator for the federal government.

DAVID CARGNELLO is a researcher with interests in ethics and public affairs. He obtained his doctorate in philosophy from the University of Oxford (Balliol College) and is currently completing a master's degree in public administration at Carleton University.

AMANDA CLARK is assistant professor at Carleton University's School of Public Policy and Administration and a Trudeau Scholar. Her work focuses on the intersections of civic engagement, digital technologies, and public administration.

PHILIP CROSS worked for thirty-six years at Statistics Canada, the last few as its chief economic analyst. He wrote Statistics Canada's monthly assessment of the economy for years, as well as many feature articles for the *Canadian Economic Observer*. After leaving Statistics Canada, he worked for the Macdonald-Laurier Institute and is a member of the Business Cycle Dating Committee at the C.D. Howe Institute.

RUBY DAGHER is a PhD candidate at the School of Public Policy and Administration at Carleton University. She has also taught international development courses at Carleton University and the University of Ottawa. Prior to teaching, Ruby worked at the Canadian International Development Agency from 2006 until 2012.

G. BRUCE DOERN is Distinguished Research Professor in the School of Public Policy and Administration at Carleton University and professor emeritus in the Politics Department at the University of Exeter.

PAUL DUFOUR is fellow and adjunct professor with the Institute for Science, Society, and Policy at the University of Ottawa, and is principal of PaulicyWorks, a science policy consulting firm in Quebec.

CRAIG JONES holds a PhD in political economy from Queen's University and teaches at Carleton University. He was executive director of the John Howard Society of Canada from 2007 to 2010. For six years he worked as a health policy analyst with the Queen's Centre for Health Services and Policy Research and the Centre for Studies in Primary Care. Currently he is executive director of the National Organization for the Reform of Marijuana Laws in Canada (normal.ca).

IRYNA KRYVORUCHKO is assistant professor in the Johnson-Shoyama Graduate School of Public Policy at the University of Regina. She is an economist with research interests in the economics of charities, applied microeconomics, public economics, and tax policy.

IAN LEE is assistant professor in the Sprott School of Business at Carleton University.

JOHN LESTER is an executive fellow with the School of Public Policy at the University of Calgary. A former federal government economist, he was also director of research for the Expert Panel Review of Federal Support to Research and Development. Prior to that assignment, he managed the Tax Evaluations and Research Group at Finance Canada.

KARINE LEVASSEUR is associate professor in the Department of Political Studies at the University of Manitoba.

EVERT LINDQUIST is director and professor at the School of Public Administration at the University of Victoria and editor of *Canadian Public Administration*.

CRAIG MACNAUGHTON is a graduate of Carleton University's master of public administration program. He works as a policy analyst in the federal government.

JENNIFER MCKEE specialized in innovation, science, and environment at Carleton University where she obtained her MPA degree. She has a BA degree from Harvard University.

KATHRYN O'HARA is an associate professor in Carleton University's School of Journalism and Communication where she holds the CTV Chair in Science Broadcast Journalism. For twenty-seven years before coming to Carleton she worked as a producer, reporter, and program host on radio and television, mainly, though not exclusively, in public broadcasting.

KEN RASMUSSEN is professor of public management at the Johnson-Shoyama Graduate School of Public Policy at the University of Regina. He has published extensively in the area of public management and most recently co-authored the book, *Public Policy and Governance: A View from the Provinces* (University of Toronto Press, 2013). He is also currently president of the Canadian Association of Programs in Public Administration.

MATT RETALLACK has bachelor's and master's degrees in water resources engineering, more than ten years of water policy research experience, and is currently working on his PhD in public policy at Carleton University. His research focuses on social and economic dimensions of integrating ecosystem services within water governance institutions.

ANDREA ROUNCE is an assistant professor of political studies at the University of Manitoba and the academic director of the Manitoba Institute for Policy Research (MIPR).

BOB SLATER is currently adjunct professor in Environmental Policy at Carleton University. He is also president of Coleman, Bright, and Associates, a consulting firm that operates internationally specializing in sustainable development issues, and a senior fellow with the International Institute for Sustainable Development. Dr Slater occupied several senior positions at Environment Canada, including senior assistant deputy minister, assistant deputy minister of policy, assistant deputy minister of environmental protection, and director general for Ontario Region at Environment Canada.

JENNIFER SPENCE is a PhD Candidate at Carleton University's School of Public Policy and Administration. She is an experienced public service manager with more than eighteen years working with Fisheries and Oceans Canada, Public Works and Government Services Canada, the Royal Canadian Mounted Police, and the Canadian Public Service Agency.

CHRISTOPHER STONEY is associate professor in the School of Public Policy and Administration at Carleton University and the director of the Centre for Urban Research and Education (CURE).

GLEN TONER is professor in the School of Public Policy and Administration at Carleton University.